# CONGRESS

## AND LAW-MAKING

# CONGRESS
## AND LAW-MAKING

### RESEARCHING THE LEGISLATIVE PROCESS

### SECOND EDITION

ROBERT U. GOEHLERT
AND
FENTON S. MARTIN

ABC-CLIO

SANTA BARBARA, CALIFORNIA
OXFORD, ENGLAND

**Library of Congress Cataloging-in-Publication Data**

Goehlert, Robert, 1948–
    Congress and law-making.

    Includes bibliographies and indexes.
        1. Legal research—United States.   2. Legislation—
United States.   3. Legislative histories—United States.
I. Martin, Fenton S.   II. Title.
KF240.G63   1988        328.73′077′072        88-22355

ISBN 0-87436-509-0 (alk. paper)

10  9  8  7  6  5  4  3  2  1

Design by Tom Reeg

ABC-Clio, Inc.
Riviera Campus
2040 Alameda Padre Serra, Box 4397
Santa Barbara, California 93140–4397

Clio Press Ltd.
55 St. Thomas' Street
Oxford, OX1 1JG, England

This book is Smyth-sewn and printed on acid-free paper ∞.
Manufactured in the United States of America

# Contents

# Figures and Tables

## FIGURES

# TABLES

# Preface to the Second Edition

This edition of *Congress and Law-making* has been considerably revised and expanded. The volume has been reorganized and enlarged from four chapters to nine. The most important change is a new, detailed section in Chapter 1 that should help readers understand how a bill progresses through all the stages of the legislative process. We have also expanded the section in Chapter 1 on how to compile a legislative history by including a section on committee membership.

New chapters include the following: Chapter 2, Federal Legislation, which includes information on how to find and interpret statutes; Chapter 3, Federal Administrative Law, which describes how to use the *Federal Register* and *Code of Federal Regulations*; Chapter 4, The Congressional Budget Process; Chapter 5, Congressional Support Agencies, which discusses the work and publications of the Congressional Budget Office, the Congressional Research Service, the Office of Technology Assessment, and the General Accounting Office; and Chapter 6, Foreign Affairs and Treaties.

The remainder of the volume focuses on secondary sources that can be used to study Congress. Not only have we included new editions of works cited in the first volume, but we have added many new items. We have added new sections on dictionaries, encyclopedias, newsmagazines, newsletters, news services, indexes, databases, audiovisual materials, television coverage, oral histories, and archives. We added to the chapter on campaigns and elections by including new material on interest groups, district data, and data archives. We have also provided an extensive glossary.

# CONGRESS
## AND LAW-MAKING

# Introduction

## AIM AND SCOPE

This guide is designed to help users trace congressional legislation and to familiarize them with the major sources of information about Congress. It provides a basic introduction to the tools of research and how they can be used to gain better insight into Congress and its workings. Tracing legislation has become easier as commercial publishers have started to provide greater bibliographic control of government publications. New reference tools make it easier to trace legislation. Nevertheless, an understanding of congressional decision making requires considerable effort and probing, time and patience, and the tools cited in this guide will require firsthand examination, for congressional reference works and bibliographies can be bewildering. This book does not describe at length all of the complexities involved in congressional research, although almost every aspect of it is touched upon. It does give the necessary information to begin an independent pursuit of the user's own educational needs. We believe researchers can proceed on their own course of study once they are equipped with this background information.

It is not unusual for a student to spend hours researching, only later to find out by accident that using a particular bibliographic tool would have saved considerable time. Almost every researcher has had the experience of serendipitously discovering a new reference tool. The main reason for compiling this guide is to systematically present the basic tools used in legislative tracing in a clear and concise manner. We hope this guide makes researchers more aware of the resources available.

1

## GUIDES TO RESEARCH

This volume will provide a discussion of documents relating to the Congress but will not cover all the other government publications relating to the executive branch or other agencies. Discussions of documents have been kept as simple as possible and do not go into great detail concerning all the technical and bibliographic aspects of documents and the tools used to identify them. There is no need to cover ground that has already been treated in other volumes, nor is it possible to mention every reference tool associated with document use in a guide designed as an introduction to resources on the Congress. Because we have concentrated on providing information on both documents and commercial publications, we have had to be selective in our discussion of documents. For the student and researcher who wants to know more about documents, there are numerous excellent guides. The first five annotated entries listed below are the best guides to documents, both for current and historical materials. After those guides are listed a variety of other, more specialized research guides. All of these can be useful, and students and researchers should take the time to review them in order to know when to consult them.

Following the guides to research we have outlined a number of general guides to government documents. When appropriate, we will refer to them later in the volume, but for the most part these tools are more general in nature and not the primary tools used in researching the Congress. However, students and researchers should be aware of their existence.

## Commercial Guides

Sears, Jean L., and Marilyn K. Moody. *Using Government Publications.* 2 vols. Phoenix, AZ: Oryx Press, 1986.

The first volume of this set covers searching by subjects and agencies. Each of twenty-seven chapters covers a single subject or agency, such as foreign policy, occupations, elections, or the president. Each chapter includes a search strategy as well as covering indexes, on-line databases, and general sources. The second volume covers finding statistics and using special techniques, including historical searches, legislative histories, budget analyses, and treaties. This set is an excellent tool for the first-time user of government documents.

Bitner, Harry, Miles O. Price, and Shirley R. Bysiewicz. *Effective Legal Research*. 4th ed. Boston MA: Little, Brown, 1979.

This work gives an excellent description of the legislative process and all tools related to legal research. It provides an in-depth examination and explanation of the reference works and indexes used in legislative tracing. There are also chapters on finding federal statutes, treaties and other international acts, federal administrative law, and the rules and decisions of federal courts and administrative and regulatory agencies. This volume is excellent as a guide to government documents, especially those relating to the legislative process.

Morehead, Joe. *Introduction to United States Public Documents*. 3rd ed. Littleton, CO: Libraries Limited, 1983.

Although this work is a textbook for library school students and professional librarians, it is a valuable guide for anyone interested in researching federal documents. The chapter on legislative-branch materials contains a wealth of information, including an especially detailed description of congressional publications and the reference tools used in tracing legislation. There are also separate chapters on the executive branch, regulatory agencies, and advisory commissions. The book has especially useful information on how the depository system works and on the work of the superintendent of documents and the Government Printing Office. This volume is especially useful for learning the technical aspects of documents, such as the SuDocs classification system.

Boyd, Anne Morris. *United States Government Publications*. 3rd ed. Rev. by Rae Elizabeth Rips. New York: H.W. Wilson, 1949.

Even though this work is somewhat outdated, its discussion of government publications is still useful for understanding the nature, types, and value of government publications. The work is also important when researching congressional publications in the eighteenth and nineteenth centuries.

Schmeckebier, Laurence F., and Roy B. Eastin. *Government Publications and Their Use*. 2nd rev. ed. Washington, DC: Brookings Institution, 1969.

This well-known and respected reference work covers all government publications. It contains extensive information on all forms of publications published by the government and, like the Boyd volume, has much information not found elsewhere. Though the volume does not include information about the numerous reference tools published in the last two decades,

Schmeckebier does provide an excellent description and analysis of documents published prior to 1900.

Folsom, Gwendolyn B. *Legislative History: Research for the Interpretation of Laws*. Charlottesville: University Press of Virginia, 1972.
This well-written handbook is for beginning researchers. It contains important chapters on the history of the legislative process, basic sources of information documenting the process, and a step-by-step method of researching legislative histories.

Meyer, Evelyn S. "Reference Guides to Congressional Research." *RQ* 22 (Fall 1972): 30–36.
This is a short guide to sources of information on the Congress and tools used for legislative tracing. Each source is briefly annotated, providing a synoptic description of its value and general format.

Shannon, Michael Owen. *To Trace a Law: Use of Library Materials in a Classroom Exercise*. ERIC Document ED 11 341. Washington, DC: Educational Resources Information Center, 1976.
This volume is a basic guide to legislative history for the novice. It is designed to familiarize students with the legislative process by asking them to choose a topic of interest and trace a bill as it becomes law. The guide provides descriptions of the standard reference works through which the student can find information on laws, legislators, and legislative procedures.

Nabors, Eugene. "Legislative History and Government Documents— Another Step in Legal Research." *Government Publications Review* 3 (Spring 1976): 15–41.
The author presents a formula approach to developing legislative histories. All of the actions involved in the legislative process are perceived as the behavior of a system. The author has constructed an abstract model representing the legislative process that can be used as a means to charting legislative histories.


There are many other research guides to political science and government publications that also contain sections or chapters on congressional research. Most of these guides would be available in any college or university library. Several of them are listed below.

Andriot, John L. *Guide to U.S. Government Publications*. rev. ed. McLean, VA: Documents Index, 1988.

Brock, Clifton. *The Literature of Political Science: A Guide for Students, Librarians and Teachers.* New York: R. R. Bowker, 1969.

Freides, Thelma. "A Guide to Information Sources on Federal Government Agencies." *News for Teachers of Political Science* 18 (Summer 1978): 6–13.

*Government Reference Books: A Biennial Guide to U.S. Government Publications.* Littleton, CO: Libraries Unlimited, 1968/1969– .

Holler, Frederick L. *Information Sources of Political Science.* 4th ed. Santa Barbara, CA: ABC-Clio, 1986.

Jacobstein, J. Myron, and Roy M. Mersky. *Fundamentals of Legal Research.* 3rd ed. Minneola, NY: Foundation Press, 1985.

Lu, Joseph K. *U.S. Government Publications Relating to the Social Sciences: A Selected Annotated Guide.* Beverly Hills, CA: Sage Publications, 1975.

Mason, John B. *Research Resources: Annotated Guide to the Social Sciences.* Santa Barbara, CA: ABC-Clio, 1968–1971. 2 vols.

Palic, Vladimir M. *Government Publications: A Guide to Bibliographic Tools . . . , Incorporating Government Organization Manuals: A Bibliography.* New York: Pergamon Press, 1977.

Robinson, Judith S. *Subject Guide to Government Reference Books.* Littleton, CO: Libraries Unlimited, 1985.

Schwarzkopf, LeRoy C. *Guide to Popular U.S. Government Publications.* Littleton, CO: Libraries Unlimited, 1986.

Van Zant, Nancy P. *Selected U.S. Government Series: A Guide for Public and Academic Libraries.* Chicago: American Library Association, 1978.

Vose, Clement E. *A Guide to Library Resources in Political Science: American Government.* Washington, DC: American Political Science Association, 1975.

Weinhaus, Carol, ed. *Bibliographic Tools:* Volume II, *Legislative Guide.* 4th ed. Cambridge, MA: Harvard University, Program on Information Technologies and Public Policy, 1976.

Williams, Wiley J. *Subject Guide to Major United States Government Publications*. 2d ed. Chicago: American Library Association, 1987.

Wynar, Lubomyr R. *Guide to Reference Materials in Political Science*. Littleton, CO: Libraries Unlimited, 1967.

Zwirn, Jerold. *Congressional Publications: A Research Guide to Legislation, Budgets, and Treaties*. 2d ed. Littleton, CO: Libraries Unlimited, 1988.

## Document Guides

The following publications are general guides to government publications. The first six guides are especially useful for identifying documents of the eighteenth and nineteenth centuries. For more information regarding the use of these tools, consult the guides in the previous section, especially the works by Morehead, Boyd, and Schmeckebier.

Poore, Ben P. *Descriptive Catalog of the Government Publications of the United States, September 5, 1774–March 4, 1881*. Washington, DC: U.S. Government Printing Office, 1885.

This publication attempted to list all governmental publications, but many department publications were omitted. It is a chronological, annotated list of government publications dated from September 1774 to March 1881. It is known as *Poore's Descriptive Catalog*.

Ames, John G. *Comprehensive Index to the Publications of the United States Government, 1881–1893*. 2 vols. Washington, DC: U.S. Government Printing Office, 1905.

This is known as *Ames' Comprehensive Index*. Entries are arranged alphabetically by subject. There is an index of personal names. Some departmental publications were omitted.

Greely, Adolphus W. *Public Documents of the First Fourteen Congresses, 1789–1817. Papers Relating to Early Congressional Documents*. Washington, DC: U.S. Government Printing Office, 1900.

This is a chronological list of government publications. It includes all messages and state papers of the presidents during the period in question. There is an index of names. Additional information is provided in *Supplement, 1904*, which includes a preliminary list of papers of the first two Congresses.

*Checklist of United States Public Documents, 1789–1976.* Arlington, VA: U.S. Historical Documents Institute, 1976.
This is the most comprehensive single bibliographical source for U.S. government documents. The entries provide full bibliographic citations for all of the entries in the *1789–1910 Checklist,* the *Document Catalog,* the *Monthly Catalog, 1895–1976,* and the shelf list of the Government Printing Office's Public Documents Library.

Lester, Daniel, and Sandra Faull, comps. *Cumulative Title Index to United States Public Documents, 1789–1976.* Arlington, VA: U.S. Historical Documents Institute, 1978. This lists all of the titles in the *Checklist of United States Public Documents, 1786–1976.*

*Catalog of the Public Documents of the [53rd to 76th] Congress and All Departments of the Government of the United States [for the Period of March 4, 1893, through December 31, 1940].* Washington, DC: U.S. Government Printing Office, 1896–1945.
This is known as the *Document Catalog.* It was the first truly systematic record of U.S. public documents. It is the only complete list of executive orders from 1893 to 1940. It also contains proclamations. The entries are in alphabetical order. There are entries for authors, subjects, and some titles. This catalog has been discontinued.

U.S. Superintendent of Documents. *Monthly Catalog of United States Government Publications.* Washington, DC: U.S. Government Printing Office, 1895– .
The *Monthly Catalog* is the *Reader's Guide* of U.S. government publications. While it is not inclusive of all publications, it does index, by author, title, subject, etc., the majority of the most important publications issued by the federal government. The *Monthly Catalog* is best used in searches for information related to electoral reform, election laws, campaign contributions, etc. For statistical sources, the *Monthly Catalog* is not as productive as the *American Statistical Index* or the *Catalog of United States Census Publications* (see pp. 148–49).

The following four publications serve as indexes to the *Monthly Catalog* for the years it had no indexing or later cumulative indexing.

Kanely, Edna A., comp. *Cumulative Subject Index to the Monthly Catalog of United States Government Publications, 1895–1899.* 2 vols. Arlington, VA: Carrollton Press, 1977.

Buchanon, William A., and Edna A. Kanely, comps. *Cumulative Subject Index to the Monthly Catalog of United States Government Publications, 1900–1971.* Arlington, VA: Carrollton Press, 1973.

*Monthly Catalog of United States Government Publications Cumulative Index, Set 1: 1976–1980.* 6 vols. Phoenix, AZ: Oryx Press, 1987.

*Monthly Catalog of United States Government Publications Cumulative Index, Set 2: 1981–1985.* 6 vols. Phoenix, AZ: Oryx Press, 1987.

Parish, David W. *Changes in American Society, 1960–1978: An Annotated Bibliography of Official Government Publications.* Metuchen, NJ: Scarecrow Press, 1980.

This book describes important government publications in the last twenty years. It is arranged under broad subject areas and lists publications from congressional committees.

# 1. The Legislative Process and How To Trace It

## THE LEGISLATIVE PROCESS

Tracing the passage of a bill through Congress is an intricate process. It requires a full understanding of law-making procedures and an awareness of the informal politics that influence congressional decision making, e.g., lobbying and logrolling. The concessions and compromises involved in drafting legislation, some of which take place outside Capitol Hill, are as important as the debates within both chambers of Congress. Thus, a description of the formal steps by which a bill becomes law is not a complete picture of the legislative process, but it is fundamental in tracing legislation.

Briefly, legislation is passed into law in the following way. A member of one of the houses of Congress introduces a bill. It is referred to a committee and then to a subcommittee. The subcommittee may hold hearings on the bill and amend it. The committee issues a report on it. The bill is then ready for floor action, where it may be debated and amended. If it passes, the bill is sent to the other house, where it goes through the same process. Often, each chamber is simultaneously working on the same or a similar bill. When both houses have passed their versions of a bill, they can reconcile any differences by agreeing to or modifying the amendments of the other chamber or by sending the bill to a conference committee. The conference committee attempts to hammer out a bill acceptable to both bodies. Once both the Senate and House of Representatives agree on the specific language, the legislation is sent to the president for his approval and signature into law. If the president vetoes the bill, the Congress may have the option of trying to override his veto. But it is not always this simple; the pages to follow attempt to show what complexities may be involved.

## The Congress

The Senate consists of 100 members, two from each state. A senator must be at least thirty years of age, a U.S. citizen for nine years, and a resident of the state in which he is elected. The term of office is six years, and one-third of the Senate membership is elected every two years. The terms of senators from the same state are staggered so that they do not end at the same time. The House of Representatives consists of 435 members elected every two years from districts within the fifty states. Representatives are apportioned among the states on the basis of their total populations. A representative must be at least twenty-five years of age, a U.S. citizen for seven years, and a resident of the state in which he is elected.

A Congress lasts for two years and is divided into two annual sessions. Unlike other legislative bodies, both the Senate and the House of Representatives have equal legislative functions and powers. Bills may originate in either the House or the Senate, with one exception: All revenue-raising bills originate in the House. General appropriation bills also originate in the House. The Senate may propose or concur with amendments to these bills, as it does on others. The Constitution authorizes each chamber to determine the rules of its proceedings. The House of Representatives adopts its rules on the opening day of each Congress. The Senate, which considers itself a continuing body, operates under rules that it periodically amends.

### Sources of Legislation

The drafting of bills is an art that requires considerable skill and expertise. Sometimes a draft is the result of several years' study by a commission designated by the president or a cabinet officer. Likewise, congressional committees sometimes draft bills after studies and hearings that have gone on for several years.

Sources of legislation are unlimited, and drafts of bills originate in many places. Most common is the draft written by a member of Congress. The concept may emanate from his election campaign or his experience after taking office. The office of legislative counsel (offices exist in both chambers) can assist in casting the member's idea in the proper form.

Lobbyists, such as businesses, public interest groups, or associations, often provide the technical assistance for drafting a bill. Constituents often request that a bill be introduced. Sometimes a legislator introduces a bill "by request" even if the member does not personally support the measure. The executive branch also recommends legislation, which in turn is introduced by members, usually with the notation "by request." Executive departments send proposed bills to Congress. These proposals are normally introduced by the chairman of the committee or subcommittee that has jurisdiction, or by the ranking minority member when the president's opposition party is in the majority. The president defines his legislative program in the State of the Union and budget messages and other messages throughout the year. Committees can also write their own bills. Appropriations and revenue bills generally originate this way. Sometimes a committee makes so many amendments to a bill under consideration that it finally drafts a version incorporating all the amendments that is referred to as a "clean bill."

## Forms of Congressional Action

Once legislation is drafted, it is introduced in Congress in one of four principal forms, including

1. the bill
2. a joint resolution
3. a concurrent resolution
4. a simple resolution

The most frequently used form in both houses is the bill.
A bill that has been agreed to in identical form by both House and Senate becomes law only after

1. presidential approval
2. failure by the president to veto the bill, i.e., to return it with his objections to the house in which it originated within ten days while the Congress is in session
3. overriding of a presidential veto by a two-thirds-majority vote in each house

A bill does not become law without the president's signature if the members of Congress by their adjournment prevent its return with his objections. This action is referred to as a "pocket veto."

## Introduction of a Bill

In the past, a senator had to gain recognition from the presiding officer to introduce a bill. Today, what normally happens is that a senator submits the text of the bill to an official in the Senate chamber. Bills are numbered consecutively as they are introduced, labeled with the sponsor's name, and sent to the Government Printing Office for publication. Senators may introduce an unlimited number of bills.

Representatives introduce bills by dropping them into the "hopper," a box on the clerk's desk. The bill is assigned a number that is noted at the end of the House section of the *Congressional Record* for that day. The Congressional Research Service is required to write a description of each bill not to exceed 100 words and publish it in the *Congressional Record* as soon as possible after introduction.

In both the Senate and House it is common practice for originators of a bill to send a "Dear Colleague" letter to the other members, explaining the purpose of the proposed bill and asking them to cosponsor the bill. This practice adds to the impact of a bill's introduction and gives other members and the public a chance to see who supports a bill. Cosponsorship is not binding. Cosponsoring members may request to have their names withdrawn or may oppose a bill when it gets to the floor. Members may also add their names as cosponsors any time after a bill has been introduced. In both chambers there is no limit on the number of members who may cosponsor a bill. Cosponsors are listed after the primary sponsor on the cover of the bill. Cosponsorship is noted in a specific section of the *Congressional Record*, but bills are not reprinted to show cosponsors added after the date of introduction.

### Referral

The parliamentarians of the chambers assign bills to committees with the appropriate jurisdictions. Jurisdictions are outlined in the rules of each chamber and are also determined by the precedents of past Congresses. Jurisdictions can overlap, and bills are often drafted to take advantage of vague jurisdictional lines. Both chambers have the same options for committee referral:

1. exclusive referral, i.e., the bill is to be considered by only one committee without any deadline for reporting back to the chamber
2. joint referral, i.e., the bill is to be considered by two or more committees simultaneously, and a deadline could be set for reporting back to the chamber

3. split referral, i.e., different sections of a bill are referred to two or more committees, usually with a deadline for reporting back to the chamber
4. sequential referral, i.e., the entire bill goes to one committee, then to another, then to another, and the last committee has a deadline for reporting the bill back to the chamber

In the House, the Speaker has the option of appointing an ad hoc committee to consider specific legislation. The Speaker also specifies all the majority members of select and ad hoc committees. To do this, the Speaker must have the approval of the full House, normally a perfunctory requirement when the Speaker's party is in the majority. In the case of a House-passed bill coming to the Senate, the bill may be placed directly on the calendar without being referred to a committee. In the House, a Senate-passed bill must go to a committee unless a similar House bill has already been reported and placed on the calendar.

The most important phase of the legislative process is the consideration given by committees. It is in committees where the most intensive scrutiny is given to bills and where individuals can testify. There are twenty-one standing committees in the House and sixteen in the Senate, as well as several select committees. Select committees are generally investigative and do not consider bills. In addition, there are several standing joint committees, composed of members from both House and Senate. Each committee has jurisdiction over certain legislative subject matters. The rules provide for approximately 220 different classifications of bills that are to be referred to the respective committees in the House and approximately 200 in the Senate. Bills are increasingly subject to multiple referrals, which complicates the task of legislative tracing.

Membership on House committees is divided between the two political parties in proportion to their total membership in the House. A member usually seeks election to the committee that has jurisdiction over a field in which he/she is most qualified and interested. Many members are recognized experts on the subject addressed by their committee or subcommittee. Members rank in seniority in accordance with the order of their appointment to the committee. The rules of the House require that committee chairmen be elected from nominations submitted by the majority party caucus at the beginning of each Congress. In the Senate, chairmen are elected by either a party caucus or conference vote. Each committee is provided with a staff. For standing committees, the professional staff is appointed on a permanent basis. Standing committees may also appoint consultants on a temporary basis, if necessary.

# The Legislative Process in the House

## Consideration by Committee

Under House rules, the chairman of the committee to which a bill has been referred must assign the bill to the appropriate subcommittee within two weeks of its introduction, unless a majority of the members of the majority party on the committee vote to have the bill considered by the full committee. Most subcommittees have specified jurisdictions. One of the first actions taken in the subcommittee is the transmittal of copies of the bill to the General Accounting Office and departments and agencies concerned with the subject matter of the bill with a request for their views on the necessity or desirability of the bill. Executive departments and agencies submit their reports on the necessity and desirability of the bill to the Office of Management and Budget, which determines whether their reports and the bill are consistent with administration policy.

Standing committees are required to have regular meeting days at least once a month, but the chairman may call for additional meetings. Three or more members of a standing committee may file with the committee a written request that the chairman call a special meeting. If the chairman fails within three calendar days after the filing of the request to call the requested meeting, a majority of the members of the committee may call the special meeting. When a bill reaches a committee it is placed on the committee's legislative calendar. These calendars are published annually or semiannually by most committees and can be invaluable reference tools.

## Hearings

For important bills, committees and subcommittees will set a date for public hearings. Each committee is required to make a public announcement of the date, place, and subject matter of a hearing at least one week before the hearing, unless the committee determines that there is good cause to begin the hearing earlier. If the committee plans to begin the hearing less than a week after the announcement, it must make a public notification to that effect at the earliest possible time. Public announcements are published in the *Daily Digest* portion of the *Congressional Record* as soon as possible. A notice, usually in the form of a letter, is frequently sent to individuals, organizations, and agencies that are known to be interested in the hearing.

Committee and subcommittee hearings are required to be public except when the committee or subcommittee, in open session and with a majority present, determines by roll-call vote that some or all of the hearing shall be closed to the public. Reasons for voting a meeting closed include issues of national security, possible disclosure of trade secrets, and the need to protect the identity of law enforcement agents or informers or preserve the confidentiality of personnel matters. Even if a hearing is voted closed, no senator or representative, whether on the committee or not, may be barred from the hearings.

## Witnesses

The bill may be read in full at the opening of the hearing. After a brief introductory statement by the chairman and sometimes by the ranking minority member, the witnesses are called. Committees and subcommittees require that witnesses who appear before them file in advance a written statement of their proposed testimony and that they limit their presentations to a brief summary. All House committee and subcommittee rules provide for the application of the five-minute rule in the questioning of witnesses, i.e., five minutes for each member with each witness. Minority party members of the committee or subcommittee are entitled to call witnesses of their own to testify on a bill during at least one day of the hearing. The committee or subcommittee may invite testimony from department or agency officials, special interest groups, academics, experts, or interested citizens. Witnesses may be compelled by subpoena to appear. Senators or representatives not on the committee may and often do testify. Groups and individuals that have not been invited may request the opportunity to testify.

Frequently hearings are held with witnesses "by invitation only." In such cases, other statements are usually accepted for inclusion in the printed transcript of the hearing. Hearings provide the opportunity for witnesses to submit letters, statements, and other forms of written material for the record. The record stays open for a specified number of days for other legislators, public organizations, and individuals to submit additional material. Senators and representatives always have the opportunity to edit the transcripts of hearings to change their remarks.

Hearings are sometimes recessed subject to the call of the chairman. Thus the record may not be closed for some time. Depending on how long the record is left open and on printing schedules, it may be a matter of weeks or months before the transcript of a hearing is printed. There is a general rule for appropriations hearings that the printed hearings be available before the bill is called up on the floor.

## Mark-up Session

After a hearing is completed, the committee or subcommittee usually will consider the bill in a session that is known as the mark-up session, when each line of a bill is discussed and analyzed. The views of both sides are studied in detail, and at the conclusion of deliberation a vote is taken to determine the action of the subcommittee. It may decide to report the bill favorably to the full committee, with or without amendments, or unfavorably, or suggest that the committee postpone action. Each member of the subcommittee has a vote. All meetings, including the mark-up of bills, must be open to the public except when the committee or subcommittee, in open session with a majority present, determines by roll-call vote that some or all of the meeting shall be closed.

## Committee Action

The full committee may repeal any of the subcommittee's actions. It may hold additional hearings before considering the subcommittee's recommendations. Normally the full committee marks up the bill as it was reported by the subcommittee. (Reporting a bill means submitting findings and recommendations.) In considering the report the full committee may

1. report the bill back to its chamber as it was introduced
2. report the bill amended and append those amendments that were adopted during mark-up
3. report the bill unfavorably
4. report a "clean bill" embodying the amendments adopted in mark-up
5. vote to table the bill

A bill dies if it is not reported back to its chamber by the end of a Congress. If there were numerous amendments to a bill the committee could draft a "clean bill" that can be introduced, reported, and placed on the calendar all on the same day. This method is used to save time during floor debate on a bill, as each committee amendment does not have to be considered separately. Committee amendments can be considered together in a single vote, but this requires unanimous consent. If a member should object, separate votes could be forced on each amendment.

If the final committee vote is favorable to a bill, it is then "ordered reported." It may be a matter of days, weeks, or months before the bill is "reported," i.e., an actual written report is filed in the chamber. In the course of a lengthy mark-up, committees generally prepare documents called drafts, working papers, or prints. They are valuable because they represent versions of the bill that may differ significantly from the bill as it is finally introduced.

The result of each roll-call vote in any meeting of a committee must be made available by that committee for inspection by the public. Among the information available in roll-call vote results is

1. a description of each amendment, motion, order, or other proposition
2. the names of the members voting for and against the amendment, motion, order, or proposition, and whether they voted by proxy or in person
3. the names of those members present but not voting

With respect to each roll-call vote by a committee on a motion to report a bill or resolution, the total number of votes cast for and against the reporting of the bill or resolution must be included in the committee report.

## Reports

Reports are extremely valuable documents in a legislative history. They are used by the courts, executive departments, and the public as sources regarding the intent and purpose of a bill. They are numbered consecutively as they are filed, e.g., House Report 100-1, House Report 100-2, etc. The report number contains a prefix that indicates the number of the Congress.

If the committee votes to report the bill favorably to the House, one of the members is designated to write the committee report. The report is a justification for the bill being reported. It includes

1. purposes and scope of the bill
2. section-by-section analysis of the bill
3. proposed changes in existing law
4. explanations of committee amendments
5. opinions of departments and agencies whose comments were solicited
6. minority views, i.e., members who disagree with the majority of the committee in reporting bill
7. the committee's oversight findings and recommendations
8. a summary of the oversight findings and recommendations made by the Committee on Government Operations
9. the statement required by the Congressional Budget Act of 1974, if the bill provides new budget authority or new or increased expenditures
10. the estimate of costs for carrying out the bill, prepared by the director of the Congressional Budget Office whenever the director has submitted such to the committee prior to the filing of the report

Each report must contain a detailed analytical statement as to whether the enactment of the bill into law may have an inflationary impact. Each report must carry an estimate of the costs that would be incurred in carrying out the provisions of that bill in the fiscal year reported and in each of the five succeeding years or for the duration of the bill if less than five years. These provisions do not apply to committees on appropriations. In the case of a bill involving revenues, the report need contain only an estimate of the gain or loss in revenues for a one-year period.

The bill is printed when reported, and committee amendments are indicated by showing new matter in italics and deleted matter in stricken-through type. The report number is printed on the bill and the calendar number is shown on both the first and back pages of the bill. Bills voted on favorably by a committee must be reported immediately after the vote. A majority of the members of the committee may file a written request with the clerk of the committee for the reporting of the bill. When the request is filed, the clerk must immediately notify the chairman of the committee of the filing of the request, and the report on the bill must be filed within seven days after the day on which the request is filed.

Theoretically a bill cannot be considered in either chamber unless the report has been available to members for at least three days. In practice, this rule is often waived by unanimous consent. In the House, there is also the option of getting a special waiver from the Rules Committee.

### Legislative Review by Standing Committees

Under the rules of the House, each standing committee (other than the committees on appropriations and Committee on the Budget) is required to review and study the application, execution, and effectiveness of the laws dealing with the subject matter over which the committee has jurisdiction as well as to review and study the operation of federal agencies having responsibility for the administration and evaluation of those laws. The purpose of the review and study is to determine whether laws created by Congress are being carried out in accordance with the intent of Congress and whether those laws should be continued, changed, or eliminated. Each committee having oversight responsibility is required to review any conditions that may indicate the necessity or desirability of passing new or additional legislation within the jurisdiction of that committee. Each standing committee also reviews and studies the impact of tax policies on matters within its jurisdiction.

At the start of each Congress, a representative of the Committee on Government Operations meets with representatives of other House committees to discuss the oversight plans of those committees and to assist in coordinating all of the oversight activities. Within sixty days after Congress convenes, the committee reports to the House the results of those discussions and recommendations.

## Calendars

There are five calendars in the House. These calendars are issued each day the House is in session in a comprehensive document called *Calendars of the United States House of Representatives and History of Legislation*. The calendars contained in this comprehensive House document are

1. the Union Calendar, which contains all public bills that raise revenue or make appropriations
2. the House Calendar, which contains all public bills not dealing directly or indirectly with raising revenue or making appropriations
3. the Consent Calendar, which contains noncontroversial bills that have already been referred to either the House or the Union Calendar, to expedite consideration
4. the Private Calendar, which contains bills for the relief of individuals with claims against the U.S.
5. the Discharge Calendar, which contains motions to discharge committees from further consideration of a bill

Any bill having an effect on the Treasury goes on the Union Calendar. Theoretically, the Union Calendar is the calendar of the Committee of the Whole, because bills listed on it are first considered by that committee. The House may resolve itself into the Committee of the Whole, consisting of 100 or more members, to consider bills presented to it by the Rules Committee when a quorum is not present. The committee then reports such bills back to the House for a final vote.

Bills on the House Calendar have no effect on the Treasury and generally are administrative and procedural matters. They are not usually considered by the Committee of the Whole, but rather, directly by the House.

Any member may file a request with the clerk to place a particular bill on the Consent Calendar to expedite such legislation. Unanimous consent is required to pass these bills. This means that the objection of one member can result in blocking a bill's passage. The Consent Calendar is called the first and third Monday of each month. The first time a bill is called up under the Consent Calendar, one member's objection can delay its consideration. The second time around, the objection of three members can have the bill stricken from the Consent Calendar, although its place on the House or Union Calendar would remain the same.

The Private Calendar contains bills that deal with individual matters like claims against the government or immigrants' requests to be exempted from certain requirements. The Private Calendar is called on the first and third Tuesday of each month, and private bills are usually passed without debate.

The Discharge Calendar is not a list of bills, but of petitions or motions to discharge a legislative committee or the Rules Committee from further consideration of a bill. A majority of House members must sign the petition before it is placed on the Discharge Calendar, where it must then remain for seven legislative days, giving the committee a final opportunity to act on the bill. On the second and fourth Monday of each month, excluding the last six days of the session, a member who has signed the petition may move that the committee be discharged from further consideration of the bill. Twenty minutes of debate, equally divided between opponents and proponents, is in order. If the motion to discharge is agreed to by a majority of the members, the consideration of the bill becomes a matter of high privilege, i.e., the House may decide to consider the measure immediately or place it on a calendar. Although rarely successful, the discharge petition may be used to force the following actions:

1. the release of any public bill that has been before a standing committee for thirty days
2. the release of any reported bill that has been before the Rules Committee for seven days
3. the granting of a special rule by the Rules Committee allowing for the consideration of a bill that has been before a standing committee for thirty days

## Rules Committee

Some bills pending on the House and Union calendars are more important than others, and it is necessary to have a system allowing their consideration ahead of those that do not require immediate action. Because all bills are placed on those calendars in the order in which they are reported to the House, the latest bill reported would be the last to be taken up if calendar number were the sole determining factor. The Rules Committee was created to expedite the consideration of important bills. This committee has specific jurisdiction over resolutions (called "rules") relating to the order of business of the House and has the power to report those resolutions that take bills out of calendar order. Most of the committee's work is deciding whether or not to grant these rules to bills that might be delayed on one of the calendars. After a committee has reported a bill, the following procedures are taken to get a special resolution from the Rules Committee.

The chairman of the legislative committee reporting a bill, the bill's sponsor, and other committee members appear before the Rules Committee seeking support for a resolution providing for the bill's immediate consideration. The Rules Committee, if it decides that the bill should be considered, reports a resolution to the House that

1. provides for immediate consideration of the bill
2. sets forth a time allotment for debate
3. determines who controls the debate
4. waives points of order against the bill
5. regulates the amending process, e.g., forbids all amendments, allows only amendments proposed by the relevant committee ("closed rule"), or allows amendments from the floor ("open rule")

A rule approved by the Rules Committee must be reported to the House within three legislative days of approval. The report must lie over in the House for one day unless two-thirds of the House members present and voting decide to take the rule up immediately. Since reports of the Rules Committee are privileged, the Speaker must recognize the Rules Committee member designated to call up a rule at any point in the order of business. If the member reporting the rule does not call it up within seven days after reporting, any member of the Rules Committee may do so as a question of privilege. The rule can be debated for one hour, with time divided equally between proponents and opponents.

There are several other methods of obtaining consideration of bills that either have not been reported by a committee or, if reported, for which a special resolution or rule has not been obtained. These methods include

1. motion to suspend the rules
2. calendar Wednesday
3. privileged matter

## Motion to Suspend the Rules

On Monday and Tuesday of each week and during the last six days of a session, the Speaker may entertain a motion to suspend the operation of the regular rules and pass a bill or resolution. Arrangement must be made in advance with the Speaker for a member's motion to be recognized. Before being debated in the House, the motion must be seconded by a majority of the members present. A second is not required on a motion to suspend the rules when printed copies of the proposed bill or resolution have been available for one legislative day before the motion is considered. The motion to suspend the rules and pass the bill can be debated for forty minutes, twenty by the proponents and twenty by the opponents. If amendments are to be added to a bill considered under suspension, those amendments must be included in the original motion to suspend and pass. No amendments are allowed from the floor. To assure that only bills with wide support are considered in this manner, a two-thirds vote is required for passage. If a bill fails to pass under suspension, it can be brought up later through regular procedures.

## Calendar Wednesday

On Wednesday of each week, unless the procedure is dispensed with by unanimous consent or a two-thirds majority of the members voting, a quorum being present, the standing committees are called in alphabetical order. A committee may call up for consideration any bill reported by it on a previous day and pending on either the House or Union Calendar. Only two hours of general debate are allowed and action must be completed on that same legislative day. The procedure is not allowed during the last two weeks of a session. A vote of a simple majority of the members present is sufficient to pass the measure.

## Privileged Matters

Under the rules of the House, certain matters are regarded as privileged matters and may interrupt the order of business. Also, at any time after the reading of the *Journal*, i.e., approval of the previous day's proceedings, a member, by direction of the Appropriations Committee, may move that the House resolve itself into the Committee of the Whole for the purpose of considering the privileged matter of bills raising revenues or general appropriation bills. (General appropriation bills may not be considered in the House until three calendar days after printed committee reports and hearings on them have been made available to the members.) The limit on general debate is generally fixed by unanimous consent. Examples of other privileged matters are conference reports, amendments to bills by the Senate, veto messages from the president, and resolutions privileged pursuant to statute. The member in charge of such a matter may call it up at any time for immediate consideration. Generally, this is done after consultation with both the majority and minority floor leaders so that the members of both parties will have advance notice and not be taken by surprise.

## Consideration by the House

Once consideration of a bill is obtained by one of the above methods, it is then considered by the entire chamber with the opportunity for debate and the offering of amendments. In order to expedite the consideration of bills and resolutions, the House often resorts to a parliamentary practice that enables it to act with a quorum of only 100 members instead of the normal majority of 218, resolving itself into the Committee of the Whole to consider a bill. The Committee of the Whole is a House procedure that allows the chamber to operate under special rules and expedite business. All bills on the Union Calendar involving taxes or appropriations must be first considered in the Committee of the Whole. Members debate and vote on the motion that the House resolve itself into the Committee of the Whole. If the motion is passed, the Speaker leaves his chair after appointing a chairman to preside.

## Debate in Committee of the Whole

The special resolution or rule reported by the Rules Committee to allow for immediate consideration of a bill fixes the length of the debate in the Committee of the Whole. The length may vary according to the importance of the bill. As provided in the resolution, the control of the time is equally divided between the chairman and the ranking minority member of the committee that reported the bill. Members seeking to speak for or against the bill usually make arrangements in advance with the member in control of the time on their respective side. Others may ask the member speaking at the time to yield to them for a question or a brief statement. Permission is often granted a member by unanimous consent to extend his remarks in the *Congressional Record* if enough time to make a spoken statement is not available during debate. The conduct of the debate is governed by the standing rules of the House that are adopted at the opening of each Congress.

The committee's chairman and the ranking minority member of the committee that reported the bill are usually floor managers for the bill and also usually control the time. Amendments may not be offered during general debate. Once the time for general debate has passed, the bill is read for amendment under the five-minute rule, under which a member is permitted five minutes to explain his amendment, after which the member who is first recognized by the chair is allowed to speak for five minutes in opposition. There is no further debate on that amendment, thereby preventing any attempt at filibuster tactics.

Amendments must be relevant to the bill and related to the section to which they are offered, in contrast with Senate procedure. Amendments offered by the legislative committee that reported the bill are always considered first, and then, if the bill has an open rule, amendments may be offered from the floor. All amendments can be modified to the second degree. Third-degree amendments are not allowed. Substitute amendments, also amendable to the second degree, are in order. Then begins the "second reading" of the bill, section by section, at which time further amendments may be offered to a section when it is read. Each amendment is put to the Committee of the Whole for adoption.

At any time after debate is begun under the five-minute rule on proposed amendments to a section of a bill, the Committee of the Whole may, by majority vote of the members present, close debate on the section. If debate is closed on a section before there has been debate on any amendment that a member has caused to be printed in the *Congressional Record* after the reporting of the bill by the committee but at least one day prior to floor consideration of the amendment, the member who caused the amendment to be printed in the *Congressional Record* is given five minutes in which to explain the amendment, after which the first person to obtain the floor has five minutes to speak in opposition. There is then no further debate on that proposed amendment.

### Action on the Bill

At the conclusion of the consideration of a bill for amendment, the Committee of the Whole "rises" and reports the bill to the House with the amendments that have been adopted. In rising, the Committee of the Whole reverts to the House and the chairman of the committee is replaced in the chair by the Speaker of the House. The House then acts on the bill and any amendments adopted by the Committee of the Whole. The committee can recommend that the bill be recommitted or that its enacting clause be struck, actions that kill the legislation. If the previous question has been ordered, the full House immediately votes on the amendments. Ordering the previous question is a parliamentary device that cuts off debate and forces a vote on the subject at hand. There is no way to obtain another vote on amendments rejected in the Committee of the Whole unless the amendment in question is incorporated in a motion to recommit with instructions.

### Recommittal Motions

After the previous question is ordered, the bill is ready for a third time and the vote is taken on final passage. Just before the vote on final passage, a member who is opposed to the bill in its current form may offer a motion to recommit it to the legislative committee that reported it. There are two types of recommittal motions:

1. A simple motion to recommit has the effect of killing the bill.
2. A motion to recommit with specific instructions, such as to report the bill back with a particular amendment, may delay the vote on final passage.

Votes on recommital motions are often a more accurate test of support than a vote on final passage. Ten minutes of debate are allowed on motions to recommit with instructions. If the motion fails, the vote on final passage is in order.

## Quorum Calls and Roll Calls

In order to expedite quorum calls and roll calls, the rules of the House provide alternative methods for pursuing these procedures. The rules provide that in the absence of a quorum, fifteen members, including the Speaker, are authorized to compel the attendance of absent members. A call to establish a quorum of the House is then ordered, and the Speaker is required to have the call taken by electronic device, unless in his discretion he names one or more clerks to "tell" the members who are present. In that case the names of those present are recorded by the clerk and entered in the *Journal of the House,* and absent members have fifteen minutes from the ordering of the call of the House to have their presence recorded. If sufficient excuse is not given for their absence, they may be sent for by officers appointed by the sergeant-at-arms for that purpose and their attendance secured. The House then determines the conditions on which they may be discharged. Members who voluntarily appear are immediately admitted to the House, and they must report their names to the clerk to be entered in the *Journal* as present. At any time after the roll call has been completed, the Speaker may entertain a motion to adjourn, if seconded by a majority of those present as ascertained by actual count by the Speaker. House rules prohibit quorum calls on occasions such as before or during the daily prayer, the administration of the oath of office to the Speaker or any member, the reception of messages from the president or the Senate, or in connection with motions incidental to a call of the House.

## Voting Methods

All votes are decided by a simple majority except for the following cases, which require a two-thirds majority:

1. constitutional amendments
2. veto overrides
3. expulsion of members
4. suspension of the rules
5. consideration of a special resolution, i.e., a rule
6. dispensation of Calendar Wednesday or the call of the Private Calendar

In the House, several votes may be taken on the same question. Normal procedure would be to have a voice, division, and then a recorded vote. In addition, votes on amendments considered in the Committee of the Whole may be retaken when the bill and any amendments adopted in the Committee of the Whole are reported back to the full House. Generally, actions taken in the Committee of the Whole are approved by voice vote, but a separate roll-call vote may be ordered on any adopted amendment.

There are four methods of voting in the House:

1. voice vote, i.e., the chair asks for "ayes" and "nays" orally and decides the outcome on the basis of volume
2. division vote, i.e., the chair asks for "ayes" and "nays" by requesting members to rise, counts them, and announces the result
3. teller vote, i.e., members merely pass between designated "tellers" who count them and announce the results to the chair. Members' names are not recorded in teller votes
4. recorded vote, which is requested by a member, supported by one-fifth of a quorum or twenty-five members in the Committee of the Whole, and has priority over the first three procedures. In a recorded vote, electronic voting machinery is used. Results of recorded votes are printed in the *Congressional Record*.

Automatically recorded votes are also ordered when a member makes a point of order that a quorum is not present on a voice vote. Instead of answering "present," responding members vote for or against the pending question. The votes are taken by electronic device and published in the *Congressional Record*.

Beginning with the 96th Congress the Speaker gained the authority to cluster certain recorded votes. When several bills are considered under suspension of the rules, recorded votes on final passage may be postponed until all bills have been debated. The first vote has the normal fifteen-minute voting period. The time for subsequent votes that follow immediately, i.e., are "clustered," may be reduced to five minutes each.

## Pairing

Pairing is a voting procedure found in both chambers. When a member expects to be absent for a recorded or roll-call vote he/she may "pair off" with another member whose vote would have been on the opposite side of the issue as his/hers, and neither member votes. Pairs are not counted in vote totals, but they are listed at the end of a vote. A member wishing to be paired merely asks the pair clerk of his party to arrange a pair for a certain day or vote.

Pairs may be "live," i.e., one member is present and announces his/her vote but later withdraws it and announces his/her pairing with an absent member. A second form of pairing is the "simple" pair, i.e., two absent members pair on opposite sides of an issue. Examples of live and simple pairs can be seen at the end of a recorded vote when members' names are noted. The last form of pairing is "general," i.e., two absent members pair but do not announce on which side they would have voted. Live, general, and simple pairs do not affect the outcome of a vote. Pairs are gentlemen's agreements that are never broken. If the measure being voted on requires a two-thirds majority, then pairs must be composed of two members on one side of the issue to one on the other side.

## Motion to Reconsider

The vote on the final passage is usually followed by a pro forma motion to reconsider. This motion to reconsider is in turn followed by a motion to lay the motion to reconsider on the table. Once this tabling motion is agreed to, the opportunity to have second thoughts about the bill has passed. This safeguards the bill's passage, since a bill cannot be sent to the other chamber while a motion to reconsider is pending. After the tabling motion is agreed to, an engrossed copy of the bill is certified by the clerk of the House and sent to the Senate.

## Passage in Lieu

Normally one chamber approves a version of a bill that is different from that passed by the other body. The second chamber then must substitute its own version for the text of the bill that passed the other chamber, retaining only the other chamber's bill number. If the Senate has already passed a similar measure, the bill's floor manager in the House may offer a motion to take the Senate bill, delete everything after the enacting clause, and insert the language of the House bill instead. This is referred to as "passage in lieu," and it is done so that one single bill number, incorporating two conflicting versions of the bill, will be sent to conference. It is necessary because only one bill may be sent to conference. If similar bills are being considered in both the House and Senate, the bill that passes one chamber first becomes the legislative vehicle.

### Engrossment

The preparation of a copy of a bill in the form in which it has passed the House is sometimes a detailed and complicated process because of the large number and complexity of amendments that may have been adopted for the purpose of inserting new language, substituting words, or deleting sections. It is not unusual for there to be numerous amendments, including those proposed by the committee at the time the bill is reported and those offered from the floor during consideration. Each amendment must be inserted in precisely the proper place in the bill, with the spelling and punctuation exactly the same as was adopted. It is extremely important that the copy of the bill received by the Senate be in the precise form in which it passed the House. The preparation of such a copy is one of the functions of the enrolling clerk.

There is an enrolling clerk in both the House and Senate. The House clerk receives all the papers relating to a bill, including the official clerk's copy of the bill as reported by the standing committee and each amendment adopted by the House. From this material the clerk prepares the engrossed copy of the bill as passed, containing all the amendments agreed to by the House. At this point the bill is formally termed an act, signifying that it is the act of one chamber, although it is still referred to in general conversation as a bill. The engrossed bill is printed on blue paper and a certificate that it passed the House is signed by the clerk of the House. The engrossed bill is delivered by a reading clerk to the Senate.

# The Legislative Process in the Senate

### Introduction of Bills

In the Senate a legislative day is the period from the time the chamber meets after an adjournment until the time it next adjourns. While legislative day in the House is equivalent to a calendar day, the Senate may stretch a legislative day over several calendar days. What this means is that the Senate does not daily go through all the routines of a legislative day's order of business.

A legislative day begins with the reading and approval of the previous day's *Journal,* which in each chamber is the official record of legislative action. It takes unanimous consent to dispense with the reading of the *Journal.* The Senate's "morning hour" constitutes the first two hours of the legislative day. The following matters are taken up during the morning hour:

1. messages from the president
2. communications from department heads
3. messages from the House of Representatives
4. reports of standing and select committees
5. introduction of bills and resolutions
6. presentation of petitions and memorials

A senator may introduce legislation at any time but must request unanimous consent to do so once the morning hour has been concluded. During the first hour of the two-hour morning period no motion to consider any bill on the calendar is in order except by unanimous consent. During the second hour such motions may be made, but without debate. At the conclusion of the morning hour the Senate moves on to the unfinished legislative business planned by the majority leader in consultation with other Senate leaders. The presiding officer of the Senate refers any engrossed bills from the House to the appropriate standing committee. Such bills are immediately reprinted. This printing is referred to as the "act print" or the "Senate referred print."

## Committee Consideration

Senate committees give a bill the same kind of detailed consideration as House committees and may report it with or without amendment or may table it. A single committee member or a group of members who wish to express their views may file a minority report if they give notice at the time of the approval of the bill.

When a Senate committee reports a bill, it is reprinted with the committee amendments indicated by lined-through type and italics. The calendar number and report number are indicated on the first and back pages, together with the name of the senator making the report. The committee report and any minority views accompanying the bill are printed at the same time. Any senator may enter a motion to discharge a committee from further consideration of a bill that it has failed to report after what is considered a reasonable time. If the motion is agreed to by a majority vote, the committee is discharged and the bill is placed on the calendar of business under the standing rules.

All committee meetings, including hearings, must be open to the public. A majority of the members of a committee or subcommittee may, after discussion in closed session, vote in open session to close a meeting for no longer than fourteen days if it is determined that the matter to be discussed or testimony to be taken will

1. disclose matters in the interests of national defense
2. disclose trade secrets
3. disclose matters required to be kept confidential under provisions of law
4. disclose law enforcement information
5. reflect adversely on the reputation of an individual
6. represent an unwarranted invasion of the privacy of an individual
7. relate solely to internal committee staff management or procedure

### Consideration by the Senate

There are only two calendars in the Senate: the Executive Calendar, for treaties and nominations, and the Calendar of Business, for all legislation. The Senate rule providing for the privileged call of the calendar on Mondays has been disregarded for many years. Legislation normally comes up out of calendar sequence. Theoretically, under the rule any senator can offer a motion to proceed to the consideration of a bill. A simple majority is needed to pass the motion. The motion, which is not debatable during the second hour of the morning hour, is debatable at all other times. For this reason it can be easily blocked.

Controversial legislation is called up off the calendar by unanimous consent. A list of noncontroversial legislation, cleared in advance by the majority leader, is called up when few senators are on the floor and is passed by unanimous consent. Controversial legislation is frequently brought up after a formal unanimous-consent time control agreement has been negotiated by the leadership and the appropriate committee or subcommittee chairman.

There is virtually no requirement in the Senate that amendments be germane to the bill they are appended to. In the case of appropriations bills, they must be germane unless a two-thirds vote decides that this restriction may be suspended. Senators often add nongermane substantive amendments, "riders," onto bills. Sometimes they attach one entire bill onto another as a means of forcing action on a bill. An amendment may be the result of a logrolling agreement between senators. A floor manager may agree to the inclusion of an amendment out of courtesy to another senator, saying that he will take it to conference and knowing that it will die there. If an amendment is accepted by a large majority vote, it is less likely to be dropped in conference.

By parliamentary practice each bill is to receive three readings. The first is to occur at introduction under the Senate rules. The second reading is to come prior to referral, and the third reading just before a final vote on the bill. All readings are usually dispensed with by unanimous consent. A bill passed by the House is then placed directly on the calendar and is subject to normal procedures for being called up. This procedure is used frequently when the Senate is about to consider its version of a House-passed bill and wants to avoid its referral to committee.

## Debate

Debate in the Senate is generally unlimited. Limitations on debate include the following:

1. A motion during the second hour of the morning hour to take up a bill out of calendar order is not debatable.
2. On call of the calendar, each senator may speak on each measure for no more than five minutes.
3. A senator may speak no more than twice on any one question in debate on the same day without leave of the Senate, but because each amendment is considered a separate subject, the rule can be circumvented.

Senators may speak for as long as they like on any subject during consideration of a bill. Senators may not parcel out time to other senators, but they may yield temporarily for consideration of other business.

A filibuster is a tactic used by senators to delay or block action on a bill. A senator or group of senators, once they have gained the floor, can refuse to yield and block the flow of business. A bill can be filibustered after it has been called up for consideration, but the motion to call up a bill can also be filibustered. Thus, every bill may be subject to a filibuster twice. The only way to stop debate and force a time limit on a final vote is to invoke cloture.

Cloture is a petition requiring the signature of sixteen senators, and it must lie over one legislative day. Cloture requires a three-fifths-majority vote of the entire Senate, and the vote comes two days after the petition is filed. A two-thirds-majority vote is required to stop debate on a change in the Senate rules. Once cloture has been invoked, there is a 100-hour limit on debate on the pending bill. Each senator is allotted one hour if he/she chooses to use it.

Senators are also permitted to transfer all or part of their time to the majority or minority leaders or the floor managers of the bill, but no senator can have more than one hour yielded to him/her. The 100-hour limit can only be extended by three-fifths vote of the entire Senate. No amendments are in order except those introduced by 1 p.m. on the day after the cloture petition is filed, and second-degree amendments must be submitted at least an hour before the cloture vote occurs. All amendments at this time must be germane. Limits on debate are frequently imposed through unanimous-consent time control agreements. These can be negotiated prior to a bill's being taken up or after debate has already started. Unanimous-consent time control agreements often specify

1. when a bill will be called up for consideration
2. who will be the floor managers for proponents and opponents
3. how much time will be allocated per amendment
4. that amendments be germane
5. when a final vote on the measure shall occur

## Amendments

Amendments to a bill in the Senate are unlimited, unless limited beforehand by unanimous consent. Committee amendments are taken up first and can be amended to the second degree. Sometimes the Senate by unanimous consent agrees to all the committee amendments so that the amended bill can be considered as an original text. One substitute amendment may be offered at the same time an amendment or an amendment-to-the-amendment is under consideration. The amending process is important to senators on tax bills, since they cannot originate tax bills and can only act on House bills.

There are two kinds of amendments in the Senate, printed and unprinted. Printed amendments are introduced in advance of being offered to a bill and are listed in the *Congressional Record*. They can be introduced weeks before a bill reaches the Senate floor. Unprinted amendments may be drafted on the Senate floor and usually are not available prior to floor consideration. The choice between the two types of amendments is a choice of tactics, the second type incorporating the element of surprise.

## Voting

After action on amendments is completed, a bill is ready for engrossment and the third reading, which is usually dispensed with by unanimous consent. The bill can then be voted on in one of three ways:

1. voice vote
2. division vote
3. roll-call vote, whereby a call vote occurs when one-fifth of those present request it

Only roll-call votes are recorded. A request for a division (standing) vote, when members stand up and are counted, must be seconded, and only the vote totals are recorded.

The Senate, unlike the House, cannot revote except by unanimous consent. Roll-call votes in the *Congressional Record* show the results of pairing. Passage is not final until a senator moves to reconsider the measure and the motion is tabled or voted down. Otherwise the matter could be reopened. A senator who voted with the prevailing side, or one who abstained from voting, may make the motion to reconsider within two days after final passage. If the measure was passed without a recorded vote, any senator could move to reconsider. In the unusual circumstance that a motion to reconsider is granted, the second consideration constitutes a final action.

If the bill originated in the Senate, the Senate sends an engrossed copy to the House, prepared and certified by the secretary of the Senate. If the bill originated in the House, the Senate sends back the original engrossed House bill along with the engrossed Senate amendments and a request that the House concur with them.

# The Final Steps

## The Conference

If the Senate amendments are substantial or controversial, a House member may request unanimous consent to take the bill with the Senate amendments from the Speaker's table, disagree to the amendments, and request a conference with the Senate to resolve the disagreeing votes of the two chambers. If there is objection to such a request, it becomes necessary to obtain a special resolution from the House Rules Committee unless the Speaker recognizes a member for a motion, authorized by the committee having jurisdiction over the subject matter of the bill, to disagree to the amendments and ask for a conference. If there is no objection to the request, or if the motion is carried, the Speaker then appoints the conferees and a message is sent to the Senate advising it of the House action.

The request for a conference can be made only by the chamber in possession of the official papers. Occasionally the Senate, anticipating that the House will not concur in its amendments, votes to insist on its amendments and requests a conference on passage of the bill prior to returning the bill to the House. Several days' time may be saved by the designation of the Senate conferees before the bill is returned to the House. The question of which chamber requests the conference is not without importance, because the chamber asking for the conference acts last on the report to be submitted by the conferees.

## Appointment of Conferees

The Senate rules state that the chamber elects the conferees, but normally, the presiding officer in the Senate appoints them based on the recommendations of the committee chairman. The conferees are approved by unanimous consent. In the House the Speaker has authority to appoint the conferees but also relies on the advice of the committee chairman. The Democratic Caucus Rules require that the Democrat/Republican ratio in the House be reflected in the selection of House members to each conference committee. A listing of the House and Senate conferees can be found in the *Congressional Record* or the House Calendar.

The size of the House and Senate delegations may vary, since each chamber's conferees vote separately. A simple majority of the chamber's conferees decides whether to accept or reject the other chamber's language. Proxy voting is not unusual at this final stage in the legislative process. Normally the House and Senate committee chairpersons alternate roles in presiding over the conference meetings.

## Meetings of Conferees

The meetings of the conferees are traditionally held on the Senate side of the Capitol. In 1977, the House amended its rules to require that conference meetings be open, unless the House in open session determines by a roll-call vote of a majority of those members voting that some or all of the meeting will be closed. When the report of the conference committee is read in the House, a point of order may be made that the conferees did not comply with this requirement. If the point of order is sustained, the conference report is considered rejected by the House and a new conference is requested.

There are generally four forms of recommendations available to the conferees when reporting back to their respective chambers:

1. the Senate recede from all or certain of its amendments
2. the House recede from its disagreement to all or certain of the Senate amendments and agree thereto

3. the House recede from its disagreement to all or certain of the Senate amendments and agree thereto with amendments
4. the House recede from all or certain of its amendments to the Senate amendments

The complete report may be composed of one or all of these recommendations with respect to various amendments. Occasionally the conferees find themselves unable to reach an agreement with respect to one or more amendments and report back a statement of their inability to agree. These amendments may then be acted on separately. If they are unable to reach any agreement, the conferees report that fact to their respective chambers, and the amendments revert to their status previous to the conference. New conferees may be appointed in either or both chambers. The House may also instruct the conferees as to the position they are to take.

After House conferees on any bill or resolution in conference between the two chambers have been appointed for twenty calendar days and have failed to make a report, the House rules provide for an immediate motion to instruct the House conferees or discharge them and appoint new conferees. During the last six days of a session, it is a privileged motion to move to discharge, appoint, or instruct House conferees after the conferees have been appointed thirty-six hours without having made a report.

## Rules

Conferees are limited to action on matters in dispute between the two chambers as stated in the rules. Conferees may not strike out or amend any portion of a bill not amended by the second chamber. No new material may be introduced that is not germane to the differences between the two chambers. (The House rules do not permit any nongermane language.) Changes in dollar amounts contained in the bill must fall between figures previously agreed to by each body.

In reality, rules are often circumvented. It is possible for one chamber to strike all the text after the enacting clause and to substitute its own bill. Consequently the entire bill can be rewritten by the conferees. In the event the House concurs with Senate language that is considered new material or nongermane language, the committee chairman will request a rule for the conference report from the House Rules Committee that waives all points of order so that no member could challenge the conference report on grounds that the House conferees exceeded their authority.

Since the language decided upon by the House and Senate conferees is not subject to floor amendments, added importance is given to the conference deliberations. Besides the need to reach compromises in language that will be acceptable to both chambers, conferees are very much aware of the need to satisfy lobbyists. To complicate matters, conferees on major bills that have progressed slowly through the legislative process and make it to the conference stage late in the second congressional session receive added pressure to get the bills through the system.

## Conference Reports

When the conferees, by majority vote of both the House and Senate groups, have reached complete agreement or find that they are able to agree with respect to some but not all amendments, they write their recommendations in a report that must be signed by a majority of the conferees appointed by each chamber. The conferees in the minority have no authority to file a statement of minority views in connection with the report. The report is required to be printed in both chambers and must be accompanied with an explanatory statement prepared jointly by the conferees. The statement must be detailed enough to inform both chambers as to the effect the amendments contained in the report will have on the bill. The engrossed bill and amendments and one copy of the report are delivered to the body that is to act first on the report, i.e., the chamber that had agreed to the conference requested by the other.

When conference reports are filed in disagreement, usually the House and Senate conferees have reached agreement on the compromise language but the House conferees are precluded from agreeing because they have violated one of the House rules, i.e., those on new material or nongermane amendments. There must be separate votes on those amendments that are in disagreement. If the amendments reported in disagreement cannot be agreed to on the floors of both chambers, then the conference procedure begins anew on the amendments remaining in disagreement. When a conference report is sent back to conference, the entire report is subject to revisions. Amendments and the final conference report must be agreed to in identical form before the bill can be sent to the president.

The presentation of the report in the Senate is always in order except when the *Journal* is being read or a point of order or motion to adjourn is pending, or while the Senate is voting or determining a quorum. The report is not subject to amendment in either chamber and must be accepted or rejected in its entirety. If the time for debate on the adoption of the report is limited, the time allotted must be equally divided between the majority and minority parties. If the Senate, acting first, does not agree to the report, it may by majority vote order it recommitted to the conferees. When the Senate agrees to the report its conferees are thereby discharged and the original papers are delivered to the House of Representatives with a message advising the House of its action.

The presentation of the report in the House of Representatives is always in order except when the *Journal* is being read, while the roll is being called, or when the House is taking a division vote. The report is considered in the House and may not be sent to the Committee of the Whole on the suggestion that it contains matters ordinarily requiring consideration in that committee. It is not in order to consider either a conference report or an amendment proposed by the Senate to a bill reported in disagreement between the two chambers until the third calendar day after the report and accompanying statement have been filed in the House. Consideration then is in order only if the report and accompanying statement have been printed in the daily edition of the *Congressional Record* for the day on which the report and statement were filed. These provisions do not apply during the last six days of the session. Nor is it in order to consider a conference report or such amendment unless copies of the report and accompanying statement, together with the text of the amendment, have been available to members for at least two hours before the beginning of consideration. It is in order to call up for consideration a report from the Rules Committee making in order the consideration of a conference report or such amendment, notwithstanding the latter restriction. The time allotted for debate on a conference report or such amendment is equally divided between the majority and minority parties. If the House does not agree to a conference report that the Senate has already agreed to, the report may not be recommitted to conference because the Senate conferees are discharged when the Senate agrees to the report.

## *Enrollment*

When the bill has been agreed to in identical form by both chambers, either without amendment by the Senate, or by House concurrence in the Senate amendments, or by agreement in both chambers to the conference report, a copy of an enrolled bill, i.e., a final perfect copy, is presented to the president. The preparation of an enrolled bill includes all amendments, either by way of deletion, substitution, or addition, agreed to by both chambers. The enrolling clerk of the House receives the original engrossed bill, the engrossed Senate amendments, the signed conference report, messages from the Senate, and a notation of the final action by the House for the purpose of preparing the enrolled copy. From these he must prepare the final form of the bill, as it was agreed to by both chambers, for presentation to the president.

The enrolled bill is printed on parchment paper, with a certificate on the reverse side of the last page, to be signed by the clerk of the House if the bill originated in the House of Representatives, or by the secretary of the Senate if it originated in the Senate. The enrolled bill is examined for accuracy by the Committee on House Administration or by the secretary of the Senate. When the House committee is satisfied with the accuracy of the bill, the chairman of the committee attaches a slip stating that the committee finds the bill truly enrolled and sends it to the Speaker of the House for his signature. All bills are signed first by the Speaker and then by the president of the Senate. The Speaker and the president of the Senate may sign bills only while their respective chamber is sitting unless advance permission is granted to sign during recess or after adjournment. After both signatures are affixed, the bill is ready for presentation to the president.

## Presidential Action

In the case of most major bills, the White House has been closely monitoring them from the time of their introduction through the conference committee process. Once the original enrolled bill is delivered to the White House, the president has ten days (not including Sundays) to act. To approve legislation, the president signs the bill, usually writing "approved" and the date. The bill becomes law the day it is signed unless specified otherwise in the act. When Congress is in session, the bill becomes law if the president takes no action within ten days. The pocket veto can be used only during final adjournment at the end of a Congress. The bill dies when the president does not sign the bill and does not register his objections. To veto a bill, the president returns it to the chamber of origin, accompanied by his veto message stating his objections. The president's veto covers the entire bill and cannot be confined to separate items within a bill.

## Congressional Reaction to a Vetoed Bill

A vetoed bill and the accompanying message are returned to the chamber where the bill originated. A veto override is a privileged matter and can be considered on the floor immediately. Action may be delayed because of efforts to secure the necessary votes. If there is not enough support for a vote to override a veto, the vetoed bill will usually be referred to a committee and there will be no immediate floor action. If the veto is successfully overridden by the first chamber, the second chamber then considers the bill by identical procedure. If the president's veto is sustained, the bill dies. When both chambers vote to override a veto, the bill becomes law notwithstanding the objections of the president.

## Publication of the Law

Each law is assigned a public law number. Public law numbers run in sequence starting at the beginning of each Congress: P.L. 100-1 would be the first public law enacted in the 100th Congress. The statute is first published as a "slip law." A slip law contains a brief legislative history of a law, i.e., committee report, references in the *Congressional Record*, and dates of floor consideration. Finally, the law is sent to the Statutes Branch of the National Archives in the General Services Administration and is placed in the *United States Statutes at Large* and the *United States Code*.

# SUMMARY

To sum up, the following minimal outline traces a bill as it passes through Congress:

1. A bill is introduced by a member or members of Congress either in the House or the Senate.
2. The bill is assigned a number and referred to the committee or committees having jurisdiction over the legislation.
3. The bill is either considered by the committee or refused further study. While in committee the bill may be amended or even entirely rewritten. Additionally, hearings may be held concerning the ramifications of the bill.
4. A committee mark-up is scheduled and the bill is analyzed.
5. After deliberation by the committee, the bill is referred to the chamber calendar. Bills favorably recommended by a committee are accompanied by a report.
6. The terms of floor consideration are framed and approved.
7. The bill is submitted to the floor of the chamber for possible debate on the merits of the legislation. In the House, legislation is brought up on the floor by privileged status or by adoption of a rule by the Rules Committee; in the Senate, by negotiation or unanimous consent.
8. If the bill is passed it is then sent to the other chamber for consideration. Much legislation, however, starts as similar bills in both houses.
9. The bill undergoes the same process as in the original chamber in which it was introduced (steps 1–7).
10. If the House and Senate versions of the bill differ, the bill is sent into

conference, where a compromise is hammered out and amendments
are agreed to.
11. A conference report is drafted.
12. The conference report is debated by each chamber and approved.
13. The president either signs the bill into law or he vetoes it. The
    president has ten days (Sundays excluded) to act upon a bill; if the
    president does not act within ten days, the bill becomes law without
    his signature, providing Congress is in session. If Congress adjourns
    before the ten-day limit, the bill does not become law; this is what is
    referred to as a "pocket veto."

# SOURCES RELEVANT TO THE LEGISLATIVE PROCESS

While there is no easy way to become adept at legislative tracing, one way to
make tracing easier is to recognize the relationship between the steps of the
legislative process and ensuing congressional publications. For each level in
the legislative process, corresponding publications may exist. For example,
when a committee holds hearings, the researcher must try to ascertain if the
proceedings were published.

Table 1 (see p. 239) presents legislative steps and the publications that
may result from each congressional activity. After becoming familiar with
the essential steps in the legislative process, the researcher can start to
examine in more detail the precise pathways by which bills journey through
Congress. The researcher can then learn through actual tracing some of the
variations that may occur in the course of the legislative process.

For additional information, several good sources provide extended treat-
ments and rich background material.

Congressional Quarterly. *Guide to Congress*. 3rd ed. Washington, DC:
Congressional Quarterly, 1982.

Cummings, Frank. *Capitol Hill Manual*. 2d ed. Washington, DC: Bureau of
National Affairs, 1984.

Oleszek, Walter. *Congressional Procedures and the Policy Process*. 2d ed.
Washington, DC: Congressional Quarterly, 1984.

Ripley, Randall. *Congress: Process and Policy*. 3rd ed. New York: Norton,
1983.

Willett, Edward F. *How Our Laws Are Made*. Rev. ed. Washington, DC: U.S. Government Printing Office, 1986.

The parliamentary procedures used in the House and the Senate can be found in publications on rules and the compilations of prior decisions published by each body. For the Senate, these sources comprise the following:

U.S. Congress. Senate. Committee on Rules and Administration. *Senate Manual Containing the Standing Rules, Orders, Laws and Resolutions Affecting the Business of the United States Senate*. Washington, DC: U.S. Government Printing Office, 1967– . [Revised biennially]

U.S. Congress. Senate. *Senate Procedure: Precedents and Practices*. Washington, DC: U.S. Government Printing Office, 1977.

For the House, these sources include

U.S. Congress. House. *Constitution, Jefferson's Manual and the Rules of the House of Representatives*. Washington, DC: U.S. Government Printing Office, 1797– . [Revised biennially]

Deschler, Lewis. *Deschler's Precedents of the United States House of Representatives: Including References to Provisions of the Constitution and Laws, and to Decisions of the Courts*. U.S. Congress. H. Doc. 94-661. 1977– .

Deschler, Lewis. *Procedure in the United States House of Representatives. 97th Congress: A Summary of the Modern Precedents and Practices of the House. 86th–97th Congress*. Washington, DC: U.S. Government Printing Office, 1982.

*Procedure in the U.S. House of Representatives, 1985 Supplement: Annotations of the Precedents of the House for the 97th and 98th Congresses*. Prepared by the Office of the Parliamentarian, U.S. House of Representatives. Washington, DC: U.S. Government Printing Office, 1986.

Hinds, Asher C. *Hinds' Precedents of the House of Representatives of the United States, including Reference to Provisions of the Constitution, the Laws, and Decisions of the United States Senate*. Washington, DC: U.S. Government Printing Office, 1907, vols. I–V.

Cannon, Clarence. *Cannon's Precedents of the House of Representatives of the United States, including Reference to Provisions of the Constitution, the*

*Laws and Decisions of the United States Senate.* Washington, DC: U.S. Government Printing Office, 1935–1941, vols. VI–XI.

Almost every textbook on American government will have a chapter on the Congress and a section on how a bill becomes a law.

# Congressional Publications

Before one can begin to trace legislation, it is essential to become well versed in the terminology one will encounter. Congress publishes a copious amount of material, much more than just bills and laws. Included among the different kinds of works are directories, manuals, and legislative calendars. Publications initiated by Congress can be products either of Congress as a whole or of a particular committee or subcommittee. From the standpoint of legislative tracing, the publications directly resulting from the legislative process are the most significant. They are the documents that accrue as a bill passes through Congress.

## Bills

Bills are the form used for most legislation, whether permanent or temporary, general or specific, public or private. They may originate in either chamber, except for revenue-raising bills, which must be introduced in the House. Appropriations bills, by convention, all originate in the House. The numbers of bills introduced in the House are prefixed with "H.R.," and in the Senate, "S." Bills are numbered consecutively as they are introduced from the beginning of each two-year congressional term.

## Joint Resolutions

Joint resolutions are designated "H.J.Res." or "S.J.Res." In reality there is little difference between a bill and a joint resolution, as a joint resolution goes through the same procedure as a bill and has the force of law. Joint resolutions differ from bills in that they are usually introduced to deal with limited matters, e.g., a single appropriation. Like a bill, a joint resolution requires the approval of both houses and the signature of the president, except when it is used to propose an amendment to the Constitution.

## Resolutions

Resolutions are designated "H.Res." or "S.Res." Often resolutions are referred to as "simple resolutions," in contrast to joint resolutions. Resolutions concern only the business of a single house, e.g., the creation and appointment of committees or the instigation of a special investigation. For the most part resolutions deal with the rules of a house or are used to express the sentiments of a house. Resolutions have no legislative effect outside the house in which they originate. Resolutions become operative upon passage by that house and do not require approval by the other house or the signature of the president.

## Concurrent Resolutions

Concurrent resolutions are designated "H.Con.Res." or "S.Con.Res." They are used for matters affecting the business of both houses. Unlike a bill or joint resolution, they do not require the signature of the president. Like simple resolutions, concurrent resolutions do not have the effect of law.

## Hearings

Hearings contain the oral testimony and written materials submitted to committees of Congress in public sessions designated for hearing witnesses. Witnesses before hearings include specialists, experts, important government officials, prominent private citizens, and spokesmen for organizations and groups that may be affected by the bills under consideration. Hearings are designated by an alphanumeric notation known as the SuDocs (Superintendent of Documents) class number.

## Committee Prints

Committee prints are documents requested by committees and compiled by their research staffs, outside consultants, or the Congressional Research Service. Committee prints are authorized by a particular committee at the time of a hearing. Used for background information in consideration of a bill, committee prints are often of a technical or research nature. They often give the summation of staff findings, histories of previous legislation and congressional efforts, and the implications of the bill should it pass. Committee prints are also given a SuDocs classification number. Not all committee prints are offered to the depository libraries or are for sale by the superintendent of documents. Often one has to request the print directly from the committee or by writing to one's congressman. To say the least, the distribution of committee prints is quite unpredictable. As committee prints are usually printed in a limited quantity, it is sometimes difficult to obtain them.

## Reports

Reports are designated "H.Rept." or "S.Rept." At the time a committee sends a bill to the floor, a written report containing the justification for its action accompanies the bill. The report denotes the scope and purpose of the bill and includes any amendments or written communications submitted by departments or agencies of the executive branch. A report favors the passage of a bill, whereas a committee does not report its recommendations when it disapproves of a bill. As a noun, "report" refers to the actual document. As a verb, "report" refers to the process, as in "reporting a bill," i.e., submitting the committee's findings and recommendations to the parent chamber. It should be emphasized that reports are an extremely important element in legislative tracing, for they provide an explanation of a bill's intent and aim.

## Proceedings

Proceedings are the printed record of the daily debates, statements, and actions taken by each house. The *Congressional Record* is the printed account of the proceedings of both the House and Senate. There are also separate *Journals* for the House and Senate, which are the printed proceedings for each house. The *Journals* are published at the end of each session.

## Conference Reports

If the two chambers cannot agree on the provisions of a bill, conferees appointed by the House and Senate work to resolve conflicts between different versions of the bill and hammer out a compromise. When the conferees have harmonized the House and Senate versions of the bill, a conference report is prepared. The compromise bill must then be approved by each house before it is sent to the president. Conference reports use the imprint of the chamber where the bill originated, e.g., H.R.1234.

## Slip Laws

When a bill has been enacted into law it is first officially published as a slip law, i.e., a separately published law in unbound single-sheet or pamphlet form. Once a bill has received presidential approval it takes two or three days for the slip law to become available.

## United States Statutes at Large

*United States Statutes at Large* is a chronological arrangement of all the laws enacted by Congress in each session. While the laws are not arranged by subject matter, they are indexed.

## United States Code

The general and permanent laws of the United States are consolidated and codified under fifty titles in the *United States Code*. The titles are arranged by subject, the first six titles dealing with general subjects and the remaining forty-four titles arranged alphabetically by broad subject area. Every six years the code is revised, and after each session of Congress a supplement is issued.

## Presidential Messages

When a president signs or vetoes a piece of legislation, he usually issues a brief statement concerning its value or deficiencies. During the time a bill is proceeding through Congress, the president may also make statements concerning the merits of the bill or criticizing Congress for its handling of the bill.

The next step is learning how to recognize the publications that relate to a particular bill. Specific "handles" help in identifying documents. For example, the designation H.R.16373 enables one to isolate a single bill. Reports will have report numbers, i.e., H.Rept.93-1416. Laws will have public law numbers, i.e., PL93-579. Congressional hearings and prints, as well as documents from executive departments and agencies, will have SuDocs numbers. Getting the SuDocs number is like getting the call number for a book.

Table 2 (see p. 240) provides an example of a legislative profile of the sort a researcher should strive to construct. When actually tracing legislation, it may prove useful to draw up a work sheet similar to Table 2 to record the history of a law. Another form one could use is Table 3 (see pp. 241–45). This form includes all the basic information one needs to gather. The cover sheets of actual documents are reproduced in Figures 1–10.

# Compiling a Legislative History

We have seen how a bill passes through Congress and the publications that result from the sequence. What has not yet been covered are the tools that are used to trace the course of a bill through Congress and to identify what publications exist. There are numerous such tools, some published by the federal government and others produced by private commercial companies. In this section these resources will be briefly described. The concise annotations provided do not really do justice to these publications, for many of them are very complex. The intent of this section is not to provide elaborate instructions for their use, but only to acquaint the user with their existence and purpose. It should be stressed once again that the best way to gain full knowledge and command of these tools is through repeated use. At the end of this section the reader will be presented with a detailed outline of how to trace legislation utilizing these bibliographic guides.

When using the tools it is important to keep in mind the distinction between guides to legislative action and guides to printed publications. A guide to legislative action allows the user to reconstruct a history of a bill's passage through Congress, i.e., to find the date it was introduced, referred to committee, reported to the chamber, voted upon, etc. Guides to printed publications enable the user to identify the proper citations necessary for finding the documents related to the bill being researched. This distinction is largely a conceptual one, for many tools do both. The *Congressional Record* is both a guide to legislative action and an index to the floor proceedings it contains. The distinction is useful, however, for it reminds the user of the procedure of first tracing the steps of a law and then finding specific citations to publications.

## Guides to the Legislative Process

### Periodicals and Indexes

The following resources are listed in approximate order of usefulness in terms of how a bill proceeds through Congress.

*Bibliographic Guide to Government Publications: U.S.* Boston: G.K. Hall, 1976– .
This guide lists documents cataloged by the Research Libraries of the New York Public Libraries and by the Library of Congress. The annual editions serve as supplements to the *Catalog of Government Publications of the Research Libraries of the New York Public Libraries* (40 vols. Boston: G.K. Hall, 1972).

*Public Affairs Information Service Bulletin.* New York: The Service, 1975– .

A subject guide to American politics in general, indexing government publications, books, and periodical literature. It includes citations to many hearings, and it indexes the *National Journal, CQ Weekly Report, Congressional Digest* and, selectively, the *Weekly Compilation of Presidential Documents.* All of these journals are invaluable guides to legislative action on a current basis. A fifteen-volume *Cumulative Subject Index to the PAIS Annual Bulletins* covers the years 1915–1974. *PAIS* is cumulated quarterly and annually.

*Congressional Index.* Washington, DC: Commerce Clearing House, 1937/38– .

This weekly publication indexes congressional bills and resolutions and lists their current status. The index is designed to enable the user to follow the progress of legislation from initial introduction to final disposition. It contains a section on voting records in which all roll-call votes are reported. The guide provides a sequential history of legislation and is a good tool for following a bill through Congress. Vetoes and subsequent congressional actions are recorded.

*Digest of Public General Bills and Resolutions.* U.S. Library of Congress, Congressional Research Service. Washington, DC: U.S. Government Printing Office, 1935– .

This is normally published each session in five cumulative issues with biweekly supplements. It provides a brief synopsis of public bills and resolutions and records the introduction of a bill or resolution, committee it was referred to, and last action taken. Arrangement is by bill number, with a subject index.

*Congressional Record: Proceedings and Debates of the Congress.* Washington, DC: U.S. Government Printing Office, 1873– .

This is a daily record of the proceedings of Congress, including a history of legislation. It consists of four sections: (1) proceedings of the House, (2) proceedings of the Senate, (3) extensions, i.e., written submissions, and remarks, and (4) the *Daily Digest* of the activities of Congress. The proceedings are indexed by subject and name. The "History of Bills and Resolutions" section is arranged by bill and resolution number. While the *Congressional Record* provides a sequential history, it does not provide as much information as the *Congressional Index.* Consequently, the *Index* is often easier to use. The *Congressional Record* is important for finding roll-call votes and congressional action on vetoed bills. The *Record* is not a literal transcription of the floor debates. Legislators or their staff have a chance to edit it before it goes into print, and again before it goes into the bound volumes. Therefore the daily edition is more accurate than the bound volume. Normally this distinction makes little difference, but in hard-fought debates, as in final passage of legislation, there may be considerable editing. Prior to the publication of the *Congressional Record,* the floor proceedings were published in the *Annals of Congress, Register of Debates in Congress,* and the *Congressional Globe.*

*House Journal.* U.S. Congress. Washington, DC: U.S. Government Printing Office, 1789– .

*Senate Journal.* U.S. Congress. Washington, DC: U.S. Government Printing Office, 1789– .
  These are the official minutes of each chamber of Congress, published at the end of a session. Both *Journals* have a "History of Bills and Resolutions," in which legislative actions are arranged by number, title, and action. The two *Journals* each have a name, subject, and title index.

*Calendars of the United States House of Representatives and History of Legislation.* U.S. Congress. Washington, DC: U.S. Government Printing Office, 1951– .
  The *Calendar* is published daily when the House is in session, with each issue being cumulative. Each Monday there is a subject index to all legislative action to date in both the House and Senate. House and Senate bills passed or pending are arranged numerically in a table. Because this series is cumulative it is a useful guide to legislative action.

*Congress in Print.* Washington, DC: Congressional Quarterly, 1969– .
  This tool lists the publications of the congressional committees as they come into print. It lists hearings, reports, prints, staff studies, calendars, etc.

*Congressional Monitor.* Washington, DC: Congressional Quarterly, 1965– .
  The *Congressional Monitor* is published each day Congress is in session. Each issue of the *Monitor* lists committee actions and witnesses scheduled for the day. A "Weekly Legislative Status Report" is issued every Friday, and bills are indexed by bill number. This is the fastest reporting service covering congressional action. Congressional Quarterly also publishes *Congress in Print: A Weekly Alert to Just-Released Committee Hearings, Prints and Staff Studies,* which provides an up-to-the-minute listing of new publications, including Congressional Budget Office and General Accounting Office reports.

*Congressional Record Scanner.* Washington, DC: Congressional Quarterly.
    This daily publication abstracts and reorganizes the *Congressional Record* for easy reading. It is easier to use than the *Congressional Record* in most cases.

*CIS/Index: Congressional Information Service/Index to Publications of the United States Congress.* Washington, DC: Congressional Information Service, 1970– .
    This is an inclusive monthly index to all congressional publications. It abstracts all forms of publications emanating from the legislative process. Materials are indexed by subject, names, committees, bill numbers, report numbers, document numbers, and names of committee chairmen. Because *CIS/Index* abstracts reports, hearings, and other congressional documents, the researcher can save valuable time by reading the synopses of publications. For most researchers, *CIS/Index* should be the first place to look when tracing legislation. There are quarterly cumulative indexes, and at the end of the year the *CIS/Annual* is issued. There is also the *CIS Five-Year Cumulative Index 1970–1974, CIS Four-Year Cumulative Index 1975–1978, CIS Four-Year Cumulative Index 1979–1982,* and *CIS Four-Year Cumulative Index 1983–1986.* A guide to using *CIS/Index* and *Abstracts,* the *CIS/Index User Handbook,* is available in most libraries that subscribe to *CIS/Index* or can be obtained from the Congressional Information Service. A *CIS/Index* database is also available on-line through ORBIT (System Development Corporation) for computer searching.

*CIS U.S. Congressional Committee Prints Index: From the Earliest Publications through 1969.* Bethesda, MD: Congressional Information Service, 1980.
    This index covers an estimated 15,000 committee prints issued during the period 1830 through 1969. The index provides complete bibliographic data for each print and a detailed index of names and subjects, including individual names, names of organizations, names of bills and laws, and issuing committees.

*CIS Index to Unpublished U.S. Senate Committee Hearings: 8th Congress—88th Congress 1823–1964.* 5 vols. Bethesda, MD: Congressional Information Service, 1986.
    This index covers 7,000 transcripts issued during the period 1824 through 1964. The index provides complete bibliographic data for each hearing plus three indexes. There is an Index by Bill Numbers and Titles. The Index by Personal Name lists individuals who testified, who were the subject of testimony, or who submitted papers. The Index of Subjects and Organiza-

tions provides access to information by subject or policy area, including the names of committees, laws, and organizations.

*CIS U.S. Congressional Committee Hearings Index.* 42 vols. Bethesda, MD: Congressional Information Service, 1981.

This index covers more than 40,000 titles published during the period from 1833 to 1969. The index provides complete bibliographic data as well as a list of witnesses, their affiliations, page location of testimony, and subject descriptors. There are six indexes: Index by Personal Name, Index by Subjects and Organizations, Index by Titles, Index by Bill Numbers, Index by Superintendent of Documents Number, and Index by Report and Documents Number. CIS has also published a *CIS U.S. Congressional Hearings Index 1833–1969 User Handbook.*

*Monthly Catalog of United States Government Publications.* Washington, DC; U.S. Government Printing Office, 1895– .

This is an important index for identifying many congressional publications. It is especially useful for finding committee hearings and reports. The *Monthly Catalog* has a subject index as well as an index arranged by government author. Carrollton Press has published a *Cumulative Subject Index to the Monthly Catalog of U.S. Government Publications, 1900–1971.*

*GPO Sales Publication Reference File.* Washington, DC: U.S. Government Printing Office, 1977– .

The *Publication Reference File* is a "document in print," for it catalogs all federal publications currently sold by the Superintendent of Documents. Documents are arranged by subjects, titles, agency, series and report numbers, key words, authors, stock numbers, and SuDocs classification numbers. The *PRF* is issued on 48X microfiche and is available to depository libraries. The *PRF* is easy to use and is the first place to look to identify new or recent documents.

*Cumulative Index of Congressional Committee Hearings.* Washington, DC: U.S. Government Printing Office, 1935– .

The *Cumulative Index* and its supplements can be used for tracing hearings prior to the publication of *CIS/Index.* The *Cumulative Index* provides access by bill number, subject, and committee. Greenwood Press has published on microfiche a *Witness Index to the United States Congressional Hearings 25th–89th Congress (1839–1966).*

*United States Code Congressional and Administrative News.* St. Paul, MN: West Publishing Company, 1939– .

This monthly service reprints the full text of all public laws and reproduces the *U.S. Statutes at Large*. The service also includes selected presidential messages, executive orders, and proclamations, listed by number, date and subject. It also reprints selected House and Senate documents. In addition it provides information on the status of legislation, contained in seven tables. One of the tables provides a complete legislative history of all bills passed into law. As the series is cumulative, it is an excellent tool for legislative tracing.

*Weekly Compilation of Presidential Documents*. Washington, DC: U.S. Government Printing Office, 1965– .
Published every Monday, this compilation covers the preceding week. It is an up-to-date source of information, including the full text of messages, speeches, press conferences, executive orders, and statements made by the president. All bills signed or vetoed are listed. A cumulative index is published with each issue.

*Public Papers of the Presidents of the United States*. Washington, DC: U.S. National Archives and Records Administration, 1958– .
Published annually, the text of the volumes includes oral and written statements of the president. Materials are selected from communications to Congress, public speeches, press conferences, public letters, messages to heads of state, and executive documents. Since this series is edited, there are some discrepancies between the *Public Papers* and *Weekly Compilation of Presidential Documents*. KTO Press has published *The Cumulated Indexes to the Public Papers of the Presidents*. At present the five-volume set spans the Truman to Carter presidencies. KTO Press expects to issue volumes as each president's administration is completed. Besides containing the texts of documents, each volume indexes the complete public papers of a presidential administration. Formerly it was necessary to use each individual volume of *The Public Papers of the Presidents of the United States*.

*Presidential Vetoes: List of Bills Vetoed and Action Taken Thereon by the Senate and House of Representatives, 1789–1976*. Washington, DC: U.S. Government Printing Office, 1978.

*Presidential Vetoes, 1977–1984*. Washington, DC: U.S. Government Printing Office, 1985.
These handy reference works list vetoes chronologically by congressional session and presidential administration. The vetoes are entered by bill number and include the citation to the *Congressional Record* where the message is printed.

*United States Statutes at Large: Containing the Laws and Concurrent Resolutions Enacted* . . . Washington, DC: U.S. Government Printing Office, 1789– .

The *Statutes at Large* is a record of all laws published in their final form, giving the full text of congressional acts and resolutions passed during a congressional session. Slip laws, i.e., the texts of individual acts, are published separately as they are passed. Slip laws contain legislative histories on the inside back cover and are indexed in the *U.S. Monthly Catalog*. Since 1963 the *Statutes at Large* has contained a section entitled "Guide to Legislative History of Bills Enacted into Public Law."

*United States Code.* Washington, DC: U.S. Government Printing Office, 1926– .

The *Code* is a compilation of all federal laws in force. The laws are arranged by subject under fifty "titles." The index volume contains a table of all title and chapter headings and a subject index to all sections. The Office of the Federal Register has published two useful guides, *How to Find U.S. Statutes and U.S. Code Citations* and *The Federal Register: What It Is and How to Use It; A Guide for the User of the Federal Register–Code of Federal Regulations System,* which are helpful for learning how to use the *Statutes* and *Code.*

Johnson, Nancy P., comp. *Sources of Compiled Legislative Histories: A Bibliography of Government Documents, Periodical Articles, and Books.* Littleton, CO: Fred B. Rothman, 1979.

This looseleaf volume and supplements includes major legislative histories from the First to the Ninety-sixth Congresses. There are histories arranged by topic and author, and title and act indexes.

*Federal Register.* Washington, DC: U.S. National Archives and Records Service, 1936– .

*Code of Federal Regulations.* Washington, DC: U.S. National Archives and Records Service, 1949– .

These include executive orders, reorganization plans, and presidential proclamations of legal significance. *Title 3, CFR* is a compilation of presidential documents.

*Congressional Quarterly Weekly Report.* Washington, DC: Congressional Quarterly, 1946– .

This weekly journal provides an excellent summary of what happened last week in Congress.

*National Journal.* Washington, DC: Government Research Corporation, 1980– .

This weekly journal is essential for background information and analysis of policy issues in both the Congress and the executive branch.

## Other Resources

**American Enterprise Institute Legislative Analyses.** This series of analytical reports published by the American Enterprise Institute provides background information on current bills before Congress. These reports cover all major legislation, including topics such as deregulation, campaign finance reform, unemployment, etc.

**Committee Calendars.** These calendars list committee and subcommittee membership, committee publications, legislation referred to the committee, and any action taken on it. These calendars also list the legislative jurisdiction of the committee and its subcommittees and the committee rules. Some committee jurisdictions and rules are published in separate committee prints.

**Informal Congressional Groups.** Several informal groups have regular publications. The most useful are the Democratic Study Group's *Legislative Report,* the Environmental Study Conference's *Weekly Bulletin,* and the House Republican Conference's *Legislative Digest.* For more information on informal groups, see Chapter 8, pp. 179–80.

**Support Agencies.** The Congressional Budget Office, Office of Technology Assessment, Congressional Research Service, and General Accounting Office often publish studies that may be in response to legislation. (See Chapter 5.)

## Legislative Tracing

Not until one has compiled several legislative histories will one feel confident of knowing the best strategy to use for tracing a bill through Congress. Often a researcher is not sure where to start or becomes lost somewhere in the process. The following outline is designed as a guide through legislative tracing step by step. It should be emphasized that the key to legislative tracing is obtaining a bill or statute number. With one of these numbers it is relatively easy to compile a legislative history and identify all of the relevant documents. The other major way of tracing legislation is by subject. But again, it is sometimes best to isolate a group of bills on a particular subject and trace the bills by their numbers.

Getting the bill or statute number is not difficult. Because most of the guides to legislative action are indexed in a variety of ways (names of individuals, committees, report numbers, etc.), a single piece of information about a bill or law can be used to identify its number. Knowing who introduced a bill or to which committee it was referred can lead to the bill or statute number through use of a name index or committee index. If no specific information about a bill or law is known, it becomes necessary to use a subject approach. The subject indexing in the guides is quite good. Even if one has only a general knowledge of the substance of a bill or statute, a subject index will lead to its number.

## Tracing Outline

These are the steps to follow in tracing a bill through Congress.

If the bill has been passed into law, get the statute number and go to any of the following indexes to get the legislative history:

*Congressional Quarterly Almanac* or *CQ Weekly Report*
*CIS/Annual*—"Index of Bill, Report and Document Numbers"
*U.S. Code Congressional and Administrative News* —"Table of Legislative History"
*Congressional Record, Daily Digest*—"History of Bills Enacted into Law"
*Congressional Index*—"Bill Status Table"
*Digest of Public General Bills and Resolutions*—"Public Law Listing"
*Federal Index*—"Calendar of Legislation"
*Calendars of the United States House of Representatives and History of Legislation*—"Index Key and History of Bill"
*U.S. Code Annotated*—"Annotations and Legislative History"
*U.S. Code Service*—"Annotations and Legislative History"
*House Journal*—"History of Bills and Resolutions"
*Senate Journal*—"History of Bills and Resolutions"
*Slip Law*—"Legislative History"

If a bill is still in Congress, get the bill number and go to the following guides to determine the present status of the bill:

*Congressional Quarterly Weekly Report*
*Congressional Index*—"Bill Status Tables"
*Digest of Public General Bills and Resolutions*—"Synopsis of Bills"
*Congressional Record*—"History of Bills and Resolutions"
*Congressional Record, Daily Digest*—"Subject Index of Bills Acted Upon"
*CIS/Index*—"Index of Bill, Report and Document Numbers"

*Calendars of the United States House of Representatives and History of Legislation*— "Index Key and History of Bill"
*U.S. Code Congressional and Administrative News*— "Public Laws Table"
*Federal Index*— "Calendar of Legislation"

If the bill number or statute number is not known, go to the subject, author, or other category indexes in the following guides to determine the bill number or statute number:

*CIS/Index*
*CQ Weekly Report* or *CQ Almanac*
*Congressional Index*
*Congressional Record*
*Calendars of the United States House of Representatives and History of Legislation*
*Digest of Public General Bills and Resolutions*
*Statutes at Large*
*U.S. Code and Administrative News*

Follow the bill through Congress, recording which actions transpired and which publications were issued. Committee activities and publications, hearings, and prints can be traced through

*CIS/Index*
*CQ Weekly Report*
*Congressional Monitor*
*Congress in Print*
*Cumulated Index of Congressional Committee Hearings*
*Monthly Catalog of U.S. Government Publications*
*PAIS*
*CIS U.S. Congressional Committee Prints Index*
*CIS Index to Unpublished U.S. Senate Committee Hearings*
*CIS U.S. Congressional Committee Hearings Index*

House, Senate, and conference committee reports can be traced through

*CIS/Index*
*CQ Weekly Report*
*Congressional Index*
*Congressional Monitor*
*Calendars of the United States House of Representatives and History of Legislation*

*Congressional Record*
*Monthly Catalog of U.S. Government Publications*
*U.S. Code Congressional and Administrative News*

Floor proceedings and debates can be followed through

*CIS/Index*
*Congressional Record*
*CQ Weekly Report*
*Congressional Monitor*
*Congressional Record Scanner*
*Federal Index*

Roll-call votes are recorded in

*CIS/Index*
*CQ Almanac*
*CQ Weekly Report*
*Congressional Roll Call*
*Congressional Record*
*Congressional Index*
*Federal Index*
*House Journal*
*Senate Journal*

Presidential statements are printed or indexed in

*CIS/Index*
*CQ Weekly Report*
*Federal Index*
*Weekly Compilation of Presidential Documents*
*Public Papers of the President of the United States*
*Cumulated Index to the Public Papers of the Presidents*

Slip law approval is recorded in

*CIS/Index*
*CQ Weekly Report*
*National Journal*
*Congressional Record*
*Congressional Index*
*Calendars of the United States House of Representatives and History of
    Legislation*

*U.S. Code Congressional and Administrative News*
*Congressional Monitor*

Laws are printed in

*U.S. Code Congressional and Administrative News*
*Statutes at Large*
*United States Code*

Veto messages are referenced in

*CIS/Index*
*CQ Weekly Report*
*Congressional Record*
*Calendars of the United States House of Representatives and History of
    Legislation*
*Weekly Compilation of Presidential Documents*
*Monthly Catalog of U.S. Government Publications*

Congressional votes on vetoes are recorded in

*CQ Almanac*
*CQ Weekly Report*
*Congressional Record*
*Congressional Index*
*Congressional Roll Call*

For analysis and commentary on bills as they pass through Congress,
proceed to

*CQ Weekly Report*
*National Journal*
*Washington Post*
*New York Times*
*Major Legislation of the Congress*

## Elements of a Legislative History

A complete legislative history would include the following:

1. A history of related legislative activities and publications both prior
   and subsequent to the bill in question. This information is useful in
   charting changes in social trends and congressional attitudes.

2. A chronological account of how a bill is passed through Congress, including dates, committees, actions taken, and votes.
3. An examination of documents relating to the passage of a bill, including
   a. Executive communications
   b. House calendar
   c. Bill as introduced in the House
   d. Hearings
   e. Bill as reported by House committee
   f. House committee report
   g. House debate
   h. Legislation as passed by the House
   i. Senate committee report
   j. Senate debate
   k. Senate floor amendments
   l. Senate-passed version of the legislation
   m. Conference committee print
   n. Conference committee report as filed in the Senate
   o. Conference committee report
   p. Slip law
   q. Presidential messages
4. Materials and recommendations made by executive departments concerning the bill.
5. Materials and recommendations made by special interest groups participating in the legislative process.
6. Any relevant court cases and decisions that relate to the interpretation of the law.
7. Useful secondary analysis and histories.

Table 4 (see pp. 246–52) provides a detailed information checklist that can be used to remember what should be looked for as a bill goes through Congress, though not all the information will be needed for each tracing. The table also contains a sample vote tally sheet. Two more tables show at a glance where to look to find the status of a bill (Table 5; see p. 253) and a legislative history (Table 6; see p. 254).

## Committee Membership

One of the most frequently asked questions is what committees a particular member of Congress sits on or what the membership of a committee is. The problem is not that it is difficult to find the information but that it may be inaccurate. Committee and subcommittee assignments change, even within a congressional session. While the information available in a particular source may have been accurate at the time it was printed, the membership of a committee could have subsequently changed.

The best source for identifying who sits on a committee and how many committees a member of Congress belongs to is Congressional Quarterly's *100th Congress Committees*. This volume lists every committee's members, majority and minority staff directors, phone numbers, hearing rooms, and responsibilities. It also provides each member's office and phone number and committee assignments. Unfortunately, this series only starts with the 99th Congress. For committee assignments in the past one can use the *CQ Weekly Report* or the *Almanac of American Politics, Congressional Staff Directory, Congressional Yellow Book, Official Congressional Directory,* or *Politics in America*. Most standing committees periodically issue cumulative calendars that provide the names of committee members.

The directories listed above are discussed in more detail in Chapter 7. In addition to the above sources, two other sources related to committees are extremely useful:

Stubbs, Walter, comp. *Congressional Committees, 1789–1982: A Checklist.* Westport, CT: Greenwood Press, 1985.

This volume lists over 1,500 committees, arranged in alphabetical order by the key word in the title of the committee. For each committee the following information is supplied: (1) committee name; (2) SuDocs classification number; (3) date the committee was established; (4) former name of committee; (5) *Congressional Record* citation to establishment; (6) resolution of the Senate; (7) date of committee termination; and (8) *Congressional Record* citation on termination. This is also a chronological list of committees and subject index.

Ornstein, Norman J. *Vital Statistics on Congress.* 1987/88 ed. Washington, DC: Congressional Quarterly, 1987.

This statistical handbook, issued every two years, contains a section on committees. It includes data on the number and type of committees in the House and Senate over the last thirty years and committee assignments for representatives and senators over the last thirty years. It also includes majority party chairmanships for House and Senate committees and subcommittees. These statistical data will be invaluable for anyone interested in committees.

If one is interested in how a committee voted on a bill that has been reported, this information is contained in the actual House and Senate reports.

Tracing the Privacy Act of 1974

Earlier, the legislative history for the Privacy Act of 1974 (PL 93-579) was provided in Table 2. When compiling a legislative history, if the bill number or public law number is known it is fairly easy to find a legislative history already compiled. Each of the tools listed in the very first step of the Tracing Outline provides legislative histories. Figures 11 through 16 are the legislative histories for the Privacy Act of 1974 that are included in some of the tools listed in the first section of the Tracing Outline and Table 6 (see p. 254).

The legislative history from the 1974 *CIS/Annual* (Part One: "Abstracts of Congressional Publications and Legislative Histories," p. 912) is shown in Figure 11 (see p. 229). The legislative history in the final edition of the *Daily Digest*, January 10, 1975, is given in Figure 12 (see p. 230). Figure 13 (see p. 231) reflects the history given by the *U.S. Code Congressional and Administrative News* for the 93d Congress, 2d session, 1974. A similar legislative history also appears in the *U.S. Statutes at Large* (Figure 14; see pp. 232–33), but it is better to use the *U.S. Code Congressional and Administrative News* because it is published much earlier than the *Statutes at Large*. The *Digest of Public General Bills and Resolutions* (93d Congress, 2d session, final issue, pt. 1, pp. 179–80) provides a legislative history in outline form (Figure 15; see p. 234). On the inside back cover of the slip law for the Privacy Act of 1974, the legislative history is printed (Figure 16; see p. 235). Obviously, it is not always possible to find a ready-made legislative history, which is the case if the law has been passed recently or is still in the legislative process. The very first section of the Tracing Outline (p. 54) enumerates those indexes one can go to for a legislative history that has already been compiled.

The Privacy Act of 1974 can also be traced through a subject approach. The subject heading "Privacy" in the subject index of the *CIS/Annual* will lead the user to Figure 11. Looking under "Privacy" in the index to the *CQ Almanac* would lead the researcher to a three-page synopsis of the Privacy Act (*CQ Almanac*, vol. 30, 1974, pp. 292–94). The index to the *CQ Weekly Report* for 1974 lists eight entries under the heading "Federal Data Banks." One of the entries is a special report entitled "Privacy: Congress Expected to Vote Controls" (*CQ Weekly Report*, vol. 32, pp. 2611–14). The subject index to *National Journal* (vol. 6, nos. 27–62) has the descriptor "Privacy" as a subheading under "Civil Liberties." That entry refers the researcher to an article entitled "Justice Report/Protection of Citizens' Privacy Becomes Major Federal Concern" (*National Journal*, October 12, 1974, pp. 1521–30). The annual index for the 1975 *U.S. Monthly Catalog* provides seventeen citations to hearings, reports, and other documents under the subject heading "Privacy."

If interested in prior publications on the topic of privacy, the researcher could also check the *Cumulative Subject Index to the Monthly Catalog of United States Government Publications, 1900–1971,* where thirty-five citations are listed under the heading "Privacy." The *Public Affairs Information Service Bulletin* (vol. 60, 1973–1974) lists twenty-seven items under "Privacy." Four of those citations are to federal documents, two are articles in the *National Journal,* and one an article in the *CQ Weekly Report.*

When conducting a subject search, make a conscious effort to think carefully about all possible appropriate subject headings. Pay close attention to "see" references, for they act as directional signs to other related headings. As shown above, three different subject headings proved fruitful. In a subject approach to legislative tracing you will always get a reference to some document or background article. Once you have tracked down that information, you should have little trouble identifying the bill number or public law number. With either number in hand, the tools described earlier can be used to compile a legislative history. All the bibliographic tools used in legislative tracing are always indexed by bill number and/or law number.

Bills take varying lengths of time to pass through Congress. It is unusual for important pieces of legislation to pass in a single year, or even in a single Congress. Many bills span a great number of years (and will have different numbers in each Congress).

The historical roots of a bill may also span a prolonged period of years. The Privacy Act of 1974 was the culmination of a legislative history extending back to 1965. Between 1965 and 1972, beginning with the 89th Congress and ending with the 92nd, a total of 342 legislative proposals related to privacy were introduced in Congress. Consequently, there is a wealth of government publications about privacy. Since 1965, hundreds of committee hearings, prints, and executive publications have been issued.

Citing just a few such publications will underscore the importance of searching for related documents issued prior to the bill itself. The President's Commission on Federal Statistics issued in 1971 a two-volume report entitled *Federal Statistics* (Washington, DC: U.S. Government Printing Office, 1971), containing chapters entitled "Privacy and Confidentiality," "Statistics and the Problem of Privacy," and "Findings and Recommendations on Privacy and Confidentiality." In July 1973 the Secretary's Advisory Committee on Automated Personal Data Systems of the U.S. Department of Health, Education and Welfare issued a report, *Records, Computers and the Rights of Citizens* (Washington, DC: U.S. Government Printing Office, 1973). A year later the Senate Subcommittee on Constitutional Rights released the six-volume *Federal Data Banks and Constitutional Rights: A Study of Data Systems on Individuals Maintained by Agencies of the United States Government* (Washington, DC: U.S. Government Printing Office, 1974). In addition to a survey of government agencies, the first volume includes informative introductory sections, including "Historical Context" and "Legislative Context." These documents, along with countless others, provide reams of valuable testimony, investigative reports, historical essays, statistics, surveys, recommendations, and findings.

Congress has not completed its work when a bill becomes law. It then takes on the responsibility of evaluating the implementation and impact of the law. Every congressional committee is charged with watching over the agencies and programs within its purview. This is a part of the legislative process, just as were the activities that led to the bill's passage. In June 1975 the House Committee on Government Operations published its hearings on the Privacy Act, *Implementation of the Privacy Act of 1974: Data Banks* (Washington, DC: U.S. Government Printing Office, 1975).

Legislative tracing entails searching for documents, both congressional and executive, published after a bill has been signed into law. Seven months after the Privacy Act of 1974 became law, *Privacy, A Public Concern: A Resource Document* (Washington, DC: U.S. Government Printing Office, 1976) was issued under the Office of the President. The document was based on the proceedings of a seminar on privacy sponsored by the President's Domestic Council Committee on the Right of Privacy and the Council of State Governments. In September 1976 a joint committee print, *Legislative History of the Privacy Act of 1974, S. 3418 (Public Law 93-579)* (Washington, DC: U.S. Government Printing Office, 1976) was issued by the Senate Committee on Government Operations and House Subcommittee on Government Information and Individual Rights. This huge document, almost 1,500 pages long, recounted the history of the Privacy Act of 1974 and discussed developments since its enactment. In 1977, the Privacy Protection Study Commission, established by the Privacy Act of 1974, issued its first in a series of reports, *Personal Privacy in an Information Society.*

After having examined and applied the tools of legislative tracing, researchers can decide for themselves which references best fulfill their needs and with which they feel most comfortable. Each tool has advantages: Some are more comprehensive; others are published more frequently and quickly. Often the choice of guides depends upon what the researcher is seeking. In some situations, the judgment is dictated by time. When tracing legislation in process, the researcher must use those tools that record the progress of a bill as it occurs. Speed and frequency of publication make the *Congressional Monitor, Congressional Index, CQ Weekly Report, National Journal, Calen-*

*dars of House and History of Legislation, CIS/Index,* and the *Congressional Record* best suited for current legislative tracing.

## Congressional Series

In previous sections we have discussed the publications of Congress as they related to legislative tracing, but the Congress is also the issuing agency for many noncongressional publications, especially documents associated with the presidency. For example, the *Economic Report of the President* is issued as a congressional document. Other publications issued in the House and Senate document series are the reports made to the Congress by the president. The annual *GAO Reports to be Made to Congress* is itself issued as a House document. In the next four subsections we will briefly discuss the kinds of presidential documents that can be found in the congressional series.

### House and Senate Journals

The kinds of presidential documents that can be found in the *Journals* include addresses, messages, and communications to the Congress in general. Veto messages can be found in the *Journal* of the chamber in which the bill was initiated. Both *Journals* use similar, but not identical, subject indexing; for the House of Representatives it is "President," and for the Senate, "President of the United States."

### Congressional Record

The kinds of presidential documents found in the *Congressional Record* include addresses, executive orders, proclamations, messages, and statements. Presidential documents and actions are indexed under "President of the United States." One can also use a subject approach to finding presidential materials.

### The Serial Set

The Serial Set is a series of publications that are selected and compiled under the direction of Congress. Begun in 1789, the Serial Set as a whole constitutes a historical record of the work and accomplishments of the Congress as well as noncongressional materials. All of the documents in the Serial Set, while differing in terms of origin, are printed in the series by reason of their value to the Congress in fulfilling its duties and responsibilities. In general, the Serial Set collection, also on microfiche, consists of the following types of publications:

1. congressional journals
2. congressional manuals, directories, and other internal documents
3. congressional reports on public and private bills
4. special investigatory reports conducted by or commissioned by congressional committees
5. recurring reports to be made to Congress by executive departments and agencies
6. executive publications ordered by Congress for inclusion
7. memorial addresses
8. annual or special reports of nongovernmental bodies required by law to report to Congress

Some of the documents issued in the Serial Set, such as the *Congressional Directory, House Manual,* and *Senate Manual,* are sold through the superintendent of documents to provide for greater distribution to the public.

The best access to Serial Set publications is through the Congressional Information Service's *CIS U.S. Serial Set Index.* The twelve-part index covers the period from 1789 to 1969. The index includes a comprehensive subject index, an index of names of individuals and organizations who were named as recipients of private relief or were the subjects of related actions of Congress, a numerical list of reports and documents, and a schedule of Serial Set volumes. Congressional Information Service publishes a *CIS U.S. Serial Set Index 1789–1969 User Handbook.* It is available from CIS and should be available in libraries that hold the CIS series. While the *CIS U.S. Serial Set Index* is quite easy to use, the Serial Set collection does have a number of idiosyncracies. Seeking the help of a documents librarian when trying to identify a document will often save time.

### Senate Documents

The Senate executive document series comprises messages from the president to the Senate Foreign Relations Committee regarding the texts of treaties and other international agreements. The Senate Foreign Relations Committee, meeting in closed session, reviews the materials and issues its report and the materials to the Senate as a Senate executive document.

## Finding Aids

The best finding aids for the *Congressional Record, House Journal,* and *Senate Journal* are the indexes contained in each of those tools. The *Congressional Index, CIS/Index,* and *Federal Index* can also be used for identifying materials in the *Congressional Record*. The Senate executive documents are indexed in the *Monthly Catalog* and *CIS/Index*.

# 2. Federal Legislation

## FEDERAL REGISTER SYSTEM

The General Services Administration (GSA), established in 1949 as an independent agency, was set up to oversee the management of federal documents. GSA consists of five services, among which is the National Archives and Records Administration. The chief objective of this service is the preservation and management of federal records, and within it is the Office of the Federal Register. The publication of federal records is what is referred to as the Federal Register System. On the following pages we will describe these publications. In Chapter 3 we will explain in detail how the *Federal Register* and *Code of Federal Regulations* are used to find particular kinds of information.

U.S. Office of the Federal Register. *Federal Register.* Washington, DC: U.S. Government Printing Office, 1936– .
The first section of the *Federal Register,* a daily publication, includes executive orders, proclamations, and other presidential materials such as memoranda from the president to the heads of departments or agencies, directives for officials, letters, and reorganization plans for agencies. New federal advisory committees are also recorded. Notices of each meeting of advisory bodies are published.

U.S. Office of the Federal Register. *Code of Federal Regulations.* Washington, DC: U.S. Government Printing Office, 1938– .
Executive orders, proclamations, and administrative regulations are codified in the *Code of Federal Regulations.* It is subdivided into fifty titles

by broad subject areas of federal regulations. Each title is subdivided into chapters, parts, and sections.

U.S. Office of the Federal Register. *The Federal Register: What It Is and How to Use It: A Guide for the User of the Federal Register, Code of Federal Regulations System.* Rev. ed. Washington, DC: U.S. Government Printing Office, 1986.

This guide explains the *Federal Register* and the *Code of Federal Regulations*. It contains dozens of illustrations depicting all of the relevant parts of the two publications.

U.S. Office of the Federal Register. *Title 3, The President.* Washington, DC: U.S. Government Printing Office, 1938– .

This annual work, which is part of the *Code of Federal Regulations,* is commonly referred to as "The President." The full texts of executive orders and proclamations are given in one chapter. Another chapter includes documents of the executive office of the president.

U.S. Office of the Federal Register. *Title 3A.* Washington, DC: U.S. Government Printing Office, 1972– .

This annual volume, which is part of the Code of Federal Regulations, is known as "The President Appendix." It contains the texts of proclamations, executive orders, and other presidential documents.

U.S. Office of the Federal Register. *United States Statutes at Large. . . .Containing the Laws and Concurrent Amendments to the Constitution.* Washington, DC: U.S. Government Printing Office, 1875– .

This is a compilation of public and private laws. Some presidential materials are included, such as a list of proclamations, full texts of these proclamations, and a list of reorganization plans. There is a subject index to these materials. This work was preceded by various editions of *Laws of the United States.*

U.S. Office of the Federal Register. *Weekly Compilation of Presidential Documents.* Washington, DC: U.S. Government Printing Office, 1965– .

This work is published every Monday and covers the previous week. It contains texts of messages to the Congress (budget, economic, and State of the Union addresses), texts of proclamations and executive orders, and transcripts of presidential news conferences. It also contains presidential speeches, statements, letters, remarks of welcome to foreign leaders, and similar materials made public in the form of White House press releases. Letters, memos, and reports to the president from cabinet members and other officials when released by the White House press office are included. This provides an up-to-date source for presidential policies and activities. There is an index of contents and a cumulative index to prior issues. There are semiannual and annual indexes as well.

U.S. Office of the Federal Register. *Public Papers of the President of the United States.* Washington, DC: U.S. National Archives and Records Service, 1958– .

Materials in this annual publication are arranged in chronological order with a subject index. It contains texts of the president's messages to Congress, public addresses, messages to heads of state, released statements on various subjects, and transcripts of news conferences. Some White House releases are not included in the main portion of the text. These releases are reports of presidential task forces, awards for Congressional Medals of Honor and Presidential Unit Citations, and presidential reports to Congress. These are located in several appendixes at the ends of the volumes. Proclamations and executive orders and materials of other officials are listed in Appendix B of each volume. Many of the items are annotated, and each volume has an index. The series begins with President Truman, but there are volumes available on President Hoover's administration.

U.S. Office of the Federal Register. *United States Government Manual.* Washington, DC: U.S. Government Printing Office, 1935– .

This annual manual is the official handbook of the federal government. It gives information on the agencies and departments of all three branches of government, as well as on quasi-official agencies, international organizations and boards, committees, and commissions. The history, programs, and activities of these agencies are described, and a list of the principal officials is given. Under the section on Congress the offices of Congress, standing committees of Congress, and lists of senators and representatives are found. There is a separate name index and a subject index. The volume's earlier title was *U.S. Government Organization Manual.*

# FINDING STATUTES

If the president signs a bill or a bill becomes law without his signature, the enrolled bill is sent from the White House to the General Services Administration for printing. If a bill is passed by both houses over the objections of the president, the chamber that last overrides the veto transmits it to the

GSA. There it is assigned a public law number and paginated for the *United States Statutes at Large* volume covering that session of the Congress. The public laws are numbered in sequence starting with the beginning of each Congress. Since 1957 the laws have been prefixed for ready identification by the number of the Congress.

The first official publication of a statute is in the form of a slip law, i.e., a separately published unbound pamphlet. The heading indicates the public law number, the date of approval, and the bill number. Since 1976, the heading has also indicated the *United States Statutes at Large* citation. If the statute has been passed over the veto of the president or has become law without his approval, a statement is inserted in place of the usual notation of approval.

The Office of the Federal Register supplies annotations in the margins of slip laws giving the citations to statutes mentioned in the text and other explanatory notes. Since 1974, the notes have given the citations to the *United States Code,* enabling a reader to immediately determine where the statute appears in the *Code.* Since 1975, slip laws have included a concise legislative history of the law consisting of the committee report numbers, the names of the committees, the dates of consideration and passage in each chamber, and the reference to the *Congressional Record.* Since 1971, a reference to presidential remarks has been included in the legislative history by citing the *Weekly Compilation of Presidential Documents.*

## Using the *United States Statutes at Large*

In order to provide a permanent collection of the statutes of each session of the Congress, the *United States Statutes at Large* is prepared by the General Services Administration. Each volume contains a complete index and a table of contents. From 1956 through 1975, the volumes contained a table of earlier laws affected, and from 1963 through 1974, they contained a table showing the legislative history of each law. The latter table was discontinued in 1975, as the legislative histories now appear at the back of each slip law.

## Using the *United States Code*

The *United States Code* is a codification of the statutes of the United States arranged according to subjects under fifty title headings. The purpose of the *Code* is to present the current status of laws in a concise and usable form without requiring one to use numerous volumes of the *Statutes at Large* containing every amendment. Revised editions of the *Code* are published every six years and cumulative supplements are printed at the end of each session of the Congress.

The research procedure chart given in Table 7 (see pp. 255–61) is designed to enable a user to obtain accurate and current citation of the *Statutes at Large* and the *Code*. Users should read the items from left to right. The first column contains the references that require further citing. These are (1) Revised Statutes section, (2) date of law, (3) name of law, (4) number of law, (5) *Statutes* citation, and (6) *Code* citation. The second, third, and fourth columns identify the volumes in which the citations are located. The fifth column lists other finding aids, which are especially useful for citing recent legislation.

## Indexes

As the *Statutes at Large* and the *Code* comprise the official record of statutory law, they are the primary sources and indexes for finding laws. But there are several commercial reference series that can also be used to locate statutes, either by number or popular name, and to determine the present legality of a statute. These tools can be used by themselves, but it is always best to use them in conjunction with the *Statutes at Large* and the *Code*.

*Shepard's Acts and Cases by Popular Names: Federal and State*. Colorado Springs, CO: Shepard's Citations, 1968– .

Federal statutes are often referred to by their popular names. This service, a quarterly publication, lists statutes in alphabetical order by popular name and cites their location in the *Statutes at Large* and *Code*. It also provides the same access for state acts. Federal cases referred to by popular names can be accessed by using the section that references one to the *United States Supreme Court Reports* and *National Reporter System*.

*Shepard's United States Citations: Statute Edition*. Colorado Springs, CO: Shepard's Citations, 1955– .

This citator, published irregularly, allows one to determine the validity of an act or judicial decision by providing citations to earlier and later statutes and cases as well as other legal sources. A student or researcher can determine the current status of a decision or act by identifying which amendments, other enactments, or legal decisions have affected a particular statute or decision.

*United States Code Annotated.* St. Paul, MN: West Publishing Company, 1927– .

Although this annual set reprints the *United States Code,* the statutes are accompanied by extensive annotations, legal notes, and analytic comments on the specific statute and its legislative history. This supplemental material is invaluable for anyone interested in researching the original intent and later interpretation of the statute.

*United States Code Service.* Rochester, NY: Lawyers' Cooperative Publishing Company, 1972– .

This service is very similar to the *United States Code Annotated.* Published irregularly, it reprints the *United States Code* and includes annotations, notes, and legislative histories. One of the volumes in the set, the *United States Code Guide,* is especially useful. It can be used to relate the code to several other reference tools, including the *United States Supreme Court Reports, Lawyers Edition,* and *American Jurisprudence.*

As these four reference sets are complex tools, one should consult some of the following guides to find more detailed descriptions of how they work and the various ways they can be used.

Cohen, Morris L. *How to Find the Law.* 8th ed. St. Paul, MN: West Publishing Company, 1983.

Dickerson, Reed. *The Interpretation and Application of Statutes.* Boston, MA: Little, Brown, 1975.

*How to Use Shepard's Citations: A Detailed Presentation of the Scope and Functions of Citation Books and Services Published by Shepard's Citations.* Colorado Springs, CO: Shepard's Citations, 1975.

Statsky, William P. *Legislative Analysis and Drafting.* 2d ed. St. Paul, MN: West Publishing Company, 1984.

Also, Harry Bitner's *Effective Legal Research* (Boston: Little, Brown, 1979) and Myron Jacobstein and Roy M. Mersky's *Fundamentals of Legal Research* (Mineola, NY: Foundation Press, 1987) have excellent chapters on how to use the four services.

# INTERPRETING STATUTES

Judicial decisions, both by the Supreme Court and lower courts, are important in determining whether a particular statute or presidential action is constitutional or not. As decisions by the courts affect statutory law and administrative law, it is important to be able to identify decisions and know how to follow judicial interpretations.

## Constitution

Any analysis of statutes and the rules, regulations, and orders that constitute administrative law must start with the Constitution. The powers of the president are specified in the Constitution. While there are gray areas of legality, executive orders and proclamations are not to supersede statutes. Consequently, it is important to have an understanding of the Constitution to know what the powers of the president are, as well as how statutes are made. The best single source for understanding the Constitution is what is commonly referred to as the *Constitution Annotated*.

U.S. Library of Congress. Congressional Research Service. *Constitution of the United States of America, Analysis and Interpretation: Annotations of Cases Decided by the Supreme Court of the United States to . . .* Washington, DC: U.S. Government Printing Office, 1913– .
   This publication is updated irregularly, and supplements are issued every two years. As it contains extensive case annotations and scholarly analysis and interpretations, this work is the best compendium on the Constitution.

Mitchell, Ralph. *CQ's Guide to the U.S. Constitution: History, Text, Index, Glossary.* Washington, DC: Congressional Quarterly, 1986.
   This Constitution in a nutshell contains a detailed alphabetical index by topic that makes it easy to find the specific part of the Constitution and amendments for which one is looking. It also contains an excellent glossary of legal terms.

## Dictionaries

Anderson, William S., ed. *Ballentine's Law Dictionary, with Pronunciations.* 3rd ed. Rochester, NY: Lawyers Co-operative Publishing Company, 1969.

Black, Henry C. *Black's Law Dictionary*. 5th ed. St. Paul, MN: West Publishing Company, 1979.

Gifis, Steven H. *Law Dictionary*. 2d ed. Woodbury, NY: Barron's Educational Series, 1984.

Kling, Samuel G. *The Legal Encyclopedia and Dictionary*. New York: Pocket Books, 1970.

Radin, Max. *Radin Law Dictionary*. Rev. ed. Dobbs Ferry, NY: Oceana Publications, 1970.

Chandler, Ralph C., Richard A. Enslen, and Peter G. Renstrom. *The Constitutional Law Dictionary*. 2 vols. Santa Barbara, CA: ABC-Clio, 1985–1987.

Volkell, Randolph Z. *Quick Legal Terminology*. New York: Wiley, 1979.

## Encyclopedias

Levy, Leonard W., ed. *Encyclopedia of the American Constitution*. 4 vols. New York: Free Press, 1986.

This four-volume set is the only encyclopedia specifically about the Constitution. Articles are by 262 contributors, including lawyers, political scientists, historians, and journalists. There are more than 2,200 articles about constitutional history, concepts and terms, Supreme Court cases, and public acts. The encyclopedia includes a guide to legal citations and a chronology of 100 significant dates in constitutional history as well as a subject index and index of cases.

*American Jurisprudence*. 2d ed. San Francisco, CA: Bancroft-Whitney, 1962– .

This multivolume encyclopedia contains treatises covering U.S. federal and state laws. Each volume is indexed, and there is also an index to the whole set. There are annual supplements.

*Corpus Secundum Secundum*. New York: American Law Book Company, 1937–1960, 1961.

Over 400 articles on U.S. law are arranged under topical headings in this work. Citations are given to law cases. They are indexed in each volume as well as in a separate index. There are annual supplements.

*The Guide to American Law: Everyone's Legal Encyclopedia.* 12 vols. St. Paul, MN: West Publishing Company, 1983.

This encyclopedia contains entries for over 5,000 topics, including articles on legal cases, statutes, terms and concepts, and notable persons. Each volume is individually indexed; the last volume indexes and cross-references the entire set.

*The Guide to American Law Yearbook, 1987: Everyone's Legal Encyclopedia.* St. Paul, MN: West Publishing Co., 1987.

# Bibliographies

Hall, Kermit L. *Bibliography of American Constitutional and Legal History, 1896–1979,* 5 vols. Millwood, NY: Kraus International Publications, 1984.

This five-volume work cites over 18,000 major writings on the history of U.S. legal culture from 1896 through 1979. It covers books, dissertations, and scholarly journal articles published in English in the United States. The bibliography is organized into seven parts: (1) general surveys and texts, (2) institutional, (3) constitutional doctrine, (4) legal doctrine, (5) biographical, (6) chronological, and (7) geographical.

Ontiveros, Suzanne R., ed. *The Dynamic Constitution: A Historical Bibliography.* Santa Barbara, CA: ABC-Clio, 1986.

This bibliography includes more than 1,370 citations to books, articles, and dissertations. There are annotations for the articles but not the books and dissertations. The bibliography is arranged in five chapters, each with an introductory survey. The first chapter provides citations to materials that are historiographies, and the following four chapters are by time period. The volume includes an author and a title index.

Chambliss, William J., and Robert B. Seidman. *Sociology of the Law: A Research Bibliography.* Berkeley, CA: Glendessary Press, 1970.

This bibliography contains some material on the Supreme Court and constitutional law, but it is most useful for finding citations to jurisprudence, judicial review, and more theoretical aspects of judicial behavior.

Andrews, Joseph L. *The Law in the United States of America: A Selective Biographical Guide.* New York: New York University Press, 1965.

This bibliography selectively lists and annotates legal publications. There are two parts, the first listing primary materials and the second, secondary works. The entries are found under broad subject headings.

Reams, Bernard D., and Stuart D. Yoak. *The Constitution of the United States: A Guide and Bibliography to Current Scholarly Research.* Dobbs Ferry, NY: Oceana Publications, 1987.

This unannotated bibliography includes citations to essays, articles, books, and government documents about the Constitution and all the amendments. The citations are arranged by branches of government and each amendment.

Millet, Stephen M. *A Selected Bibliography of American Constitutional History.* Santa Barbara, CA: ABC-Clio, 1975.

This bibliography contains citations to the origins and development of the Constitution, the history of amendments, and the role of the Supreme Court, Congress, and the president in the judicial system.

Mason, Alpheus T., and D. Grier Stephenson. *American Constitutional Development.* Arlington Heights, IL: AHM Publishing Corporation, 1977.

This is an excellent guide to the literature on constitutional law and statutory interpretation. The citations are taken mostly from the field of legal studies, but there are some citations from the social sciences and humanities.

McCarrick, Earlean M. *The U.S. Constitution: A Guide to Information Sources.* Detroit, MI: Gale Research Company, 1980.

This guide covers all aspects of constitutional law, including its development, amendments, and the role of the Supreme Court and individual justices. It is better for finding citations to books than to journal literature.

## Guides

*Guide to the U.S. Supreme Court.* Washington, DC: Congressional Quarterly, 1979.

This one-volume guide is more like an encyclopedia on the Supreme Court. It is a massive handbook divided into five chapters covering the origins and development of the Court, the Court and the federal system, the Court and the individual, pressures on the Court, and the Court at work. It also includes a section on the justices, providing background information, and a section on major decisions of the Court, summarizing major decisions since 1789.

Elliott, Stephen P., ed. *A Reference Guide to the United States Supreme Court.* New York: Facts on File, 1986.

This volume includes four chapters on the Supreme Court, including the role of the Court, constitutional power of the branches, the division of power between the federal government and the states, and individual rights. There is an excellent section on landmark cases providing good summaries, and biographies of the justices. There are numerous appendixes, including an alphabetical listing of chief justices, an alphabetical listing of associate justices, two chronological tables for the chief justices and associate justices providing basic information about their careers, a listing of sitting Courts, and a chronological listing of landmark cases. The volume also includes a short bibliography and subject index.

## Casebooks

Supreme Court decisions are first issued as "slip opinions." These are published within three days and are available in depository libraries. In addition to the slip opinions there are several casebooks a researcher can use for finding Supreme Court decisions.

U.S. Supreme Court. *United States Reports*. Washington, DC: U.S. Government Printing Office, 1790– .

The *Reports*, an annual publication, contain the official text of all opinions of the Supreme Court. Also included are tables of cases reported, cases and statutes cited, miscellaneous materials, and a subject index. All written reports and most per curiam reports of decisions are printed.

U.S. Supreme Court. *Supreme Court Reporter*. St. Paul, MN: West Publishing Company, 1983– .

This weekly nongovernmental publication contains annotated reports and indexes of case names. It includes some material not covered in the *United States Reports*, such as opinions of justices in chambers.

*United States Law Week*. Washington, DC: Bureau of National Affairs, 1930– .

This weekly periodical service includes important sections on the Supreme Court. It has four indexes, whereby if you know the subject you can use the Topical Index; if you know the name of the case, you can use the Table of Cases; if you know the docket number you can use the Docket Number Table; and if you know the date, you can use the Proceedings Section. In addition to containing the full text of all decisions, the periodical has a number of useful sections, including (1) cases filed last week,

(2) summary of cases filed recently, (3) journal of proceedings, (4) summary of orders, (5) arguments before the Court, (6) argued cases awaiting decisions, (7) review of the Court's work, and (8) review of the Court's docket.

U.S. Supreme Court. *United States Supreme Court Reports: Lawyers' Edition.* Rochester, NY: Lawyers Cooperative Publishing Company, 1790– .

All other casebooks contain the official reports, but this service contains numerous per curiam decisions not found elsewhere. The annual service also summarizes individually the majority and dissenting opinions and counsel briefs. The Index to Annotations leads one to the legal notes provided for each case.

*West's Federal Case News.* St. Paul, MN: West Publishing Company, 1978– .

This weekly publication provides summaries of cases decided in the Supreme Court but also does so for a number of other courts, including the U.S. Court of Appeals, U.S. Court of Claims, U.S. district courts, and selected cases from state courts.

Decisions of lower courts (district courts and courts of appeals) are not reported officially by the government. However, decisions of these courts are printed unofficially. The National Reporter System is a privately published edition of law reports covering most of the lower federal courts. The *Federal Reporter* contains the decisions of federal intermediate appellate courts and some selected district courts, and the *Federal Supplement* contains mainly the decisions of the U.S. district courts.

Besides publishing the decisions of the Supreme Court, the government also publishes on a regular basis the decisions of the following courts: Court of Claims, Court of Customs and Patent Appeals, Customs Court, Commerce Court, Tax Court, and United States Court of Military Appeals.

## Digests

There are several excellent reference tools that give digests analyzing the decisions of the Supreme Court. The digest sets can also be used as indexes for identifying decisions by subject and case name. *Shepard's United States Citations* also has the capability to identify every time a decision has been cited in a later case, whereby one can follow changes in legal interpretation.

Blandford, Linda A., and Patricia Russell Evans, eds. *Supreme Court of the United States, 1789–1980: An Index to Opinions Arranged by Justice.* 2 vols. Millwood, NY: Kraus, 1983.

*Digest of United States Supreme Court Reports, Annotated with Case Annotations, Dissenting and Separate Decisions since 1900.* Rochester, NY: Lawyers' Cooperative Publishing Company, 1948.

Guenther, Nancy A. *United States Supreme Court Decisions: An Index to Excerpts, Reprints, and Discussions.* 2d ed. Metuchen, NJ: Scarecrow Press, 1983.

*Shepard's United States Citations: Case Edition.* Colorado Springs, CO: Shepard's Citations, 1947– .

*Significant Decisions of the Supreme Court.* Washington, DC: American Enterprise Institute, 1969– .

*United States Supreme Court Digest.* St. Paul, MN: West Publishing Company, 1940– .

## Briefs and Records

Several tools can be used to locate the briefs and oral arguments used by counsel on both sides. The briefs and records are a valuable resource for understanding the eventual decision of a case and the interpretation of a statute or administrative rule.

*Complete Oral Arguments of the Supreme Court of the United States.* Frederick, MD: University Publications of America, 1980– . (Published annually.)

Kurland, Philip, and Gerhard Casper. *Landmark Briefs and Arguments of the Supreme Court of the United States: Constitutional Law.* Washington, DC: University Publications of America, 1975– . (Published annually.)

U.S. National Archives. *Tape Recordings of Oral Arguments Before the U.S. Supreme Court.* Washington, DC: Archives, 1955– .

U.S. Supreme Court. *Records and Briefs.* Washington, DC: 1832– .

## Secondary Sources

There are several excellent legal newspapers that regularly report on Supreme Court decisions. They are the *National Law Journal, Federal Times,* and the *Legal Times of Washington.* They also provide a wealth of information on other aspects of the judiciary, including the appointment of new judges and other personnel, judicial behavior, administrative law, regulatory politics, and legislative-executive relations. A congressional staff publication, simply entitled *Staff,* published by the Senate Committee on Rules and Administration, also includes a section in each monthly issue providing a synopsis of important federal court decisions. Besides keeping abreast of current developments by reviewing legal newspapers, a researcher can also retrospectively search for articles in those newspapers, as well as the hundreds of law journals published throughout the country, by using the *Legal Resource Index, Current Law Index,* or *Index to Legal Periodicals.*

Finally, other sources regarding interpretations of the law and legal issues are the publications of the Justice Department and General Accounting Office. *Official Opinions of the Attorneys General* and *Opinions of the Office of Legal Counsel* both are issued by the Department of Justice. In the *Decisions of the Comptroller General,* one can find legal decisions regarding the disbursement of appropriated monies. The last source, *Court Proceedings and Actions of Vital Interest to the Congress,* issued by the House Judiciary Committee, is rather specialized. Its focus is primarily on decisions affecting members of Congress, such as immunity, election disputes, and the scope of their powers.

# 3. Federal Administrative Law

## FINDING RULES AND REGULATIONS

Administrative agencies are often referred to as the fourth branch of government. As Congress has delegated some of its authority to agencies, these agencies have administrative, legislative, and judicial power to make and enforce laws. Congress can also authorize the president to make rules and regulations. In turn, the president has delegated much of his authority to the executive agencies under him to make rules and regulations.

As mentioned earlier, the Federal Register System is primarily composed of two publications, the *Federal Register* and the *Code of Federal Regulations*. These two publications contain a current compilation of all rules and regulations issued by executive departments and agencies. To comprehend the Federal Register System, one needs to understand each publication and the relationship between the two publications.

## USING THE *FEDERAL REGISTER*

For monitoring rules and regulations, the *Federal Register* is an invaluable tool, as it is the only publication that prints all rules adopted by agencies. The *Federal Register,* which is issued daily, contains documents in the following categories:

1. presidential documents—documents signed by the president and submitted

2. rules and regulations—documents having general applicability and
   legal effect
3. proposed rules—notices to the public of proposed rules
4. notices—documents other than rules that are of interest to the public
5. Sunshine Act meetings—notices of meetings published in accordance
   with the Government in the Sunshine Act

The *Federal Register* is basically a daily update of the *Code of Federal
Regulations*. When an agency adopts a new rule, it is published in the
*Federal Register.* Every time the *Code of Federal Regulations* is updated, all
of the adopted rules appearing in the *Federal Register* since the most recent
edition are inserted into the proper place in the *Code of Federal Regulations*.


## Final Rules and Regulations

The Rules and Regulations section of the *Federal Register* contains
regulatory documents that are keyed to and codified in the *Code of Federal
Regulations*. The meanings of the terms "rules" and "regulations" are
identical in the *Federal Register.* Agencies are required to give at least thirty
days' notice in the *Federal Register* that a rule has been adopted before it has
legal effect. Exceptions to this procedure are interpretive rules, statements of
policy, rules that grant exceptions, and rules for which an agency believes
good cause exists for not complying with the thirty-day rule.

When a final rule is published in the *Federal Register,* the agency is
required to include a summary of the comments received in response to the
proposed rule and any changes recommended in the comments that were
incorporated into the final rule. Sometimes an agency will adopt a final rule
and simultaneously request comments, which are not due until after the rule
has legal effect. Likewise, an agency will sometimes request comments on a
rule that did not go through the proposed rule procedure because the agency
believed the Administrative Procedure Act did not require that proposed
rules be issued.

Each document in the *Federal Register* begins with a heading that includes
the name of the issuing agency, the *Code of Federal Regulations* title and
parts affected, and a brief synopsis of the contents. Immediately after the
heading is the preamble, which accompanies the text of all proposed and
final rules. The contents of the preamble are meant to improve the clarity of
documents. The preamble must be in the following format and contain the
following items:

1. the agency proposing the action
2. the type of action
3. summary of the action
4. deadline for comments
5. address to which comments may be sent
6. the person in the agency to contact for information
7. supplementary information, including the background, rationale, and content of the action

## Proposed Rules and Regulations

With certain exceptions, all rules must be presented to the public in a proposed form before they become final. The publication of proposed rules is a notice to the public whereby interested citizens have the opportunity to participate in hearings before the adoption of final rules. The format and preamble requirements for documents in the Proposed Rules section are identical to the Final Rules section. The date given in the preamble is usually the final deadline for submission of comments. An address is provided to which comments may be sent. Proposed rules are generally documents that recommend amendments to regulations in the *Code of Federal Regulations* and request public comment on the changes. Most proposed rules are required to be published by authority of the Administrative Procedure Act or other statutes.

One of the first steps in the rule-making procedure is the petition for rule making. The petition, which is published in the Proposed Rules section because it proposes to amend parts of the *Code of Federal Regulations,* requests public comment. Another preliminary document also published in the Proposed Rules section is the advance notice of a proposed rule. Agencies issue these notices of intent early in the process in order to receive public comments as quickly as possible. These documents discuss a problem and the anticipated action of the agency. This step in the process is not required by the Administrative Procedure Act, but is used when an agency wants to get public comments before issuing a proposed rule. After reviewing comments received in response to a notice or advance notice, an agency will propose a rule if it decides that a new rule is necessary.

The Administrative Procedure Act does not require that a hearing be held in the rule-making process, but the legislation that requires the promulgation of regulations may specify that hearings be held. Even when hearings are not required, most agencies will hold hearings on any significant proposals. In order to identify each of their proceedings, agencies assign a specific number to each one. The information received by the agency pertaining to that proceeding is maintained in a file and is open to the public. These files are referred to by agencies as dockets. Dockets sometimes include material prepared by the agency staff, but the dockets are not necessarily a complete record of all that has transpired. When the agency staff releases material, a copy of the released material is placed in the file for public inspection as well.

## Notices

As stated in the *Federal Register,* notices are "documents other than rules or proposed rules that are applicable to the public." Some of the documents included in the Notices section are required by statutory authority to be published in the *Federal Register.* Documents in this section are not codified in the *Code of Federal Regulations.* The following are types of materials that are published as notices in the *Federal Register.*

1. Advisory committee meetings. The Federal Advisory Committee Act requires that advisory committees publish announcements stating the date, time, location, and purpose of their meetings.
2. Petitions and applications. These documents represent miscellaneous requests made by agencies for permission for a special authority.
3. Environmental impact statements. The National Environmental Policy Act requires that an environmental impact statement be included along with any regulation that may have an effect on the quality of the environment.
4. Delegations of authority. An agency may decide to delegate some of its authority to a different agency.

## Sunshine Meetings

The *Federal Register* publishes the agendas of open agency meetings. The Government in the Sunshine Act specifies that agencies hold open meetings and that the public be given a week's notice of the time and place of a meeting. Sunshine meetings are often avenues for finding out about a rule that an agency may propose or a final rule before it has been published in the *Federal Register.* Agencies also will list those meetings that are closed to the public. Finally, one can try to get on an agency's sunshine agenda mailing list. Usually an agency's office of information maintains a mailing list.

# Finding Aids

Every issue of the *Federal Register* includes a number of bibliographic tools, referred to as "finding aids." They are printed at the beginning and the end of the issue. In order as they appear in the *Federal Register*, these finding aids are

1. Highlights. The Highlights section is a listing on the front cover and inside front page of documents in the issue that have wide public interest. Highlights entries include the beginning page number of the document, a brief subject heading, the issuing agency's name, and a synopsis of the document.
2. Contents. The Contents section contains a complete listing of all proposed and final rules, as well as notices, arranged by agency. Each entry includes the beginning page number of the document and a brief description.
3. Meetings Announced in This Issue. This section is arranged by agency name and provides the date when each scheduled meeting is to be held.
4. *Code of Federal Regulations* Parts Affected in This Issue. This list is similar to the monthly *Cumulative List of Code of Federal Regulations Sections Affected (LSA)*, but it is only for that day's issue. It is a listing of titles and parts of the *Code of Federal Regulations* that have been or will be affected by rules contained within the issue. The proposed and final rules are published under each *Code of Federal Regulations* title and arranged by part number, including the beginning page numbers of the documents. *Code of Federal Regulations* parts can be affected by such changes as additions, amendments, and deletions.
5. Reader Aids. At the back of each day's issue is the Reader Aids section, which is intended to assist the user in finding specific information in the *Federal Register*. The reader aids include
   a. Information and Assistance. This is a listing of Office of Federal Register telephone numbers to call for specific types of questions.
   b. *Federal Register* Pages and Dates. This is a table of the inclusive pages and corresponding dates for the current month's *Federal Register*.
   c. CFR Parts Affected During. This is a cumulative list of *Code of Federal Regulations* parts affected by proposed and final rules printed so far in the *Federal Register*. This list serves the same purpose as the "List of *CFR* Parts Affected in This Issue," but it is cumulative for the month. This list is necessary for filling in the period between the most recent *LSA* and issues of the *Federal*

*Register* that have accumulated since the last publication of the *LSA*.

d. Agency Publication on Assigned Days of the Week. Some agencies publish their documents on two assigned days of the week.

e. Table of Effective Dates and Time Periods. This table is used for computing advance notice requirements and the public deadline for comments for *Federal Register* documents published during the current month. This is published in the first issue of each month.

f. *Code of Federal Regulations* Checklist. This is a list of the revision dates and current prices of *Code of Federal Regulations* volumes. This is published in the first issue each month.

g. Agency Abbreviations. This section contains the abbreviations used in the Highlights and Reminders sections. It is published in the first issue of each month.

h. Reminders. Every issue concludes with a list of reminders, including Rules Going into Effect Today and the List of Public Laws recently signed by the president. Each Wednesday the list is expanded to include the following information: Next Week's Deadlines for Comments on Proposed Rules, Next Week's Meetings, and Next Week's Public Hearings.

There is one important finding aid for the *Federal Register* that is published separately. The *Federal Register Index* is published quarterly and annually. This index is arranged by agency, providing citations to all proposed and final rules and notices that have been printed in the *Federal Register* for the last quarter or year. The *Index* also prints a list of Privacy Act publications, a Table of *Federal Register* Pages and Dates, and a Guide to Freedom of Information Indexes.


# USING THE *CODE OF FEDERAL REGULATIONS*


The *Code of Federal Regulations* is a codification of the rules published in the *Federal Register* by all of the executive departments and agencies. The *Code of Federal Regulations*, which is revised annually, is arranged into fifty titles that represent broad subject areas. Each title contains regulations pertaining to a single subject area and consists of one or more chapters. Each chapter contains a single agency's regulations. The chapters are further divided into parts, parts into sections; if necessary, sections are broken down into paragraphs. A summary of the terms, identifying symbols, and a description of each section is as follows:

| Term | Symbol | Description |
|---|---|---|
| Title | 1,2,3, etc. | Each title represents an area that is subject to federal regulation. Subtitles are arranged consecutively by capital letters, and if it is necessary, distinguishes between the regulations of the agency as a whole and its bureaus. Subtitles are also used to group related chapters. |
| Chapter | I, II, III, etc. | Chapters are arranged by upper case roman numerals, and each is normally assigned to a single issuing agency—either an entire agency or one of its bureaus. Subchapters are arranged by capital letters to group related parts. |
| Part | 1,2,3, etc. | Each chapter is divided into parts by arabic numerals. A part consists of regulations pertaining to a single function of the issuing agency or is devoted to a particular subject under the jurisdiction of an issuing agency. Subparts are arranged by capital letters to group related sections. |
| Section | 1.1, 1.2, 1.3, etc. | Each section number includes the number of the part, a decimal point, and the section number. The section is the basic unit of the *CFR* and consists of a brief account of a single proposition. |
| Paragraph | (a), (b), (c), etc. | When further division of a section is needed, sections are divided into paragraphs. |

After every three months, one-quarter of the *Code of Federal Regulations* is revised and issued on a quarterly basis. Consequently, at the end of each year the complete *Code of Federal Regulations* has been revised as of the following dates:

| Title 1 through Title 16 | January 1 |
| Title 17 through Title 27 | April 1 |
| Title 28 through Title 41 | July 1 |
| Title 42 through Title 50 | October 1 |

The revision date is printed on the cover of each volume, and the cover for each volume is a different color for quick reference. As most titles cover a broad area, the regulations of any single title will generally be contained in more than one book. Normally, all of a particular agency's regulations are contained in a single title. Every volume of the *Code of Federal Regulations* includes a Table of *CFR* Titles and Chapters, listing the subject areas of the regulations contained in each title and the name of the agency for the corresponding chapter. The authority citation following the table of contents is listed before each part. This citation provides the legislative or presidential authority under which a part or a section is issued. A source note is also given by the Office of the Federal Register. This note specifies by volume, page, and date where the codified document was published in its entirety in the *Federal Register.* Every volume of the *Code of Federal Regulations* also includes an alphabetical list of agencies whose regulations are codified within the *Code* and a citation to the title and chapter where the agency's regulations are located. And each agency's regulations include the procedures the agency is to follow in making its rules. After the codified material, each *Code of Federal Regulations* volume includes several finding aids.

The *CFR Index,* revised semiannually, is a separate volume of the *Code of Federal Regulations.* Basically, the volume consists of an index arranged by agency names and subject headings covering rules currently codified in the *Code of Federal Regulation,* with a citation to the title and section of the *Code* where the rules pertaining to a subject or agency can be found. Also included in the *CFR Index* are

1. Agency-prepared indexes for each *CFR* volume.
2. Parallel Table of Statutory Authorities and Rules. This table lists all sections of the *United States Code* and the *United States Statutes at Large* that are cited as the authority for rules codified in the *Code of Federal Regulations.* Basically, this is a three-part table designed to lead a researcher from a statute to a regulation.
3. List of *CFR* Titles, Chapters, Subchapters, and Parts. This list is the same as the "Table of *CFR* Titles and Chapters" that is contained in each *CFR* volume.
4. Alphabetical Listing of Agencies. This listing is the same as that contained in every *CFR* volume.

Finally, the *Cumulative List of Code of Federal Regulations Sections Affected (LSA)* is published monthly, and as it is cumulative it serves as an update to the *Code of Federal Regulations*. The starting date for each title in the *LSA* is the date when the *CFR* volume containing that title was last revised. The *LSA* is intended to assist users of the *CFR* in finding amendments published in the *Federal Register*. The entries are arranged by *CFR* title, chapter, part, and section, and they denote the change made. Besides the entries, the *LSA* also contains an explanation of how to use the *LSA*, a Checklist of Current *CFR* Volumes, a Parallel Table of Authorities and Rules, and a Table of *Federal Register* Issue Pages and Dates. Instead of going through numerous issues of the *Federal Register* to find out what new rules, amendments, or proposed rules have been promulgated since the *CFR* was last updated, it is best to use the *LSA*.

# COMMERCIAL GUIDES

While the *Federal Register* and *Code of Federal Regulations* are the primary tools and records relating to rules and regulations, there are several commercial indexes to finding administrative citations.

*CIS Federal Register Index*. Bethesda, MD: Congressional Information Service, 1984– .

This weekly index contains four parts. An index by subject and name provides access by subjects, geographical areas, issuing agency, industries, corporations, organizations, individual names, and legislation. There is a calendar of effective dates and comment deadlines. The index by *CFR* section numbers specifies when and where final or proposed changes to the *CFR* have been announced. Finally, there is an index by agency docket numbers. Each index entry provides the issuing agency, register issue date, type of document, and *Federal Register* page number.

*Index to the Code of Federal Regulations*. Bethesda, MD: Congressional Information Service, 1977– .

This annual service has a detailed subject index, which allows a search of all fifty titles at once. You can search a general or specific subject and be referred to all the relevant parts and subparts. There are two geographical indexes. The first indexes regulations regarding political jurisdictions such as states, counties, and cities. The second cites properties administered by the federal government, such as parks, military bases, etc. There are also two other indexes that can save time if you already have a citation. A list of descriptive headings gives headings assigned to each part of the *CFR*. A list of reserved headings lists indicates which parts of the *CFR* have been designated reserved, either for future use or because they have been vacated from use.

*Shepard's United States Administrative Citations.* Colorado Springs, CO: Shepard's Citations, 1967– .

This citator, published bimonthly with quarterly cumulations, lists all the decisions of federal agencies, boards, and commissions that are originally published in the agencies' own indexes and digests. It also includes citations to articles in law journals and various other reporting series.

# SECONDARY SOURCES

Most federal administrative agencies issue decisions and opinions that are useful for studying Congress. Some decisions and opinions eventually are contested in the Supreme Court regarding their constitutionality. For a student or researcher interested in keeping up on administrative agencies, the best periodicals to review are the *Legal Times of Washington,* the *National Law Journal,* and the *Administrative Law Review.* One should also consult several legal indexes, including the *Current Law Index, Index to Legal Periodicals,* and *Legal Resource Index.*

# 4. The Congressional Budget Process

## INTRODUCTION

Each January, the president sends a proposed budget to Congress for the fiscal year that begins the next October 1. The Office of Management and Budget (OMB) prepares the budget proposals and has the responsibility within the executive branch for supervising expenditures once a federal budget has been enacted into law. Early in the summer, OMB sends budget ceilings to the agencies of the executive branch. In September, the agencies give OMB their plans for programs and their estimates of financial requirements for the year under consideration and two additional years.

OMB then develops a preliminary budget as its analysts complete their reviews of the agencies' programs, detailing their projections for the future and identifying major issues for discussion with officials of the agencies. During the budget process, the president's economic advisers assess the economy and prepare a revised estimate of revenues and spending plans for the president. OMB then sends "directive letters," which set spending levels and priorities, to each department and agency. Officials can appeal directly to the president for changes they believe should be made in OMB's decisions, but most disagreements are settled between the director of OMB and the head of the department. In late December, the president makes his final decisions on the budget. The document is then printed, and the president prepares his budget message.

The budget proposes specific levels of spending authority and actual outlays for all government agencies. It presents in detail the basis for the president's programs. Congress can approve, modify, or reject the president's budget proposals. It can change funding levels, eliminate proposals, or add programs not requested by the president, and it acts on legislation determining taxes and other means of increasing or decreasing receipts as well as stimulating or slowing down the economy. When the new fiscal year begins on October 1, the budget has been agreed on and is in place. Should the budgeting timetable slip, Congress can enact a "continuing resolution" to provide money for any agency whose appropriations have not yet been approved.

The congressional budget process is closely related to the process through which legislation in general is enacted into law. Proposals for the spending of monies must work their way through the legislative process if they are to become law. Spending proposals are referred to House and Senate appropriations committees, which in turn refer the detail work to subcommittees. These subcommittees have jurisdiction over specific departments and agencies. The congressional reconcilation procedure is an exception to the general rule that the budget process is the same as the legislative process. Budget reconciliation, a procedure where spending by the federal government is brought into conformity with congressional budget resolutions, is an element of the Budget Control Act. The annual budget process can be a complex process; typically the Congress and executive branch are at odds with each other and budget battles go on within Congress.

Congress generally follows a two-step legislative process. First it legislates programs as proposed by its standing committees. This is known as the authorization process. Then it funds the programs as recommended by the appropriations committees. (See below.) House and Senate rules have been adopted to keep authorization and appropriation as distinct steps. In practice the process is more complex. Authorization bills may contain appropriations, and appropriation bills are sometimes passed before authorization bills. In fact, the appropriations committees are able to establish policy and act in a substantive manner.

The congressional budgetary process is the last phase of the larger annual process through which federal spending levels are established. Although the Congress has the power of the purse, the executive branch has evolved as at least an equal partner in federal spending decisions. The size and complexity of the federal budget has forced the Congress to delegate a large part of the initial task of budgeting to the executive branch.

Congress is not only in the business of allocating funds one year in advance; funding for some projects must be spread over many years. The budget is largely composed of spending and receipts that are fixed by authorization and appropriation decisions of previous years and thus is not generally subject to review.

In appropriating monies for authorized programs, what Congress acts upon is not actual expenditures but rather requests for budget authority. Government agencies are granted budget authority, and they in turn make the actual expenditures. There are basically two overlapping processes at work in each congressional budget cycle.

1. The authorization process. This process occurs when the standing legislative committees authorize the allocation of funds for specific programs. An authorization specifies the substance of the particular program and which agencies shall be responsible for implementing it. The authorization does not determine the dollar amount to be spent; this is a function of budget appropriations. Authorizing legislation can set an outside limit on the funds for a program or can authorize the appropriation of such sums as may be necessary. Certain major programs are authorized annually.

2. The appropriations process. This process usually determines how much funding each department, agency, or program is allotted. The House and Senate appropriations committees are charged with this responsibility, but most of the detail work is done in the appropriations subcommittees that have jurisdiction over specific departments and agencies. Under the Budget Control Act, the Congress each year must pass a concurrent resolution on the budget, establishing the overall level of spending, revenues, and corresponding deficit before considering any legislation authorizing new budget authority. A second budget resolution must also be approved each budget cycle prior to the beginning of the fiscal year, affirming or revising the targets of the first resolution. If the spending level envisioned in the first resolution is exceeded, the Congress can either increase the spending ceiling in the second resolution or direct a reconciliation. The reconciliation provision allows the House and Senate to order a particular committee to bring a spending measure into line with the original spending estimates.

The two-step authorization and appropriation process is often not followed. While both chambers of Congress have rules barring legislation on an appropriations measure, these rules seem to be honored more in the breach than the observance. One strategy to avoid the rules has been to earmark funds for certain purposes within agency funding. Another tactic has been to attach "riders," amendments barring funds except in certain narrow circumstances, to appropriations bills.

# BUDGET TIMETABLE

A key part of the congressional budget process is a timetable that coordinates the authorization and appropriations cycles with the overall congressional budget enacted by the first and second budget resolutions. It shapes legislative activity for the entire Congress, forcing the committees to hold hearings, mark up bills, and report legislation prior to the May 15 budget deadline. In the early months of each congressional session, activity centers in committees. In late spring and summer it shifts to the floor and to the passage of the coming year's spending legislation.

## November 10

The first step in the budget timetable is the submission by the president of the current services budget, projecting federal spending for the coming five years on the basis of continuing current programs, excluding any program initiatives. The Congressional Budget Office, established by the Budget Act to supply budget data and analysis, also prepares a five-year budget projection. All such budget projections are contingent on several assumptions, e.g., the rate of growth in the gross national product, levels of inflation, etc.

## March 15

Soon after the president submits his budget, the authorization and appropriations committees begin to hold their hearings. By March 15 they must report to the budget committees their estimates of new budget authority to be enacted for the upcoming fiscal year. Some committees hold formal mark-up sessions to draft these budget reports, and sometimes the reports are a good forecast of the committees' legislative priorities.

## April 1

By April 1, the Congressional Budget Office submits reports to budget committees.

## April 15

By April 15, the budget committees of each chamber must file their reports accompanying the first budget resolution. The first budget resolution establishes targets for

1. the level of total outlays and total new budget
2. the recommended level of federal revenues
3. the appropriate budget surplus or deficit
4. the appropriate level of public debt

## May 15

The dual May 15 budget deadline is probably the most significant of the entire process. Its first requirement is the reporting of all legislation proposing new budget authority. If a committee fails to meet this deadline, the legislation cannot be considered by the House or Senate unless a waiver is reported by the House Rules Committee or the Senate Budget Committee. The administration is required to make requests for authorizing legislation a year in advance of the May 15 reporting deadline, so that the committees are allowed a full year to deal with administration requests for authorizations. In addition, just as the authorizing bills must be reported by May 15, the appropriations bills cannot be reported before this date. Congress must complete action on the first budget resolution to satisfy the second part of the May 15 deadline requirement. Until the first budget resolution has been finalized, setting a "target" spending ceiling and revenue floor for the fiscal year, neither chamber can consider any spending or revenue bill that would take effect in that fiscal year.

## Seventh Day after Labor Day

By the seventh day after Labor Day, the Congress is required to complete action on all regular authorization and appropriations measures. The only exception to this rule is consideration of bills that have been delayed because necessary authorizing legislation was not enacted in time. Such delays have forced departments to exist on the prior year's funding levels.

## September 15

While there is no deadline for the reporting of the second budget resolution, it occurs before the annual August recess and must be finalized by September 15. The total and functional spending levels in the first resolution are "target," but those figures in the second resolution are "binding."

## September 25

Provision was made in the Budget Act for the Congress to direct committees to bring spending and revenue bills into line in the reconciliation process. The committees can be directed to report bills or resolutions embodying the changes, and the Congress must complete action on these by September 25. The Congress cannot adjourn until a second budget resolution and any reconciliation bills are completed.

The fiscal year begins October 1. The timetable laid down in the Budget Act can be summarized as follows:

| On or Before | Action |
|---|---|
| November 10 | President submits current service budget |
| 15th day after Congress meets | President submits his budget to Congress |
| March 15 | Committees and joint committees submit report to Budget Committee |
| April 1 | Congressional Budget Office submits report to budget committees |
| April 15 | Budget committees report first concurrent resolution on the budget to their houses |
| May 15 | Committees report bills and resolutions authorizing new budget authority; Congress completes action on first concurrent resolution on the budget |
| 7th day after Labor Day | Congress completes action on bills and resolutions providing new budget appropriations and new spending authority |
| September 15 | Congress completes action on second required concurrent resolution on the budget |
| September 25 | Congress completes action on reconciliation bill or resolution, or both, implementing second required concurrent resolution |
| October 1 | Fiscal year begins |

Congress has increasingly resorted to forms of spending that circumvent the two-step congressional spending process. "Backdoor spending" refers to spending that bypasses the regular appropriations process. While there is a general rule that spending for a program cannot result where there is not both a specific authorization and an appropriation of funds to carry out the program, backdoor spending has evolved as a loophole. The term "backdoor spending" actually means a number of things:

1. entitlement, i.e., programs in which the government is obligated to extend benefits to all individuals meeting certain criteria
2. borrowing authority, i.e., allowing government agencies to operate by borrowing either from the Treasury or directly from the public
3. contract authority, i.e., providing a lump sum in contract authority for facilities over several years

The Congress has begun to curb backdoor spending, but not until the Congressional Budget and Impoundment Control Act of 1974 did Congress deal with the problem. The act closed the door on all new borrowing and contract authority by requiring this form of spending to go through the appropriations process. All new entitlement legislation that breaches the limits for a particular function is automatically referred to the Appropriations Committee.

# BUDGET COMMITTEES

Under the Budget Act, budget committees were set up in the House and Senate to implement new budget procedures and monitor congressional spending actions. The primary responsibility of the budget committees is to report and see passed the two annual budget resolutions. The committees monitor the individual authorizations, appropriations, and revenue decisions taken by the Congress. This "scorekeeping" function keeps the Congress informed of progress it is making toward meeting its budget targets. Status reports are published weekly by the Senate Budget Committee and periodically by the House Budget Committee. Both committees are standing legislative committees. The Senate's sixteen committee members are chosen through normal Senate procedures, while the twenty-five House committee members comprise five from the Appropriations Committee, five from the Ways and Means Committee, thirteen from other standing committees, and one each from the majority and minority leadership. The membership of the House Budget Committee differs from other standing committees in that it is rotating. No member can serve more than two terms during any ten-year period. Since the new budget process was imposed over the authorization and appropriations cycles, the Budget Committee chairmen have played a significant part in determining a role for the committees.

# OFFICE OF MANAGEMENT AND BUDGET PUBLICATIONS

While the Office of Management and Budget is not a congressional support agency, its publications are invaluable in researching the budget process. The executive budget is primarily formulated by OMB, which issues the publications listed below. All executive budget publications are noted in the *Weekly Compilation of Presidential Documents* and are indexed in the *Monthly Catalog*.

*The Budget of the United States Government.* Washington, DC: U.S. Government Printing Office, 1972– .
    This annual publication contains the president's message on the budget. It summarizes his proposed plans for the budget and any recommended taxes.

*The Budget of the United States Government, Appendix.* Washington, DC: U.S. Government Printing Office, 1972– .
    This annual publication accompanies the OMB publication *The Budget of the United States Government*. A line-item identification of the budget, it gives detailed estimates for the budget arranged by agency and account.

*The U.S. Budget in Brief.* Washington, DC: U.S. Government Printing Office, 1972– .
    This is an abridged version of OMB's *Budget of the United States Government*. For finding information on the budget quickly, this annual publication is the one to consult.

*Major Themes and Additional Budget Details.* Washington, DC: U.S. Government Printing Office, 1983– .
    This annual publication describes how the budget affects the president's programs.

*Special Analyses, Budget of the United States Government.* Washington, DC: U.S. Government Printing Office, 1969– .

This annual publication provides an analysis of presidential programs in terms of the budget. The series contains statistical data, charts, and tables.

Other OMB publications include:

*Catalog of Federal Domestic Assistance Programs.* Washington, DC: U.S. Government Printing Office, 1965– . (Published annually.)

*Social Indicators.* Washington, DC: U.S. Government Printing Office, 1973– . (Published triennially.)

*Statistical Services of the United States Government.* Washington, DC: U.S. Government Printing Office, 1975.

*Federal Statistical Directory.* Washington, DC: U.S. Government Printing Office, 1944– . (Published irregularly.)

For information concerning the Office of Management and Budget the following work is most helpful.

Berman, Larry. *The Office of Management and Budget and the Presidency, 1921–1979.* Princeton, NJ: Princeton University Press, 1979.

# 5. Congressional Support Agencies

## INTRODUCTION

The four support agencies of Congress—the Congressional Budget Office, the Congressional Research Service, the Office of Technology Assessment, and the General Accounting Office—publish a variety of reports and studies useful for researching legislation and Congress itself. Many publications of the four agencies are listed in the *Monthly Catalog* and *GPO Sales Publications Reference File*. At the end of the description of each agency will be listed specific tools that can be used to identify publications of that agency. In addition to these tools, some publications and the testimony of officials from all four agencies are indexed in *CIS Index*. Finally, all four agencies submit an annual report to Congress that details their activities and plans.

## CONGRESSIONAL BUDGET OFFICE

To implement the new budget procedures established by the Budget Act of 1974, Congress created three new institutions, including the newest of the congressional support agencies, the Congressional Budget Office (CBO). CBO was established as the legislative branch's counterpart to the Office of Management and Budget. CBO is a nonpartisan organization that provides Congress with economic forecasts and fiscal policy analyses. Its objective is to present Congress with different public policy options and their budgetary impact. It also develops cost estimates for carrying out legislation reported by committees. Another service consists of supplying five-year cost estimates for all legislation reported by congressional committees. These projections find their way into committee reports and often into floor debate on a bill.

Each year CBO prepares a report by April 1 detailing the alternative spending and revenue levels associated with different overall budget options. During the year CBO keeps track of congressional actions on individual spending bills, comparing them with aggregate and functional spending in the first budget resolution. CBO issues periodic reports, which are available to the public, showing the status of congressional action.

CBO's cost estimates for carrying out legislation reported by committees can be found in *Congressional Budget Scorekeeping Reports* (Washington, DC: Congressional Budget Office, 1976–   ). This new series adds another dimension to legislative tracing, for it is now possible to ascertain the projected expenditures for a bill.

CBO publishes an annual *List of Publications,* which began in 1975. This catalog is cumulative, so the latest catalog will list all the publications since 1975. The *List of Publications* is arranged in both chronological and subject listings, including topics such as the economy and fiscal policy, federal budget, commerce, trade and industry, social programs, national security, and government operations. The *American Statistical Index* (Washington, DC: Congressional Information Service, 1973–   ) can also be used to identify CBO publications.

## CONGRESSIONAL RESEARCH SERVICE

The Library of Congress was established in 1800 as a congressional resource. While it still has a special relationship to Congress, its function as a congressional resource is mainly in conjunction with an agency known as the Congressional Research Service (CRS).

CRS works exclusively for members of Congress and congressional committees. CRS reports, known as "multiliths," can only be obtained through a representative, senator, or committee office. Sometimes a multilith will be published by a congressional committee in the form of a committee print.

Another service provided by CRS, which is available by subscription from the Government Printing Office, is the *Digest of Public General Bills and Resolutions.* The *Digest* summarizes all legislation introduced in each session of Congress, providing the sponsor of the legislation, cosponsor, identical bills, short title, subject index, and brief factual description. The *Digest* is printed in five cumulative issues each year, supplemented by biweekly updates.

In addition to the multiliths and the *Digest*, CRS provides a number of other services, including

1. special legal research and analysis
2. special projects conducted by senior specialists
3. storage on-line in a special computer system of information useful to the Congress

SCORPIO, as the computer system is called, can be accessed directly in many congressional offices by computer terminal. SCORPIO on-line files contain a bill digest, major legislation of each Congress, and "issue briefs" on significant public policy issues. The public can access the SCORPIO files by using terminals located in the Library of Congress, and an arrangement has been worked out through which organizations can buy time on the system.

Selected publications of CRS are available on microfilm in the series *Major Studies of the Legislative Reference Service/Congressional Research Service: 1916–1974* and yearly supplements *Major Studies and Issue Briefs of the Congressional Research Service*. The original collection and each supplement comes with a printed guide providing a title/author guide and subject index. These sets cover such areas as legal and constitutional issues; the Congress; energy and environmental issues; social, health, and educational issues; government and political issues; foreign and defense issues; and economic and labor studies.

The *CRS Studies in the Public Domain* is a subject listing of CRS reports and studies published in some form, usually congressional hearings and prints, by the Government Printing Office. It covers topics such as economic affairs, educational and public welfare, environment and natural resources, foreign affairs, government and law, and science and technology. This annual series started in 1978.

Since 1980, CRS has also published a journal, *Congressional Research Service Review*, ten times a year. Aimed at individuals interested in congressional affairs, it focuses on public policy issues. Another useful tool is the CRS journal *Major Legislation of the Congress*, published fifteen times a year. It is designed to provide summaries of congressional issues and major legislation. Each issue is cumulative, and the final issue, published at the end of each Congress, is meant to be used as a permanent reference tool.

# OFFICE OF TECHNOLOGY ASSESSMENT

The Office of Technology Assessment (OTA) was established in 1973. OTA has conducted a number of assessments in such areas as energy, food, health, transportation, oceans, materials resources, etc. OTA relies to a large extent on teams of specialists assembled from government, academia, and industry to prepare its assessments. It is governed by a twelve-member congressional board, a director and an Advisory Technology Assessment Council. Requests for assessments can originate with the chairman of a congressional committee, a congressional member of the OTA board, or with OTA's director.

OTA reports are available from the Government Printing Office. OTA's *List of Publications,* which began in 1978, gives an annotated listing of publications by broad subject areas, including energy, industry, technology, employment, international security and commerce, biological applications, food and renewable resources, health, communication and information technology, oceans and the environment, science, education, and transportation. These research reports are excellent materials for anyone doing research on legislation relating to those topics.

# GENERAL ACCOUNTING OFFICE

The General Accounting Office (GAO) is the largest and second oldest of the congressional support agencies. GAO was established by the Budget and Accounting Act of 1921 to audit spending by federal departments and agencies. It is organized along broad functional lines and divided into ten audit divisions. The agency is engaged in monitoring federal spending to ensure that programs are being implemented efficiently and in accordance with legislative intent. As a result of additional responsibilities mandated by the Legislative Reorganization Acts of 1946 and 1970 and the Congressional Budget and Impoundment Control Act, GAO has been changed into an investigative arm of the Congress, providing Congress with numerous audits and studies requested by congressional committees and members of Congress, studies directed by statute, testimony at congressional hearings, and commentary on new legislation.

GAO publishes an extensive series of "blue cover" reports on the operation of various government programs. About one-third of the more than 1,000 annual reports issued by the comptroller general are in response to requests by congressional committees and members of Congress. Some GAO reports are transmitted in the form of letters to committee chairmen, but they are usually available to the general public. A monthly publication, *GAO Documents,* that lists GAO reports is issued by the agency and is published in the *Congressional Record.* The agency also publishes a biannual booklet, *General Accounting Office Publications,* listing reports submitted to Congress the previous year. Also, a computerized subject index of GAO reports issued since July 1, 1973, is maintained in the GAO library.

Often referred to as the watchdog of Congress, GAO was created in part to assist Congress in fulfilling its oversight responsibilities. Students should always check to see whether GAO has published a report on the particular area of government operations they are researching. The *GAO Review,* a quarterly journal, contains articles on the activities of GAO and Congress. Title VIII of the Budget Act of 1974 requires GAO to identify, compile, and disseminate information to Congress for use in fulfilling its oversight and budget monitoring responsibilities. Accordingly, GAO publishes the yearly Congressional Sourcebook Series, a set of three volumes. *Requirements for Recurring Reports to the Congress* monitors and specifies such requirements made by all branches of the federal government. *Federal Program Evaluations* identifies and discusses evaluation reports conducted by or for executive departments, agencies, and federal commissions. *Federal Information Sources and Systems* identifies and describes such sources and systems on fiscal, budgetary, and program data in executive agencies. Each of the sourcebooks is well indexed and is an excellent directory and guide to federal programs and information.

# 6. Foreign Affairs and Treaties

This section describes the tools one uses in researching foreign affairs in general and the treaty-making process. Because of their international aspect, the treaty-making process allows for greater latitude than the legislative process. Any international compact, regardless of whether it is called a treaty, convention, accord, protocol, etc., that is submitted by the president to the Senate for approval is a treaty. In this chapter, we will discuss how to identify treaties and gather background information regarding them.

## DEPARTMENT OF STATE PUBLICATIONS

The Department of State, so named in 1789 following the election of President Washington, is the oldest department of the executive branch. Under the Constitution, the whole of the diplomatic corps is headed by the president. Historically, the department, along with its secretary, has been one of the most important parts of the government and extension of the president.

The Department of State is one of the most voluminous publishers in the executive branch. Its publications cover many aspects of foreign affairs and diplomacy. The best indexes for identifying State Department publications are the *Monthly Catalog* and *GPO Sales Publications Reference File*. Of all the publications issued by the Department of State, the two most useful for studying the Congress, especially in regard to treaties and executive agreements, are listed below.

U.S. Department of State. *Department of State Bulletin*. Washington, DC: U.S. Government Printing Office, 1939– .

From 1939 to 1977 the *Bulletin* was a weekly publication with semiannual indexes. Since 1977 it has been issued monthly, with an annual index. As the official record of foreign policy, it is an invaluable tool for studying treaties. Sections in each issue give notice of the ratification of treaties and announce executive agreements. In addition to being self-indexed, the *Bulletin* is also indexed in *Public Affairs Information Service Bulletin*, the *Index to U.S. Government Periodicals*, and *Reader's Guide to Periodical Literature*.

U.S. Department of State. *The Foreign Relations of the United States, Diplomatic Papers*. Washington, DC: U.S. Government Printing Office, 1861– .

This series, which is usually published on an annual basis, contains records on foreign policy and diplomatic practice. A variety of materials can be found in this set, including presidential documents, some treaties, and diplomatic correspondence and reports.

# TREATIES

Whether referred to as an accord, protocol, compact, or convention, any international agreement submitted to the Senate by the president is a treaty. Basically a treaty is an agreement between two or more nations that is governed by international law.

Four compilations provide complete texts of all treaties and executive agreements from 1776 to the present. These four works are all a student needs to find a treaty.

U.S. Department of State. *Treaties in Force*. Washington, DC: U.S. Government Printing Office, 1929– .

This annual publication, referred to as *TIF*, lists treaties and agreements currently in effect to which the United States is a party. The first part lists bilateral treaties and other agreements in order by country and then by topic. The second part lists multinational agreements arranged by subject and then by country under the subject. The series also cites superseding treaties and terminations of treaty articles and notes amendments and supplementary treaties. For keeping up to date, one can use the monthly *Department of State Bulletin*.

U.S. Department of State. *Treaties and Other International Acts Series.* Washington, DC: U.S. Government Printing Office, 1945– .

This series, referred to as *TIAS,* is a continuation of the *Treaty Series,* covering the years 1908–1945, and the *Executive Agreement Series,* covering the years 1929–1945. Each text is published separately in pamphlet form about six to twelve months after it has come into force. The text is in English and the language of the other country. Also included are important dates in the treaty's development, the president's proclamation, and correspondence.

U.S. Department of State. *United States Treaties and Other International Agreements.* Washington, DC: U.S. Government Printing Office, 1950– .

This annual publication, referred to as *UST,* is the text of treaties and agreements proclaimed during the preceding year. It contains a subject and country index. The texts are printed in the language of the original instrument. Before 1950 the treaties and agreements were published in the *United States Statutes at Large.* This annual multivolume set cumulates and replaces *TIAS.*

Bevans, Charles I. *Treaties and Other International Agreements of the United States of America 1776–1949.* 13 vols. Washington, DC: U.S. Government Printing Office, 1968–1976.

This compilation, the comprehensive collection of treaties, contains all of the treaty and agreement texts prior to 1950. Each volume has an index and there are cumulative analytical indexes. The set is commonly referred to as "Bevans."

# REFERENCE GUIDES

The following two sections identify some of the most useful commercial guides to treaty information.

## Finding Aids

While *TIF, TIAS, UST,* and Bevans are the primary sources for finding treaties, several commercial guides also can be used.

Kavass, Igor I., and M. A. Michael, comps. *United States Treaties and Other International Agreements Cumulative Index, 1776–1949.* 4 vols. Buffalo, NY: William S. Hein, 1975.
This set can be used to identify treaties and agreements by their *TIAS* number, date, country, and subject.

Kavass, Igor I., and Adolph Sprudas, comps. *UST Cumulative Index, 1950–1970: Cumulative Index to United States Treaties and Other International Agreements, 1960–1970.* 5 vols. Buffalo, NY: William S. Hein, 1973.

Kavass, Igor I., and Adolph Sprudas, comps. *UST Cumulative Index, 1971–1975: Cumulative Index to United States Treaties and Other International Agreements, 1971–1975.* Buffalo, NY: William S. Hein, 1977.
These volumes provide the same kind of access as the above entry. The series is updated by a looseleaf service, which is cumulated every five years.

Wiktor, Christian L. *Unperfected Treaties of the United States, 1776–1976.* 6 vols. Dobbs Ferry, NY: Oceana, 1976–1984.
This set is an annotated compilation of treaties not approved by the Senate or ratified by the president.

As mentioned earlier in the discussion of the Congressional Serial Set (pp. 63–64), Senate executive documents are issued by the Congress and indexed and abstracted in *CIS/Index* and *CIS/Annual.* Also, *Shepard's United States Citations: Statute Edition* contains a section entitled "United States Treaties and Other International Agreements." This citator can be used to determine what modifications, renewals, terminations, revisions, and court decisions have affected a treaty.

In Table 8 (see pp. 262–64) we have summarized where one can look to find information regarding the treaty-making process. The tools listed include both text publications and bibliographic tools. Basically, the best sources for finding information about current treaty developments are the *Department of State Bulletin,* the *Weekly Compilation of Presidential Documents, Treaties in Force, Shepard's United States Citations, CIS/Index,* and the *Monthly Catalog.*

# Bibliographies

The bibliographies and guides listed below are useful in a variety of ways. In addition to providing citations to secondary materials, especially books and articles, they contain information on many of the treaty compilations cited previously. They also contain references to other sources of information relating to the study of foreign affairs, such as archives, manuscript collections, documentary collections, yearbooks, atlases, oral histories, and special collections. All three of these guides are superb reference tools and should be consulted when studying the role of the Congress in foreign affairs.

Burns, Richard Dean, ed. *Guide to American Foreign Relations Since 1700.* Santa Barbara, CA: ABC-Clio, 1983.

Bemis, Samuel Flagg. *Guide to the Diplomatic History of the United States, 1775–1921.* Washington, DC: U.S. Government Printing Office, 1935.

Plishke, Elmer. *U.S. Foreign Relations: A Guide to Information Sources.* Detroit, MI: Gale Research Company, 1980.

# 7. Secondary Sources

## CONGRESSIONAL QUARTERLY PUBLICATIONS

Congressional Quarterly (CQ) publishes voluminous materials on national affairs, reporting on all aspects of congressional and executive activities in publications with a reputation of being factually reliable and up to date. Many CQ publications are relatively inexpensive to acquire. In addition to reference works, CQ issues special paperbacks on current topics and has in print several paperbacks related to Congress, including *Congress Reconsidered, Congress and Its Members, Congressional Procedures and the Policy Process, Committees in Congress, Congressional Reform, Congress and Democracy, Politics of Shared Power: Congress and the Executive, Power in Congress, Campaigning for Congress,* and *How Congress Works.*

CQ also publishes a number of special-purpose newsletters, including *Campaign Practices Report, Congress in Print,* and *Congressional Insight.* Another useful CQ publication is the *Congressional Record Scanner,* which abstracts and distills the *Congressional Record.* Finally, CQ provides the Washington Alert Service (see p. 147), an on-line database that allows one to analyze voting patterns, track legislation, and get profiles of members. A catalog of publications is available on request from Congressional Quarterly, 1414 22nd St., N.W., Washington, DC 20037.

CQ's research guides are listed below.

*CQ Weekly Report,* 1946– .

This weekly recounts important congressional and political activities for the previous week, including developments in committees as well as on the floor. When covering major pieces of legislation, it provides voting records and excerpts of testimony in hearings. Lobbying activities are given considerable coverage, with special reports on the relationship between congressional voting and interest groups. Each issue usually contains an article on a special issue or major legislation pending in Congress. The *CQ Weekly Report* quickly publishes the unofficial returns for congressional elections. CQ indexes the *Weekly Report* quarterly and annually. The *Weekly Report* is also indexed in *Public Affairs Information Service Bulletin*.

*Congressional Insight, 1976– .*

This weekly newsletter supplements the *CQ Weekly Report. Congressional Insight* forecasts the outcome of pending bills and summarizes new legislation about to be introduced. *Congressional Insight* is designed to map out what will be happening in Congress in the coming weeks. It reports which bills are ready for action, being ignored, or being amended. In an attempt to convey some of the drama of congressional power struggles, *Congressional Insight* focuses on personalities in Congress, discussing their aspirations and conflicts with other legislators and the roles they play in the battle over a piece of legislation.

*Congressional Quarterly Almanac, 1945– .*

This annual edition is published each spring. The *Almanac* is more than a synthesis of material issued in the *Weekly Report,* for it summarizes and cross-indexes the previous year in Congress. Included are accounts of major legislation enacted, presidential programs and initiatives, analyses of Supreme Court decisions, election results of any federal elections held in the last year, an examination of lobbying activities, and other special reports. Like the *CQ Weekly Report,* the *Almanac* records the roll-call vote for every member of Congress.

*Congress and the Nation, 1945–1984,* 6 vols.

This reference set is a well-organized work providing quick access to descriptions of major legislation as well as national and international events. The set provides an excellent chronological history of major legislative programs and political developments during each Congress and executive administration, including biographical information, major votes, key judicial decisions, and election issues. Additional volumes in the series are to be issued at the end of each presidential term of office.

*Guide to Current American Government, 1968– .*

This series serves as a current handbook to developments in the American political system. Issued each spring and fall, it covers the general areas of the presidency, Congress, the judiciary, intergovernmental relations, and lobbies. The series can be used as an up-to-date supplement to both the *Almanac* and *Congress and the Nation*.

*Editorial Research Reports,* 1923– .
This series follows a journal format and is issued four times a month. The *Reports* provide documented research on the full range of current affairs, from the arts to welfare. Each edition attempts to give the reader both the pros and cons on the issues being discussed. Bibliographies are included to facilitate further study. The *Reports* are indexed in *Public Affairs Information Service Bulletin*.

*Congressional Roll Call,* 1970– .
This annual series of publications began with the first session of the 91st Congress. The volumes open with an analysis and legislative description of key votes on major issues, followed by special voting studies such as freshman voting, bipartisanship, voting participation, etc. The remainder of the volume is a member-by-member analysis, in chronological order, of all roll-call votes in the House and Senate. There is also a roll-call subject index. In the compilation of roll-call votes, there is a brief synopsis of each bill, the total vote, and vote by party affiliation. The indices record whether the member voted for or against, paired for or against, announced for or against, was polled by CQ as for or against, voted "present," voted "not present" to avoid a conflict of interest, or did not vote or make his/her position known. The voting indices in the *CQ Weekly Report* and *CQ Almanac* are presented in the same format.

*Guide to Congress,* 3rd ed., 1982.
As a handbook concentrating on Congress, the *Guide* explains how that body works, beginning with an account of its origins and history. There are chapters on the structure and procedures of Congress and its relations with the other branches of government. The volume is most valuable to the student or researcher who is seeking a basic and thorough understanding of how Congress operates.

*Historic Documents.* 1972– .
This annual series reprints important documents in chronological order from the preceding year. The volume includes significant presidential statements and messages, speeches, treaties, debates, court decisions, proclamations, and government reports and documents. There is a detailed subject index to all the documents included in each volume.

# ALMANACS

Most annual almanacs can be used as ready reference sources. While every almanac uses a different format, they all contain essentially the same information. Election returns since 1789 are given on a national basis, including the electoral vote, popular vote, and sometimes percentages or pluralities. For the most recent elections, the election results are broken down by state. It should be noted that almanacs vary from year to year in regard to the data presented. Usually almanacs published following an election year will include somewhat more detailed statistics, such as election results broken down by county. For quick and easy checking on congressional elections, almanacs should not be forgotten or bypassed in the search for statistics, yet for more scholarly research their use should be regarded as only the initial step.

*World Almanac and Book of Facts*. New York: Newspaper Enterprise Association, 1868– .

*Information Please Almanac*. New York: Simon and Schuster, 1947– .

*Official Associated Press Almanac*. Maplewood, NJ: Hammond Almanac, 1974 – .

# DICTIONARIES

Dictionaries can be used in a variety of ways for studying Congress. Most of all they are good tools to use for finding the answers to ready reference questions, such as a date, a definition, the name of an individual, etc. Some dictionaries are more scholarly and detailed than others, providing short essays rather than dictionary-style entries.

## Political Science

Dictionaries in the field of political science contain a variety of facts. In addition to definitions of political terms and concepts, one can find entries for legal cases, court decisions, histories of government agencies, and biographical sketches. Most dictionaries in political science contain hundreds of entries relevant to the study of Congress.

Elliot, Jeffrey M., and Ali R. Sheikh. *The Presidential-Congressional Political Dictionary.* Santa Barbara, CA: ABC-Clio, 1984.

Holt, Sol. *The Dictionary of American Government.* Rev. ed. New York: Woodhill Press, 1970.

Plano, Jack C., and Milton Greenberg. *The American Political Dictionary.* 7th ed. New York: Holt, Rinehart and Winston, 1985.

Whisker, James B. *A Dictionary of Concepts in American Politics.* New York: John Wiley, 1980.

## History

Dictionaries in the field of history can be used to find important dates, biographies, and significant historical events. When one comes across an event, name, or issue one is unfamiliar with, the fastest way to get some basic information is to check a dictionary.

Adams, James T. *Dictionary of American History.* Rev. ed. New York: Charles Scribner's Sons, 1976.

Martin, Michael R., and Leonard Gelber. *Dictionary of American History: With the Complete Text of the Constitution of the United States.* Rev. ed. Totowa, NJ: Rowan and Allanheld, 1981.

## ENCYCLOPEDIAS

Encyclopedias are excellent sources of information on the Congress, yet most students and researchers tend to overlook them in their search for information. All of the encyclopedias cited below contain lengthy essays. The entries are usually written by experts in the field, providing concise overviews and histories. The political science encyclopedias are useful not only for finding information about the Congress, but for information on research concepts and methodologies as well. These encyclopedias should be the first place one looks before searching for documents, legal cases, etc.

## Political Science

Lowenberg, Gerhard, Samuel C. Patterson, and Malcolm E. Jewel, comps. *Handbook of Legislative Research*. Cambridge, MA: Harvard University Press, 1985.

This excellent volume was intended to summarize the state of research on legislative studies both about the Congress and other legislative bodies. It includes chapters on the organization and workings of legislative bodies as well as elections, campaigning, the media, and relations with other branches of government. This is a first-rate handbook and invaluable reference work for anyone seeking a review of the literature.

*Encyclopedia of the Social Sciences*. 15 vols. New York: Macmillan, 1930–1935.

This encyclopedia contains scholarly articles on the concerns of the social sciences. The articles are usually lengthy, supply bibliographies, and are signed by the author. The entries are arranged alphabetically.

Sills, David L., ed. *International Encyclopedia of the Social Sciences*. 17 vols. New York: Macmillan, 1968.

Articles with a general subject matter are arranged alphabetically in this encyclopedia. There are cross-references and an index to aid the reader in finding materials. The articles are all written by social scientists and include material on the Congress relating to the disciplines of political science, law, history, economics, and sociology. This encyclopedia is not a revision of the earlier *Encyclopedia of the Social Sciences*.

## History

Morris, Richard B., and Jeffrey B. Morris. *Encyclopedia of American History*. 6th ed. New York: Harper and Row, 1982.

This one-volume work covers chronologically the important events in American history. There is a section devoted to biographies of important U.S. figures.

DeConde, Alexander, ed. *Encyclopedia of American Foreign Policy: Studies of the Principal Movements and Ideas*. 3 vols. New York: Charles Scribner's Sons, 1978.

This encyclopedia contains articles on U.S. foreign policy written by scholars in that field. An appendix lists important persons in American diplomatic history. There is also an index.


# NEWSPAPERS AND INDEXES


Newspapers are unrivaled for their ability to provide almost instantaneous, vivid, day-by-day reporting on congressional activities. The two best newspapers for following congressional politics are the *New York Times* (indexed in the *New York Times Index*) and the *Washington Post* (indexed in the *Washington Post Index*).

The New York Times Information Bank, which began in 1969, is a unique on-line database service. Articles published in the *New York Times*, as well as articles from more than seventy additional periodicals, are indexed and abstracted in the database. One can use the database to retrieve the bibliographic citations or the abstracts of the articles. The indexing and abstracting is selective; there is a strong emphasis on political issues and officials.

The *National Newspaper Index* indexes the *New York Times, Wall Street Journal, Christian Science Monitor, Los Angeles Times,* and *Washington Post*. This microfilm index is cumulative and is updated regularly. As it covers more than a single calendar, it is easier to use than the separate annual indexes to these newspapers. For research on current and recent issues, the *National Newspaper Index* is the first place one should look.

Another important tool is the *NewsBank Electronic Index*. This index is on CD-ROM, which makes searching for articles much easier. *NewsBank* indexes selected articles from more than 450 U.S. newspapers, beginning with January 1982. The full text of articles is available on microfiche.

All newspapers generally cover the Congress extensively, reporting on national implications of and local reactions to its activities.

*Chicago Tribune Index*. Wooster, OH: Bell and Howell, 1971– .

*Christian Science Monitor. Index to . . .* Wooster, OH: Bell and Howell, 1951– .

*Dallas Morning News Index.* Dallas, TX: Dallas Morning News Communications Center, 1960– .

*Detroit News Index.* Wooster, OH: Bell and Howell, 1976– .

*Houston Post Index.* Wooster, OH: Bell and Howell, 1976– .

*Los Angeles Times Index.* Wooster, OH: Bell and Howell, 1972– .

*Milwaukee Journal Index.* Wooster, OH: Bell and Howell, 1976– .

*New Orleans Times-Picayune Index.* Wooster, OH: Bell and Howell, 1972– .

*New York Times Index.* New York, NY: New York Times, 1913– .

*San Francisco Chronicle Index.* Wooster, OH: Bell and Howell, 1976– .

*Wall Street Journal Index.* Wooster, OH: Bell and Howell, 1955–1957. Princeton, NJ: Dow Jones Books, 1958– .

*Washington Post Index.* Wooster, OH: Bell and Howell, 1971– .

In addition to the newspaper indexes, both the *Public Affairs Information Service Bulletin* and the *Business Periodicals Index* selectively index stories from the *New York Times* and the *Wall Street Journal.*

# NEWSMAGAZINES

Weekly and monthly newsmagazines provide an excellent source for current information about the Congress. They include not only news stories but editorials and feature articles. *Newsweek* and *Time* are especially useful for weekly reports on congressional activities and actions. *Washington Monthly* and *Human Events* both focus specifically on politics in the Capitol, congressional activities, and developments in the executive branch and other agencies. *Human Events* contains sections entitled "Capitol Briefs" and "This Week's News in Washington." *Washington Monthly,* in addition to several feature articles per issue, has information on new appointments, news briefs on all activities of the government, and reviews of books on American politics. The other magazines listed below regularly carry articles on the

Congress. The journals listed include a variety of philosophical viewpoints, from liberal to conservative.

The best indexes to use for finding articles from this category of journals are the *Reader's Guide to Periodical Literature* and the *Magazine Index*. Another tool is the INFOTRAC database, a CD-ROM index that includes the *Magazine Index* and *Business Index*. INFOTRAC is updated quarterly and indexes materials back to 1980. It also indexes the *Wall Street Journal* and has an option for full text retrieval.

Although the following magazines do publish some scholarly articles on the Congress, they are not usually thought of as research journals. They are most useful for keeping up on current events and as a record of public opinion, as evidenced in their editorials and opinion articles. While they have limited value for serious research, they are valuable resources nonetheless.

*Atlantic Monthly.* Boston, MA: Atlantic Monthly Company, 1857– .

*Center Magazine.* Santa Barbara, CA: Center for the Study of Democratic Institutions, 1967– .

*Commentary: Journal of Significant Thought and Opinion on Contemporary Issues.* New York: American Jewish Committee, 1945– .

*Commonweal.* New York: Commonweal Publishing Company, 1924– .

*Conservative Digest.* Falls Church, VA: Viguerie Communications Corporation, 1975– .

*Current.* Washington, DC: Heldref Publications, 1960– .

*Harper's Magazine.* New York: Harper's Magazine Company, 1851– .

*Human Events: The National Conservative Weekly.* Washington, DC: Human Events, Inc., 1944– .

*National Review: A Journal of Fact and Opinion.* New York: National Review, Inc., 1955– .

*New Republic: A Journal of Opinion.* Washington, DC: New Republic, 1914– .

*Newsweek.* New York: Newsweek, Inc., 1933– .

*Progressive.* Madison, WI: Progressive, Inc., 1909– .

*Society: Social Science and Modern Society.* New Brunswick, NJ: Transactions Periodicals Consortium, Rutgers University, 1963– .

*Time; The Weekly Newsmagazine.* New York: Time-Life, 1923– .

*U.S. News and World Report.* Washington, DC: U.S. News and World Report, Inc., 1933– .

*Washington Monthly.* Washington, DC: Washington Monthly Company, 1969– .

# NEWSLETTERS

There are literally hundreds of newsletters and reports published by public interest and lobbying groups, representing almost every industry, business, and professional association and organization throughout the country. These newsletters range from just a few pages to rather lengthy reports. As they are intended for specific audiences, such as a union, political organization, profession, etc., their news coverage is selective and reflects the interests of the publishing agency. Their contents can include feature articles, editorials, news briefs, background studies, ratings of legislators, and lobbying information. While their formats differ, all attempt to report any important developments related to their area of interest, whether it be congressional actions, new or proposed legislation, a Supreme Court decision, or changes in regulatory rules and decisions.

The newsletters listed below are only a selected number of titles reflecting a wide range of interests. Generally, most of these newsletters are not indexed, but some of the major ones are indexed in the *Business Periodicals Index, Business Index,* and *Applied Science and Technology Index.* The best way to determine if an organization, whether it is a public interest group or industrial or business association, publishes a newsletter that focuses on national politics is to write to the organization. Many of the newsletters are distributed free; others are only available to members of the group. Academic and public libraries often subscribe to a variety of newsletters. For the student and researcher, newsletters can be a source of information on the lobbying activities of a particular interest group. Many newsletters give ratings of legislators and other leaders that can be used to generate data for a research design. Depending on how they are used, newsletters can be considered both as primary and secondary source material.

| Title | Publisher |
|---|---|
| *ADA Legislative Newsletter* | Americans for Democratic Action<br>1411 K Street, N.W.<br>Washington, DC 20005 |
| *AFL-CIO News* | American Federation of Labor and Congress of Industrial Organizations<br>815 16th Street, N.W.<br>Washington, DC 20006 |
| *ALA Washington Newsletter* | American Library Association<br>110 Maryland Avenue, N.E.<br>Washington, DC 20002 |
| *American Political Report* | American Political Research Corporation<br>4720 Montgomery Avenue<br>Bethesda, MD 20014 |
| *Congressional Monitor* | Congressional Quarterly<br>1414 22nd Street, N.W.<br>Washington, DC 20037 |
| *Congressional Round-up* | National Rural Housing Coalition<br>1346 Connecticut Avenue, N.W.<br>Washington, DC 20036 |
| *Dateline Washington* | National Conference of State Legislatures<br>444 N. Capitol Street, N.W.<br>Washington, DC 20001 |

*DSG Legislative Reports*                    Democratic Study Group
                                             1422 Longworth House Office
                                                Building
                                             Washington, DC 20515


*Energy Legislative Service*                 McGraw-Hill
                                             1221 Avenue of the Americas
                                             New York, NY 10020


*Federal Legislative Roundup*                National Association of Life
                                                Underwriters
                                             1922 F Street, N.W.
                                             Washington, DC 20006


*First Monday*                               Republican National
                                                Committee
                                             310 First Street, S.E.
                                             Washington, DC 20003


*For the People*                             Congressional Black Caucus
                                             306 House Annex
                                             Washington, DC 20515


*In Common*                                  Common Cause
                                             2030 M Street, N.W.
                                             Washington, DC 20036


*Legislative Bulletin*                       American Mining Congress
                                             1100 Ring Building
                                             Washington, DC 20036


*Legislative Lookout*                        American Association of
                                                University Women
                                             2401 Virginia Avenue, N.W.
                                             Washington, DC 20037


*Report from the Hill*                       League of Women Voters of
                                                the United States
                                             1730 M Street, N.W.
                                             Washington, DC 20036

| *Republican Research* | House Republican Research |
| *Committee Reports* | Committee |
| | 1616 Longworth House Office |
| | Building |
| | Washington, DC 20515 |

| *Washington Report* | Chamber of Commerce of the |
| | United States |
| | 1615 H Street, N.W. |
| | Washington, DC 20062 |

| *Washington Report* | National Association of |
| | Regional Councils |
| | 1700 K Street, N.W. |
| | Washington, DC 20006 |

| *Washington Report of the* | American Security Council |
| *American Security Council* | 1101 17th Street, N.W. |
| | Washington, DC 20036 |

| *Washington Week* | National Industrial Council |
| | 1776 F Street, N.W. |
| | Washington, DC 20006 |

| *What's Next* | Congressional Clearinghouse |
| | on the Future |
| | 3692 HOB Annex II, U.S. |
| | House of Representatives |
| | Washington, DC 20515 |

# NEWS SERVICES

While newspapers provide day-to-day coverage of political events, the time lag for published indexes is one of the most frustrating problems that researchers encounter. Indexes to newspapers generally are three or more months behind. Consequently, if one is interested in finding information about an event that took place a month ago, one may not be able to search newspapers through an index. It is in these situations that news services can be most useful, as they are only about two weeks behind in their publication.

*Facts on File* and *Keesing's Contemporary Archives* are often the only indexed sources available for information about very recent events. They can be used to research political campaigns in progress or to research an event such as a convention, shortly after it has happened.

*Facts on File. Weekly News Digest and Index.* New York: Facts on File, 1940– .
This is a weekly digest of world events. The entries are grouped under topics such as world affairs or national affairs. There is a cumulative index. The emphasis is on the United States; thus this is a good service for presidential politics.

*Keesing's Contemporary Archives: Weekly Diary of World Events.* London: Keesing's Publications Ltd., 1931– .
This publication offers summaries of news reports for the week. There is strong coverage of news events in the United Kingdom and Europe. It is indexed cumulatively every two weeks, three months, each year, and every two years. *Keesing's* is a useful tool for studying American foreign policy, international relations, and treaty-making.

*Editorials on File: Semi-Monthly Compilation from 140 U.S. and Canadian Newspapers.* New York: Facts on File, 1977– .
Editorials are reproduced and indexed in this reference work. This tool can be used to study public opinions and attitudes toward the Congress. It is especially useful for studying campaigns and elections and finding the newspapers' endorsements of candidates.

## LEGAL NEWSPAPERS

We have listed legal newspapers in a separate category, as they are indeed a special kind of publication. Although these newspapers are written with the legal profession in mind, they contain a wealth of information for anyone studying the Congress. They include stories about major issues, appointment of new officials, and budget increases and cutbacks, as well as political developments and controversies surrounding the Congress. For anyone following the nation's politics, these newspapers should be required reading.

*Legal Times of Washington.* Washington, DC: Legal Times of Washington, 1978– .

This weekly periodical contains accounts of current developments in the legal world.

*National Law Journal.* New York: New York Law Publishing Company, 1978– .
This is a legal newspaper geared for a general audience. It offers a weekly selective index to legal materials.

*U.S. Law Week.* Washington, DC: Bureau of National Affairs, Inc., 1931– .
This weekly newspaper has four major sections. Section one gives summaries and analyses of major court decisions. The second section deals with new court decisions and agency rulings. The third section contains information on Supreme Court decisions. The last section contains information on Supreme Court opinions.

# BIBLIOGRAPHIES

The researcher who is interested in congressional politics will have no difficulty finding materials. Perhaps the only problem the researcher will face is focusing in on a particular topic and weeding through citations and sources. The bibliographies mentioned in this section cover all kinds of materials, including books, periodical literature, and government documents. By consulting these bibliographies the researcher will have thousands of citations from which to choose.

## General

*Bibliographic Index: A Cumulative Bibliography of Bibliographies.* New York. H. W. Wilson, 1937– .
This work lists bibliographies by subject. The bibliographies listed are separate books, parts of books, periodical articles, or pamphlets. There is a semiannual index and a cumulated index each December.

## Congress

Goehlert, Robert U., and John R. Sayre. *The United States Congress: A Bibliography.* New York: Free Press, 1982.

128                                                     Secondary Sources

This is the most complete bibliography on Congress. It includes 5,620 citations to books, dissertations, journal articles, research reports, and selected documents. The citations are classified according to fourteen major topics: History and Development of Congress, Congressional Process, Reform of Congress, Powers of Congress, Congressional Investigations, Foreign Affairs, Committees, Legislative Analysis, Legislative Case Studies, Leadership in Congress, Pressures on Congress, Congress and the Electorate, Members of Congress, and the Support and Housing of Congress. The bibliography also includes a subject and author index.

Kennon, Donald R., ed. *The Speakers of the U.S. House of Representatives: A Bibliography, 1789–1984.* Baltimore: Johns Hopkins University Press, 1986.
    This bibliography is arranged in chronological order by Speaker. For each Speaker there is a brief biographical profile followed by a listing of manuscript collections. Finally, there is a bibliography of books, dissertations, and articles about and by each Speaker. The work includes a subject and author index.

The Congressional Research Service has published a number of bibliographies on Congress. Those listed below are especially useful, as they are all annotated. All of the bibliographies cover the same areas, including history, procedure, reorganization and reform, party leadership, committee system, staff and support agencies, roll-call analysis, and policy studies. All of these bibliographies are available on microfilm in the *Major Studies and Issue Briefs of the Congressional Research Service.*

Rundquist, Paul. *Congress: A Selected Annotated Bibliography.* 1982. 12p.

Cook, Mary E., Sherry B. Shapiro, and George H. Walser. *Congress: A Selected Annotated Bibliography.* 1985. 25p.

Strickland, Dan. *The United States House of Representatives: A Selected Annotated Bibliography.* 1981. 127p.

Hardy, Carol, Sherry B. Shapiro, and George H. Walser. *The United States House of Representatives: A Selected Annotated Bibliography.* 1985. 43p.

Amer, Mildred L. *The United States Senate: A Selected Annotated Bibliography.* 1981. 106p.

Hardy, Carol, Sherry B. Shapiro, and George H. Walser. *The United States Senate: A Selected Annotated Bibliography.* 1985. 32p.

By using the subject catalog of any large library and the various indexes mentioned, one can quickly find many citations to materials on Congress. There are a few bibliographies on Congress and legislative studies in general that can be used to start one's research.

U.S. Senate Historical Office. *The United States Senate: A Historical Bibliography.* Washington, DC: U.S. Government Printing Office, 1977.

Jones, Charles O., and Randall B. Ripley. *The Role of Political Parties in Congress: A Bibliography and Research Guide.* Tucson: University of Arizona Press, 1966.

Kerwood, John R., ed. *The United States Capitol: An Annotated Bibliography.* Norman: University of Oklahoma Press, 1973.

Michigan Senate Fellows. *The Legislative Process: A Bibliography in Legislative Behavior.* Lansing: Institute for Community Development, Michigan State University, 1964.

Tompkins, Dorothy L. C. *Congressional Investigation of Lobbying: A Selected Bibliography.* Berkeley: Institute of Governmental Studies, University of California, 1956.

Tompkins, Dorothy L. C. *Changes in Congress: Proposals to Change Congress, Term of Members of the House; A Bibliography.* Berkeley: Institute of Governmental Studies, University of California, 1966.

Wilcox, Allen R. *Voting in Collegial Bodies: A Selected Bibliography.* Reno: Bureau of Governmental Research, University of Nevada, 1971.

# Federal Government

Smith, Dwight L., and Lloyd W. Garrison, eds. *The American Political Process: Selected Abstracts of Periodical Literature (1954–1971).* Santa Barbara, CA: ABC-Clio, 1972.
    This work contains numerous citations on congressional politics. Since the abstracts were drawn from *Historical Abstracts* and *America: History*

*and Life,* the work is a good source for materials published in journals in the humanities, especially history. The work also includes an excellent author/subject index.

Garrison, Lloyd, ed. *American Politics and Elections: Selected Abstracts of Periodical Literature, 1964–1968.* Santa Barbara, CA: ABC-Clio, 1968.
   This work contains selected abstracts of periodical literature between 1964 and 1968. Abstracts cover more than 500 U.S. and Canadian periodicals and are divided into four subject areas: (1) political parties, (2) the electoral process, (3) voting behavior, and (4) presidential elections (between 1800 and 1968). Within each category, abstracts are arranged topically, chronologically, and in alphabetical sequence by author.

# JOURNALS

The researcher interested in congressional activities will have no difficulty finding a substantial amount of information in the plentiful journal literature. Journal articles are important because they are published faster than books and often treat narrow topics. There are many journals containing articles on the Congress, but those cited in this section regularly have such articles. While it is best to search for journal literature by using indexes, we have identified some of the major journals in political science, law, and history that are particularly useful for studying the Congress. There are also six journals, listed below, that deserve special mention because they all focus on the Congress itself or closely related subjects.

## Congress

*Congress and the Presidency: A Journal of Capitol Studies.* Washington, DC: School of Government and Public Administration, American University, 1983– .
   Formerly titled *Congressional Studies,* this journal now covers both the presidency and Congress, the interaction between the two, and national policy-making in general. Published twice a year, it contains a mix of articles from both political science and history. Besides research articles, it includes research notes, review essays, and book reviews.

*Congressional Quarterly Weekly Report.* Washington, DC: Congressional Quarterly, 1946– .

This journal recounts important congressional and political activities of the previous week, including developments in committees as well as on the floor. When covering major pieces of legislation, it often gives voting records and excerpts of testimony in hearings. Full or selected texts of presidential press conferences, and major statements and speeches are reprinted. Lobbying activities are given considerable coverage, with special reports on the relationship between congressional voting and interest groups. Each issue usually contains an article on special issues or major legislation pending in Congress. Congressional Quarterly indexes the *Weekly Report* both quarterly and annually. The *Weekly Report* is also indexed in *Public Affairs Information Service Bulletin.*

*National Journal: The Weekly on Politics and Government.* Washington, DC: U.S. Government Printing Office, 1969– .

The *National Journal* covers all areas of federal decision making. It provides excellent analyses of activities of the Congress. Each issue contains two or more feature articles on some aspect of congressional politics. In some respects the *National Journal* is similar to the *CQ Weekly Report,* but it differs in that it gives more emphasis to developments in the executive branch. Using both the *CQ Weekly Report* and the *National Journal* will provide excellent coverage of current political events. The *National Journal* is self-indexed quarterly and annually by subject, name, and organization. It is also indexed in *Public Affairs Information Service Bulletin.*

## Elections

*Campaigns and Elections: The Journal of Political Action.* Washington, DC: National Press Building, 1980– .

Though this quarterly journal is intended for individuals involved in campaign management, politicians, and interest groups, it is very useful to students and researchers. It covers a wide variety of topics, including polling, political action committees, election demographics, fund-raising and financing, media relations, and campaign techniques and strategies.

*Election Politics.* Washington, DC: Institute for Government and Politics, 1983– .

The focus of this quarterly journal is on American political campaigns and elections. It includes articles by political scientists, journalists, and campaign professionals and features a variety of articles covering topics such as PACs, finance, public opinion research, and new election processes.

*Electoral Studies.* Guild Ford, England: Butterworth, 1982– .
This triennial journal is international in scope, but it does include American election studies. As it is the first journal to exclusively cover elections, it is invaluable for anyone interested in electoral analysis, either on a comparative basis or just in the United States.

## Political Science

Virtually every journal in political science at one time or another will contain an article on Congress. The journals listed below either publish articles on Congress on a regular basis or are useful for specialized areas of study, such as public opinion. Besides journals in political science, there are many journals in the fields of economics, sociology, psychology, and policy studies that publish articles related to the study of Congress. Again, the best method for finding articles from journals in those disciplines is to use a variety of indexes and abstracting services.

*American Academy of Political and Social Sciences, The Annals.* Philadelphia, PA: American Academy of Political and Social Science, 1890– . (Published bimonthly.)

*American Journal of Political Science.* Detroit, MI: Midwest Political Science Association, 1957– . (Published quarterly.)

*American Political Science Review.* Washington, DC: American Political Science Association, Inc., 1907– . (Published quarterly.)

*American Politics Quarterly.* Beverly Hills, CA: Sage Publications, 1973– . (Published quarterly.)

*British Journal of Political Science.* New York: Cambridge University Press, 1971– . (Published quarterly.)

*Foreign Affairs.* New York: Council on Foreign Relations, 1922– . (Published five times a year.)

*Foreign Policy.* Washington, DC: Carnegie Endowment for International Peace, 1970– . (Published quarterly.)

*Journal of Law and Politics.* Charlottesville: University of Virginia, 1983– . (Published quarterly.)

*Journal of Politics.* Gainesville, FL: Southern Political Science Association, 1939– . (Published quarterly.)

*Law and Contemporary Problems.* Durham, NC: Duke University, School of Law, 1933– . (Published quarterly.)

*Legislative Studies Quarterly.* Iowa City: Comparative Legislative Research Center, University of Iowa, 1976– . (Published quarterly.)

*Policy Review.* Washington, DC: Heritage Foundation, Inc., 1977– . (Published quarterly.)

*Political Behavior.* Albany, NY: Agathon Press, 1979– . (Published quarterly.)

*Political Psychology.* New Brunswick, NJ: International Society of Political Psychology, 1979– . (Published quarterly.)

*Political Science Quarterly.* New York: Academy of Political Science, 1886– . (Published quarterly.)

*Polity.* Amherst, MA: Northeastern Political Science Association, 1968– . (Published quarterly.)

*Public Administration Review.* Washington, DC: American Society for Public Administration, 1940– . (Published quarterly.)

*Public Interest.* New York: National Affairs, Inc., 1965– . (Published quarterly.)

*Public Opinion.* Washington, DC: American Enterprise Institute, 1978– . (Published bimonthly.)

*Public Opinion Quarterly.* New York: American Association for Public Opinion Research, Columbia University, 1937– . (Published quarterly.)

*Review of Politics.* Notre Dame, IN: University of Notre Dame, 1938– .
(Published quarterly.)

*Social Science Quarterly.* Austin, TX: Southwestern Social Science Association, 1920– . (Published quarterly.)

*Western Political Quarterly.* Salt Lake City, UT: Western Political Science Association, 1948– . (Published quarterly.)

*Wilson Quarterly.* Washington, DC: Woodrow Wilson Center for Scholars, 1976– . (Published quarterly.)


# Legal

Journals in the field of law are a primary source for articles relating to the study of the Congress. Most students and researchers tend to overlook these journals unless they are doing work on some topic from a legal point of view. Although they are indispensible for legal research, they can also be useful for other approaches to the Congress, for they contain an enormous number of articles on all aspects of the Congress. It is impossible to cite all the journals that would be useful; only a few representative journals are listed here. Omitted are university journals (*Harvard Law Review, Georgetown Law Journal*), state journals (*Illinois Bar Journal, Maryland Law Review*), and some specialized journals (*Antitrust Law and Economic Review, Tax Law Review*) that can be especially important when researching a topic related to specific areas. One should always take the time to see what specialized journals exist, as they may be primary sources of information.

*Administrative Law Review.* Chicago, IL: American Bar Association, 1973– . (Published quarterly.)

*American Bar Association Journal.* Chicago, IL: American Bar Association, 1915– . (Published monthly.)

*American Journal of Legal History.* Philadelphia, PA: American Society for Legal History, 1957– . (Published quarterly.)

*Federal Bar Journal.* Washington, DC: Federal Bar Association, 1931– .
(Published quarterly.)

*Federal Rules Decisions.* St. Paul, MN: West Publishing Company, 1941– .
(Published monthly.)

*Harvard Journal on Legislation.* Cambridge, MA: Harvard Legislative
Research Bureau, 1964– . (Published triennially.)

*United States Law Week: A National Service of Current Law.* Washington,
DC: Bureau of National Affairs, 1933– . (Published weekly.)

# History

Journals in the field of history are a particularly rich resource for materials
on Congress. Obviously, anyone doing research of a historical nature will
want to use history journals, but such journals should not be overlooked
regardless of the topic or time frame of one's research. One can find articles
in history journals that are devoted to current events and topics that are
unrelated to time. For example, history journals contain a wealth of information for anyone doing research from an institutional perspective.

In addition to the major journals listed below, all of the state historical
journals (*Annals of Iowa, Kansas Historical Quarterly, Ohio History, Wisconsin Magazine of History,* to mention a few) publish articles related to the
study of the Congress. Similarly, state historical journals publish articles on
congressional actions, appointments, or policies that significantly affected
that state.

*American Heritage: The Magazine of History.* New York: American Heritage Publishing Company, 1949– . (Published bimonthly.)

*American Historical Review.* Washington, DC: The American Historical
Association, 1895– . (Published five times a year.)

*American Studies.* Lawrence, KS: Midcontinent American Studies Association, 1960– . (Published quarterly.)

*Current History.* Philadelphia, PA: Current History, Inc., 1943– . (Published monthly.)

*Diplomatic History.* Wilmington, DE: Scholarly Resources, Inc., 1977– .
(Published quarterly.)

*Historian: A Journal of History.* Allentown, PA: Alpha Theta International Honor Society in History, 1938– . (Published quarterly.)

*Journal of American History.* Bloomington, IN: Organization of American Historians, 1914– . (Published quarterly.)

*Journal of Southern History.* New Orleans, LA: Southern Historical Association, 1935– . (Published quarterly.)

*Pacific Historical Review.* Berkeley, CA: American Historical Association, Pacific Coast Branch, 1932– . (Published quarterly.)

*Prologue: The Journal of the National Archives.* Washington, DC: U.S. National Archives and Records Service, 1969– . (Published quarterly.)

# INDEXES

Indexes and abstracting services are crucial research tools of studying Congress. They are the key to finding journal literature. While almost every index will contain citations to articles on the Congress, we have selected the indexes most likely to be used in the study of Congress. But students and researchers should always check to see if there are any other indexes that would prove useful to their research. For example, to research the role of women in the Congress, *Women Studies Abstracts* would be useful; for a focus on congressional initiatives in urban problems, check *Sage Urban Studies Abstracts*; to explore congressional efforts in the area of law and order, the *Abstracts on Criminology and Penology* will be helpful, as well as several other indexes in the field of criminal justice. As many indexes are now available on CD-ROM, one should check to see if these versions are in a library. CD-ROM products can save time and effort.

## General

*British Humanities Index.* London: Library Association, 1963– .

This work indexes articles from over 275 periodicals in the humanities and social sciences. The entries in the quarterly issues are arranged by subject. In addition to indexing all of the major British journals in political science that would have articles on the Congress, the work also indexes journals such as *New Society,* the *Guardian,* etc., which can be used as sources for studying British views of the Congress and American politics.

*Business Periodicals Index.* New York: H. W. Wilson, 1958– .
This work, published monthly except August and cumulated annually, indexes articles occurring in English-language business periodicals published in the United States. It covers accounting, advertising, finance, labor, management, public administration, and general business. The index can be used two ways to study Congress: (1) finding articles reflecting what the business and industrial sectors think of congressional policies and actions and (2) following the views and actions of interest groups and associations, because the work indexes a considerable number of trade and professional magazines. This index is also available on CD-ROM.

*Magazine Index.* Menlo Park, CA: Information Access Company, 1978– .
This monthly index lists articles and reviews appearing in general U.S. magazines. It is most useful for following current events relating to the Congress and finding articles reflecting various opinions on issues. This index is also included in *Infotrac Database,* the CD-ROM service.

*Public Affairs Information Service Bulletin.* New York: The Service, 1915– .
This is a weekly subject guide to the field of American politics in general, indexing government publications, books, and periodical literature. It includes citations to many hearings. Additionally, it indexes the *National Journal, CQ Weekly Report, Congressional Digest,* and, selectively, the *Weekly Compilation of Presidential Documents.* All of these journals are invaluable guides to studying the Congress on a current basis. A fifteen-volume *Cumulative Subject Index to the PAIS Annual Bulletins, 1915–1974* has been published by Carrollton Press. *PAIS* is cumulated quarterly and annually.

*Reader's Guide to Periodical Literature.* New York: H. W. Wilson, 1905– .
This semimonthly guide indexes articles in popular periodicals published in the United States. Articles are indexed by author and subject. Each yearly cumulation of this index includes hundreds of citations about the Congress, campaigns, and elections. While one would not use this index for scholarly research, it is always worthwhile to see what it does have about the Congress. For research focusing on events within the past year, it is a vital reference tool. This guide is now available on CD-ROM.

*Social Sciences Citation Index*. Philadelphia, PA: Institute for Science Information, 1973– .

Items appearing in the *SSCI* (published three times yearly) have been cited in footnotes or bibliographies in the social sciences. The cited works are books, journal articles, dissertations, reports, proceedings, etc. There are four separate indexes: a source (author) index, a citation index, a corporate index, and the keyword subject index. Although this index is difficult to use, it does have several unique features that can be used for studying Congress. By using the corporate index, one can identify publications issued by particular organizations, such as the Brookings Institution. The source and citation indexes can be used to identify the writings of a particular scholar who has written extensively on Congress, as well as to identify other researchers who have cited his/her writings.

*Social Sciences Index*. New York: H. W. Wilson, 1975– .

This quarterly work indexes articles found in about 150 social science journals. The index covers all of the major journals in political science as well as the other social sciences. Every literature search on the Congress, regardless of the topic, should include this index. It is also available now on CD-ROM.

## Political Science

*ABC POL SCI: A Bibliography of Contents: Political Science and Government*. Santa Barbara, CA: ABC-Clio, 1969– .

Tables of contents from about 300 journals, both U.S. and foreign, are published six times a year in this bibliography. Because it is published in advance of the journals' publication dates, it is especially useful for finding very recent articles on Congress.

*Combined Retrospective Index to Journals in Political Science, 1886–1974*. 8 vols. Arlington, VA: Carrollton Press, 1978.

This work indexes articles from approximately 180 English-language political science periodicals appearing since 1886. It indexes by subject and author. As most indexes in the field of political science were only started in the past twenty years, this one is invaluable for anyone interested in articles published about the Congress in the nineteenth and early twentieth centuries. It is the only tool for systematically searching for older articles about the Congress.

*International Bibliography of Political Science*. Chicago: Aldine, 1962– .

This annual bibliography lists books, articles, reports, and other research publications classified under these six sections: political science, political thought, government and public administration, governmental process, international relations, and area studies. Entries are selected from more than 2,000 journals. This is another source for foreign-language materials on the Congress. It includes many English-language citations as well.

*International Political Science Abstracts*. Oxford, England: Basil Blackwell, 1952– .

This bimonthly work abstracts articles published in 600 English-language and foreign-language political science journals. The abstracts for the English-language journals appear in English, while the foreign-language articles are abstracted in French. This abstracting service is the best source for finding foreign-language articles about the Congress. Even if one is not interested in foreign-language material, one should check to see if this service has citations on Congress that have not appeared in other indexes.

*Sage Public Administration Abstracts*. Beverly Hills, CA: Sage Publications, 1974– .

This quarterly abstracts articles selected from approximately 200 English-language journals as well as books, pamphlets, and government publications dealing with public administration. Although this abstracting service does not have an enormous number of citations about Congress, it should be consulted when searching for information related to policy analysis, public management, bureaucratic studies, and federal programs.

*United States Political Science Documents*. 2 vols. Pittsburgh, PA: University Center for International Studies, University of Pittsburgh, 1976– .

This annual work indexes and abstracts about 120 United States political science journals. The first volume contains indexes by author, subject, geographic area, proper name, and journal title. The second volume abstracts the articles indexed in Volume 1. This is another index that should be used for studying Congress regardless of the topic. It indexes many of the newer journals in political science that are not covered elsewhere.

# Legal

*Annual Legal Bibliography*. Cambridge, MA: Harvard University Law School Library, 1961– .

This bibliography covers books and articles acquired by the Harvard University Law School Library. The entries are classified into the following groups: common law, civil law and other jurisdictions, private international law, and public international law. The entries are not annotated. This bibliography provides excellent coverage of administrative law and congressional relations with the president and Supreme Court.

*Contents of Current Legal Periodicals.* Los Angeles: Law Publications, 1975– .
The articles listed on the table of contents pages of legal journals are indexed by subject in this monthly publication. The virtue of this service is the currency of its indexing. It is most useful for finding recent legal studies on the Congress.

*Current Law Index.* Menlo Park, CA: Information Access Corporation, 1980– .
This monthly index covers legal periodicals and newspapers. Its microfilm counterpart, *Legal Resources Index,* cumulates the information found in the paper copy. *Legal Resources Index* is also available on CD-ROM, where it is called LEGALTRAC. It also indexes books and documents. These two indexes provide extensive coverage of the Congress and related topics. While most students and researchers only use these tools when interested in legal issues, the indexes should be consulted regardless of the subject.

*The Federal Index.* Cleveland, OH: Predicasts, 1976– .
This is a monthly index covering the congressional, executive, and judicial branches of government. It indexes the *Federal Register,* the *Congressional Record,* the *Weekly Compilation of Presidential Documents,* and *U.S. Law Week.* The index is cumulated annually. It is enormously useful for keeping up to date on federal policies, rules, and decisions. As a commercial index to documents and selected secondary sources it can save time when searching for legislative documents.

*Index to Legal Periodicals.* New York: H. W. Wilson, 1908– .
This monthly work indexes articles appearing in legal periodicals of the U.S., Canada, Great Britain, Northern Ireland, Australia, and New Zealand. Indexes are provided for authors, subjects, book reviews, and cases. This is another legal index that should be used in almost every literature search on Congress. As it is the oldest legal index, it can be used as a tool for historical research as well. It is also available on CD-ROM.

*Index to Periodical Articles Related to Law.* Dobbs Ferry, NY: Glanville Publications, 1958– .

This quarterly index lists by author and subject articles found in journals published by law schools, lawyers associations, and law institutes. It contains some citations to the study of Congress, but it should be used only after consulting the other legal indexes.

*Monthly Digest of Legal Articles.* Greenville, NY: Research and Documentation Corporation, 1969– .

This is another service best utilized for finding recent journal literature on the Congress.

# History

*Arts and Humanities Citation Index.* Philadelphia: Institute for Scientific Information, 1978– .

This work, published three times a year, indexes books, journal articles, theses, dissertations, reports, proceedings, congresses, and unpublished papers cited in footnotes or bibliographies in the humanities. There is an author index, citation index, subject index, and corporate index to the citations. This work can be used to find citations on Congress from history journals as well as the arts. For anyone interested in congressional activities and actions related to the arts, culture, and humanities, this index is most helpful. Though limited as an index for studying the Congress for most topics, it is the best source for the disciplines it covers.

*Combined Retrospective Index to Journals in History, 1838–1974.* 11 vols. Arlington, VA: Carrollton Press, 1978.

This work indexes over 150,000 articles published in over 200 English-language journals in history since 1838. Five of the eleven volumes cover U.S. history. There is an author index in addition to the subject index. Besides providing indexing of journals for the nineteenth century, this work is very good for biographical research on congressmen.

*America: History and Life.* Santa Barbara, CA: ABC-Clio, 1964– .

This serial bibliography covers articles, book and film reviews, and dissertations. A streamlined format adopted in 1989 incorporates four issues each year containing abstracts and citations. There is also a cumulative annual index. This abstracting service provides excellent coverage of materials in the field of history. For historical research on the Congress, one should always include this index.

*Humanities Index.* New York: H. W. Wilson, 1974– .
This is a quarterly index to English-language journals in the humanities. The articles are indexed by author and subject. This work covers the major journals in history and is best utilized in searches for citations related to the history of the Congress. This index is also available on CD-ROM.

*Writings on American History: A Subject Bibliography of Articles.* Millwood, NY: KTO Press, 1974– .
This is an annual bibliography of journal articles published on American history appearing in about 500 periodicals. The entries are arranged chronologically, geographically, and by subject. This work, while it has only an author index, not a subject index, includes a wealth of citations about the Congress. Its scope goes beyond the field of history and includes journals from political science, economics, and other social sciences. Although most researchers do not think of using this index unless they are looking for citations to history journals, it usually contains many useful citations on almost every topic related to Congress.

# DATABASES

Bibliographic databases that cover all areas of the social sciences are available at most university and other research libraries for retrieving information quickly and efficiently. Many libraries subscribe to on-line bibliographic databases such as Lockheed's DIALOG Information Retrieval Service, the Bibliographic Retrieval Service (BRS), and Systems Development Corporation's ORBIT. The two legal database systems are LEXIS and WESTLAW. The Information Bank of the New York Times includes materials from the *New York Times* and selected materials from other newspapers and magazines. Librarians are trained to use these databases and can advise the researcher as to the cost and effectiveness of the various systems. Two journals, *Online* and *Database: The Magazine of Database Reference and Review,* report on new databases, new searching techniques, and possible future developments. There are also two directories to database services.

# Directories

Williams, Martha E. *Computer-Readable Data Bases: A Directory and Data Sourcebook.* Chicago: American Library Association, 1978– .

This directory, an irregular publication updated by looseleaf supplements, identifies databases and other reference services. It includes information about the producer of the database, availability and charge rates, scope of subject matter, indexing, search programs, services offered, and any available user aids.

Schmittroth, John J., ed. *Encyclopedia of Information Systems and Services.* 6th ed. Detroit, MI: Gale Research Company, 1986.

This reference work gives descriptions of over 2,000 organizations in the United States and sixty other countries that produce, process, store, and use bibliographic and nonbibliographic data. It also identifies and discusses on-line vendors, videotext and teletext systems, telecommunication networks, and library systems.

# Selected Databases

## Current Affairs

NATIONAL NEWSPAPER INDEX. Menlo Park, CA: Information Access Corporation, 1979– .

This database indexes the *Christian Science Monitor,* the *New York Times,* and the *Wall Street Journal.* It indexes all items except weather charts, stock market tables, crossword puzzles, and horoscopes. It provides good coverage of government relations. This database is especially useful for finding articles related to current congressional activities, as well as campaigns and electioneering.

NEWSEARCH. Menlo Park, CA: Information Access Corporation, 1979– .

This database is a daily index of more than 2,000 news stories, information articles, and book reviews from over 1,400 newspapers, magazines, and periodicals. It indexes articles for the current month. At the end of the month the magazine article data are transferred to the MAGAZINE INDEX and the newspaper data are transferred to the NATIONAL NEWSPAPER INDEX. This is another excellent source for keeping up to date on congressional news stories.

MAGAZINE INDEX. Menlo Park, CA: Information Access Corporation, 1976– .
This database indexes articles from over 370 general magazines and provides good coverage of current affairs. While not as extensive in scope as the previous two databases, this resource can be useful to research major stories about Congress as well as current issues and controversies surrounding the Congress.

## Documents

CONGRESSIONAL RECORD ABSTRACTS. Washington, DC: Capitol Services, 1976– .
This database contains abstracts of items appearing in the *Congressional Record*. It covers bills, resolutions, committee and subcommittee reports, public laws, executive communications, speeches, and inserted materials. This database can speed up the process of compiling a legislative history and helps rapidly locate congressional speeches and messages.

GPO SALES PUBLICATIONS REFERENCE FILE. Washington, DC: U.S. Government Printing Office, 1971– .
This database is essentially an on-line version of the *GPO Publications Reference File* described earlier. It is best suited for finding citations to new publications, especially those that have not yet been cited in the *Monthly Catalog,* and for determining whether a particular document is still available for purchase.

FEDERAL INDEX. Washington, DC: Capitol Services, 1976– .
This database indexes the *Washington Post, Congressional Record, Federal Register,* and other documents, including rules, regulations, bills, speeches, hearings, roll calls, reports, vetoes, court decisions, and executive orders. It is the best single source for finding information about the federal government. Because it indexes a wide scope of legislative and executive documents, it is extremely useful for researching the Congress.

FEDERAL REGISTER ABSTRACTS. Washington, DC: Capitol Services, 1977– .
This database abstracts materials in the *Federal Register.* It covers government regulations, proposed rules, and legal notices, such as presidential proclamations, executive orders, and presidential determinations. For anyone studying the president as an administrator, this database is indispensible. It is an excellent index to presidential documents and administrative law in general.

GPO MONTHLY CATALOG. Washington, DC: U.S. Government Printing Office, 1976– .

This database contains records of reports, studies, etc., issued by all U.S. federal government agencies, including Senate and House hearings. It is useful for finding documents issued through the Office of the President and the Executive Office. While it is best suited for finding documents issued by departments of the executive branch, this database can also be used in compiling a legislative history.

## Social Sciences

AMERICA: HISTORY AND LIFE. Santa Barbara, CA: ABC-Clio, 1964– .

This database gives comprehensive coverage of all areas of U.S. history, international relations, and politics and government. It is the best database for finding articles dealing with the history of the Congress, biographical materials on congressmen, and campaign and election studies.

COMPREHENSIVE DISSERTATION INDEX. Ann Arbor, MI: Xerox University Microfilms, 1861– .

This database indexes American dissertations written since 1861 by subject, title, and author. For anyone, student or researcher, doing in-depth research on the Congress or a specific congressman, a search of this database will yield dozens of citations about any one topic. As there are thousands of dissertations written about various aspects of Congress, this database has a wealth of information.

PAIS INTERNATIONAL. New York: PAIS, 1976– .

Each year approximately 25,000 citations found in over 1,200 journals and over 800 books, pamphlets, government documents, and agency reports are added to this database. All fields of the social sciences including political science, public administration, international relations, law, and public policy are covered. This database is useful not only for finding materials related to current events, but for doing research on specific topics as well. As it indexes books, documents, and articles from journals such as the *CQ Weekly Report* and the *National Journal,* this database can yield a wide variety of citations to both primary and secondary sources.

PSYCINFO. Washington, DC: American Psychological Association, 1967– .

Each year citations covering psychology and related areas are chosen from over 900 journals, 1,500 books, and numerous technical reports for this database. A search can produce numerous citations to psychological and behavioral studies of the Congress. As the database contains a considerable number of materials in the fields of political behavior and psychology, it is quite useful for anyone studying the Congress on a micro level. The print version of this index, *Psychological Abstracts,* is also available on CD-ROM.

SOCIAL SCISEARCH. Philadelphia: Institute for Scientific Information, 1972– .

All areas of the social and behavioral sciences are covered in this database. Entries are chosen from the 1,000 most important social science journals as well as from 2,200 others in the natural, physical, and biomedical sciences. As this is the largest in scope of any database, both in terms of the number of journals and disciplines covered, one can find citations to almost any facet of congressional studies. Of all the databases, this one will most likely yield the greatest number of citations on any single topic related to the Congress.

SOCIOLOGICAL ABSTRACTS. San Diego, CA: Sociological Abstracts, 1963– .

Abstracts covering sociology and related areas in the social and behavioral sciences are included in this database. Entries are chosen from over 1,200 periodicals and other serial publications. In addition to citations to sociological and behavioral studies of the Congress, this database also includes citations to campaigning, elections, public opinion, and political communication as well as the impact of congressional policies and programs. The print version of this database, *Sociological Abstracts,* is also available on CD-ROM.

USPSD. Pittsburgh, PA: University of Pittsburgh, University Center for International Studies, 1975– .

Articles from approximately 120 major political science journals published in the United States are abstracted and indexed. This database can be best utilized for finding citations from the major journals in the field of political science. It is also the best database for identifying articles on the Congress from the growing number of policy studies journals.

*Legal*

LEXIS. Dayton, OH: Mead Data Central, 1973– .

This system searches through legal documents to retrieve needed information. With a LEXIS terminal and telephone, text is retrieved from a computer in Dayton, Ohio. This system can be used for finding citations to several different perspectives on the Congress, including legal analysis of policies, decision making, and regulatory politics.

WESTLAW. St. Paul, MN: West Publishing Company, 1978– .
All recent U.S. state and federal court decisions are abstracted in this database. As it covers judicial decision making and the court system, it can be used most effectively for finding citations related to the interpretation of public laws and the relationship of the Congress to the Supreme Court.

LEGAL RESOURCE INDEX. Menlo Park, CA: Information Access Corporation, 1980– .
This database indexes over 660 law journals and five law newspapers as well as legal monographs and government publications from the Library of Congress database. It provides the best overall coverage of legal materials and can be used for researching almost any topic related to Congress.

## Legislative Search Systems

CQ WASHINGTON ALERT. Washington, DC: Congressional Quarterly, 1986– .
This database provides access to congressional committee and floor schedules up to three months in the future. Each entry includes the subject, location, and time of the meeting or hearing, including the names and affiliations of witnesses. It provides daily news highlights plus summaries of floor action, including legislation introduced, actions on bills, speeches, reports filed, procedural matters, nominations, public laws, and executive communications. It gives comprehensive chronologies of all bills introduced, their history through the legislative process, current status, and all cosponsors, as well as references to the CQ Weekly Report. It also lists new Senate, House, and joint committee reports, prints, and hearings as well as general accounting reports. It records all roll-call votes taken, including a summary of the issues. Finally, it includes member profiles, including background and biographical data, committee membership, election returns and financing, key votes and rating of congressmen by interest groups, and district descriptions and data.

## STATISTICAL SOURCES

In addition to finding data about voting and election returns, students and researchers often are interested in acquiring data about such subjects as government expenditures, the number of employees in the executive department, or some economic or social trend. There are almost 8,000 federal publications containing statistical data; fortunately, there are several special statistical indexes and guides one can use to find the data one is looking for.

*Vital Statistics on Congress*. Washington, DC: American Enterprise Institute for Public Research, 1980– .

This handbook, issued biennially, contains statistical data on Congress as an institution, including membership, elections, campaign financing, committees, staff, workload, operating expenses, budgeting, and voting alignments. The data are historical, spanning more than two decades. Congressional Quarterly is also publishing a new statistical volume entitled *Vital Statistics on American Politics,* by Harold W. Stanley and Richard G. Niemi (Washington, DC: Congressional Quarterly, 1988). It includes over 200 charts and figures on the presidency, the judiciary, public opinion data, elections and campaigns, and the Congress.

## Indexes

Andriot, John L. *Guide to U.S. Government Statistics*. Arlington, VA: Documents Index, 1973.

This guide to federal statistics lists publications containing data arranged according to departments and agencies. It includes a subject index identifying the types of data published. This guide is useful for identifying broad categories of data and for determining what data departments and agencies disseminate.

U.S. Bureau of the Census. *Catalog of United States Census Publications 1790–1972*. Washington, DC: U.S. Government Printing Office, 1974.

This catalog indexes and describes all decennial census publications, as well as all other census data on government, population, business, manufacturing, etc. For publications since 1972, one should use the monthly *Catalog of U.S. Census Publications* and the yearly cumulations. The monthly catalogs also include information on machine-readable data, reports, and tabulations. As more and more census data are being made available in this format, this is an important section for anyone interested in using data in machine-readable form.

*American Statistical Index.* Washington, DC: Congressional Information Service, 1974– .

The *American Statistical Index* is issued in looseleaf format and cumulated yearly. The 1974 edition is a special volume that indexes federal statistical publications issued between 1960 and 1973. This service indexes only data produced by the federal government, including more than 400 departments and agencies. The index provides access to data by subject, title, author, agency report, report number, and category breakdown. The twenty category breakdowns enable a user to find data by census division, industry, sex, income, commodity, race, etc. The index entry includes an accession number that leads the user to the abstract. The abstract provides complete bibliographical information on the publication as well as a descriptive synopsis of the data including its coverage, time span, arrangement, and any other specific details. In addition to indexing and abstracting the publications, Congressional Information Service also makes all of the publications available for purchase on microfilm. This volume should be the first place one starts when attempting to identify federal data. There are three cumulative indexes, covering the years 1970–1974, 1975–1978, and 1979–1982. Congressional Information Service has published a useful *American Statistical Index User Guide* (1976).

*Statistical Reference Index.* Washington, DC: Congressional Information Service, 1980– .

This bimonthly reference guide is published in the same format as its companion, the *American Statistical Index.* While the design and format are basically alike, they differ in content. This index provides access to data published by the private sector, including foundations, research centers, institutes, industrial and commercial organizations, etc. While it is not useful for researching the Congress directly, the index can be used to find data about interest groups, lobbying groups, or industries affected by legislation or regulation. In this regard, for any sector of society affected by the actions of the Congress, it is possible to find statistical data. There is also a cumulative index covering the years 1980–1985.

## Databases

On-line searching for three of the reference tools mentioned in previous sections is available through various commercial vendors. The *American*

*Statistical Index* is available as ASI and the *Statistical Reference Index* as SRI. By doing a computer search on-line it is possible to identify documents with a variety of search terms, including the index terms, titles, key words from the abstracts, issuing agency, and agency report number.

The data described in the annual *Congressional District Business Patterns* (New York: Economic Information Systems, 1981– ) are also available on-line from two databases, EIS INDUSTRIAL PLANTS and EIS NON-MANUFACTURING PLANTS. These databases, developed by Economic Information Systems, include data on more than 120,000 manufacturing plants and 350,000 nonmanufacturing businesses. The two databases cover 95 percent of all domestic manufacturing and about 65 percent of manufacturing business worldwide. Data are taken from journals, directories, corporate reports, Census Bureau publications, and information received from companies.

In addition to the above on-line services, there is a statistical database available every month on diskette. DATADISK/ECONOMIC, available from Cambridge Planning and Analytics, provides 188 series covering all aspects of the economy with the latest data, projections, and historical data. While this service does not include political data, it could be extremely useful for anyone doing research on Congress and the economy.

Finally, for additional information on statistical sources see the two sections Data Compilations (pp. 187–89) and Data Source Books (pp. 207–8) in Chapter 8.


# Ratings

One of the most frequently asked questions in libraries is, "Where can I find ratings of members of Congress?" Over 100 organizations rate members of Congress on key votes. At the end of this section are listed some of the major rating organizations. Most publish their ratings in their own newsletters or magazines. The easiest way to track down ratings by a specific organization is to write and inquire where its ratings are published. The addresses and telephone numbers for the organizations listed can be found in the directories cited in Chapter 7 (see pp. 181–82). The addresses of the groups that rate congressmen and the names of their publications are listed in a Congressional Research Service report, *Organizations that Rate Members of Congress on Their Voting Records,* by Janet Hays (revised edition, 1984). This report is available on microfilm in *Major Studies and Issue Briefs of the Congressional Research Service: 1984–1985 Supplement.*

Two weekly publications, *CQ Weekly Report* and *National Journal*, both publish ratings each year. *CQ Weekly Reports* publishes the ratings and the key votes on which the rating groups evaluated congressmen. Ratings of four organizations—Americans for Democratic Action, AFL-CIO Committee on Political Education, Chamber of Commerce of the United States, and Americans for Constitutional Action—are included in *CQ Weekly Report*. Rating listings in the *CQ Weekly Report* began in 1961. Ratings by the same groups can also be found in Congressional Quarterly's annual directory, *Politics in America*. Only the ratings are given in this volume, not the key votes on which they are based. The *National Journal*, in collaboration with the *Baron Report*, conducts its own rating, published in the *National Journal* each year since 1982. They analyze votes in three areas: economic, social, and foreign and defense policy. *The Almanac of American Politics*, by Michael Barone and Grant Ujifusa (Washington, DC: National Journal, 1972– ), provides ratings, but not the key votes, for eleven groups: Americans for Democratic Action, American Civil Liberties Union, AFL-CIO Committee on Political Education, Consumer Federation of America, League of Conservation Voters, American Conservative Union, National Taxpayers Union, National Security Index of the American Security Council, Chamber of Commerce of the United States, Americans for Constitutional Action, and Committee for the Survival of a Free Congress. The addresses and telephone numbers are provided in the front of the *Almanac*. There is also one publication that rates members of Congress on legislation affecting blacks and Hispanics: the *CEA Congressional Ledger*, published by Congressional Education Associates in Washington, DC. Finally, the best reference source is the following:

Sharp, J. Michael. *Directory of Congressional Voting Scores and Interest Group Ratings*. 2 vols. New York: Facts on File, 1988.

This volume provides a comprehensive voting study and group rating data compilation for every member of Congress since the beginning of the 80th Congress in 1947. Four categories of rating scores, all generated by Congressional Quarterly, are included. They are (1) conservative coalition, (2) party unity, (3) presidential support, and (4) voting participation. The volume also presents ratings by eleven groups that represent various areas of concern, including civil liberties, consumerism, conservation, education, and taxpayer spending. The real value of this volume is that it provides ratings back to 1947, when the first ratings were done. For a congressman who has served 20 years, one can find 20 years of rating and voting scores.

National organizations that rate members of Congress are listed below.

AFL-CIO Committee on Political Action
Amalgamated Clothing and Textile Workers Union
American Association of University Women
American Bakers Association Political Activities Committee
American Civil Liberties Union
American Conservative Union
American Consulting Engineers Council
American Farm Bureau Federation
American Federation of Government Employees
American Federation of State, County and Municipal Employees
American Federation of Teachers
American Institute of Architects
American Parents Committee
American Postal Workers Union
American Security Council
Americans for Constitutional Action Research Institute
Americans for Democratic Action
Associated General Contractors of America
Atlantic Richfield Civic Action Program
Baron Report
Bread for the World
Brotherhood of Railway, Airline and Steamship Clerks, Freight
    Handlers, Express and Station Employees
Building and Construction Trades Department, AFL-CIO
Business-Industry Political Action Committee
Campaign for UN Reform
Chamber of Commerce of the United States
Christian Voice
Citizens Committee for the Right to Keep and Bear Arms
Coalition for a New Foreign and Military Policy
Committee for the Survival of a Free Congress
Common Cause
Communication Workers of America
Congressional Education Associates
Congressional Quarterly
Conservative Caucus Research, Analysis and Education Foundation
Conservatives Against Liberal Legislation
Consumer Federation of America
Council for a Competitive Economy
Council for a Livable World
Friends Committee on National Legislation

Friends of the Earth
Human Events
Independent Petroleum Association of America
International Association of Machinists and Aerospace Workers
International Brotherhood of Teamsters, Chauffeurs, Warehousemen, and
  Helpers of America
Leadership Conference on Civil Rights
League of Conservation Voters
League of Women Voters of the United States
Liberty Lobby
March for Life
National Abortion Rights Action League
National Alliance of Senior Citizens
National Association for the Advancement of Colored People
National Association of Life Underwriters
National Association of Manufacturers
National Association of Realtors
National Association of Retired Federal Employees
National Association of Social Workers
National Audio-Visual Association
National Committee for a Human Life Amendment
National Council of Senior Citizens
National Education Association
National Farmers Organization
National Farmers Union
National Federation of Independent Business
National Journal
National League of Cities
National Right to Life Committee
National Society of Professional Engineers
National Taxpayers Union
National Women's Political Caucus
National "Write Your Congressman" Club
Network, A Catholic Social Justice Lobby
Public Citizen/Congress Watch
Public Employee Department, AFL-CIO
Review of the News
Ripon Society
United Auto Workers
United States Student Association
United Steelworkers of America

United Transportation Union
Veterans of Foreign Wars Political Action Committee
Watchdogs of the Treasury
Woman Activist

# DISSERTATIONS

Literally hundreds of dissertations from various disciplines in the humanities
and social sciences have been written about Congress and individual congressmen. As dissertations are not normally acquired systematically by
libraries, one would either have to borrow them through interlibrary loan,
purchase them directly, or request their purchase by a library. Consequently,
students may not want to include dissertations in their search strategy. But
for the serious researcher, dissertations are a major source of secondary
information. The following works can be used to identify dissertations on a
desired subject.

*Comprehensive Dissertation Index.* 37 vols. Ann Arbor, MI: Xerox University Microfilms, 1973– .
    This work indexes by author and key words the entries found in *American
Doctoral Dissertations* and *Dissertation Abstracts International* (listed below). It consists of a thirty-seven-volume set covering dissertations written
between 1861 and 1977, and there are five annual supplements. This is the
best index to use for identifying a particular dissertation or for conducting a
subject search.

*Dissertation Abstracts International.* Ann Arbor, MI: Xerox University
Microfilms, 1938– .
    This monthly index abstracts dissertations completed at American and
some foreign universities. While the *Comprehensive Dissertation Index* is a
better tool for searching for dissertations by subject, *Dissertation Abstracts*
is indispensible for finding recent dissertations. *Dissertation Abstracts* is
also available on CD-ROM.

*American Doctoral Dissertations.* Ann Arbor, MI: Xerox University Microfilms, 1955/56– .
    This is a supplement to *Dissertation Abstracts International.* Entries of
additional dissertations are listed each year.

*Doctoral Dissertations Accepted by American Universities, 1933/34–1954/55.* New York: Wilson, 1934–1956.

This work lists dissertations from U.S. and Canadian universities from 1933 to 1955. The entries are arranged by subject. There is an author and a subject index.

*Masters Abstracts.* Ann Arbor, MI: Xerox University Microfilms, 1962– .

Masters theses of some U.S. colleges and universities are abstracted in this work. The entries are arranged by subject.

*Index to American Doctoral Dissertations.* Ann Arbor, MI: University Microfilms International, 1957– .

This index was issued each year as a part of *Dissertation Abstracts.* In 1963 it began being published as a separate work.

# AUDIOVISUAL MATERIALS

One of the newest resources available for the study of Congress are video cassettes. These resources allow one to get a better understanding of how Congress works by seeing the legislative process in action. "We the People," a series of twenty-six half-hour cassettes, shows the day-to-day activities of Congress, with analysis and commentary by political scientists. Among some of the topics covered are congressional elections, committee leadership, lobbying, constituent relations, lawmaking, budgeting, ethics, the courts, and relations with the president and the media. The series was produced by the American Political Science Association and WETA, a public television station in Washington. The American Political Science Association has published both a study guide and faculty guide to accompany the series.

There is not a wealth of video cassettes about Congress, but the number is steadily growing. Another very good video cassette is "An Act of Congress," produced by the Learning Corporation of America. A video cassette put out by the U.S. Chamber of Commerce on the budget process is called "Dollars! Dollars! Dollars! The Congressional Budget Process." A set of fifteen half-hour video cassettes on American government, produced by Boston's public television station, WGBH, and Harvard University, includes three video cassettes about Congress, "The Functions of Congress," "Congressional Reform," and "Congress and the President."

Audio cassettes are another source of information. The National Public Radio sells a wide variety of cassettes that relate to Congress, on topics such as women politicians, campaigning, elections, Watergate, and National Press Club speeches. For more details concerning what is available, consult the *National Public Radio Cassette Catalog*. The Robert Maynard Hutchins Center for the Study of Democratic Institutions sells over 500 radio cassettes on international relations, economic systems, social order, and government. The center has produced a number of audio cassettes dealing specifically with Congress, including "The Need for Congressional Reform," "The Legislator's Eighteen-Hour Day," "The Executive and the Legislative Branch: Power, Efficiency and Accountability," and "Towards a Stronger Congress: Institutional Devices." The center publishes an annotated catalog of its audio cassettes.

Many libraries collect video and audio cassettes; be sure to check on what is available. Some libraries will even let you check out video cassettes.

## TELEVISION COVERAGE

Records of television news coverage are available to the public through television news archives at various locations in the United States. Because governmental issues take up the major portion of newscasts, these archives can be of considerable use to the congressional scholar. In addition, there is C-SPAN, the cable TV network devoted to congressional news.

## C-SPAN

The Congressional Satellite Public Affairs Network, available on cable TV, is one of the most important developments for students of Congress. This live broadcast of congressional proceedings, which started in 1979, provides gavel-to-gavel coverage of the House, plus other public affairs programming such as National Press Club speeches, policy addresses, debates, and public policy forums and call-in programs. This coverage of Congress allows one to study it at first hand as well as gather other background information. For anyone researching Congress or a specific piece of legislation, C-SPAN helps to make the process come alive. Following are some guides for users of C-SPAN.

Greenberg, Ellen. *The House and Senate Explained: A TV Viewer's Fingertip Guide*. Dobbs Ferry, NY: Streamside, 1986.

Green, Alan. *Gavel to Gavel: A Guide to the Televised Proceedings of Congress*. Washington, DC: Benton Foundation, 1986.

Frantzich, Stephen. "C-SPAN in the Classroom." *News for Teachers of Political Science: A Publication of the American Political Science Association* 36 (Winter 1983): 2–3.

## Archives

The following news archives are open for research, and materials in the various collections can be accessed through the news indexes in this section.

Vanderbilt University. Television News Archives. Nashville, TN.
The Television News Archives at Vanderbilt University is the most complete television news archives in the United States. Holdings include a collection of evening newscasts and special news programs from the major networks since August 1968. The tapes of the news programs can be borrowed for a fee.

Public Broadcasting Service. Public Television Archives. Washington, DC.
This archive is a collection of PBS television materials.

U.S. Library of Congress. Motion Picture Broadcasting and Recorded Sound Division. Washington, DC.
This archive has in its holdings a collection of television entertainment programs and tape copies of the programs in the Television News Archives at Vanderbilt University. The library needs to receive in advance requests to use these materials, as they are in storage.

U.S. National Archives and Record Service. Motion Picture Division of Audiovisual Archives Division. Washington, DC.
This is a collection of the CBS network evening news and news special programs such as congressional speeches. These tapes may be borrowed through interlibrary loan. To gain access to these materials the *CBS News Index* or *Television News Index* can be used.

Additional information concerning various film and video collections in the Washington, D.C., area can be found in the following publication:

Rowan, Bonnie G. *Scholars' Guide to Washington, D.C. Film and Video Collections.* Washington, DC: Smithsonian Institution Press, 1980.

## Indexes

The following indexes are to television news programs:

*Television News Index: News and Abstracts.* Nashville, TN: Vanderbilt University, Television News Archives, 1968– .
The *Television News Index* is a monthly index with abstracts cumulated yearly. Terms used in the indexing are specific rather than general. The *Index* gives reference points to various subject matter on tapes as the tapes have been dated and timed.

*CBS News Index.* New York: Columbia Broadcasting System, 1975– .
The CBS Evening News, other regular news programs, and news specials are indexed in this work. Subject headings derived from actual newspaper usage are used, and the entries are abstracted into a short descriptive phrase.

Further information on television archives and indexes can be found in the following paper:

Wilhoit, Frances G. "The Network News as History: Using Television Archives." Proceedings of the American Historical Association, 59th annual meeting, Washington, DC, December 1980. Ann Arbor, MI: University Microfilms, 1981.

## ORAL HISTORIES

Oral histories are another important resource for research on Congress. They are excellent primary source material. There are two oral history collections that focus on Congress:

*United States Senate Historical Office Oral History Collection: Interviews with Senate Staff* (Sanford, NC: Microfilming Corporation of America, 1981; Wilmington, DE: Scholarly Resources, 1984).

The interviews with retired Senate staff members provide insights into Senate personalities and the operations of the Senate. Ten oral histories are completed. The transcripts are available in the Library of Congress and Senate Library. They are available for purchase on microfiche from the companies listed above.

*Former Members of Congress Oral History Collection* (Sanford, NC: Microfilming Corporation of America, 1981).

This collection of seventy-nine oral histories by both senators and representatives covers the period from 1922 to 1977. It is a rich collection that includes histories from J. William Fulbright, Melvin Laird, Wilbur Mills, and Patsy Mink, to name a few. The collection is available on microfiche from the Microfilming Corporation of America.

In addition to the above collections there are journals that have oral histories by members of Congress or collections of oral histories that include information about Congress. Two important journals for keeping up to date about oral histories are the *Oral History Review* and *Oral History Association Newsletter.* The following three guides can be used to identify other related oral history collections:

Cook, Patsy, ed. *Directory of Oral History Programs in the United States.* Sanford, NC: Microfilming Corporation of America, 1982.

Mason, Elizabeth B., and Louis M. Starr, eds. *The Oral History Collection of Columbia University.* New York: Oral History Research Office, 1979.

Halvice, Patricia P. *Oral History: A Reference Guide and Annotated Bibliography.* Jefferson, NC: McFarland, 1985.

# ARCHIVES

For the advanced researcher, archival material is a must. Archives contain original documents such as letters, memos, reports, and other forms of primary research material. The problem with archival material is how to locate the archives and what is in them. Fortunately, there are several guides that can help.

Jacob, Kathryn A., ed. *Guide to Research Collections of Former United States Senators, 1789–1982*. Detroit: Gale, 1986.

This volume, along with a supplement, was originally published by the Senate Historical Office. It contains information about the location and scope of former senators' papers and oral histories. The volume is arranged in alphabetical order by the name of the senator. Each entry includes the dates represented by the collection, number of items, description of contents, existence of finding aids, and user restrictions. Entries for oral histories include the date of the interview, number of transcribed pages, and any restrictions. It also notes whether any portraits, photographs, or other memorabilia are available. There are two appendixes: one lists senators by state with information on party membership, offices held, and birth and death dates, and the other lists collections by the name of the repository. For information about new collections one should check *Senate History*, a newsletter published by the Senate Historical Office.

McDonough, John J., comp. *Members of Congress: A Checklist of Their Papers in the Manuscript Division, Library of Congress*. Washington, DC: Library of Congress, 1980.

This volume includes entries for 1,109 senators, representatives, and delegates to the Continental Congress. Entries are arranged in alphabetical order with brief biographical information and a description of materials in the manuscript collection. One appendix lists members by state, another by the Congress in which they served.

*National Inventory of Documentary Sources in the United States*. Cambridge, MA: Chadwyck Healy, 1983– .

This massive microfiche collection is divided into four parts: (1) Federal Records: The National Archives, the Presidential Libraries, and the Smithsonian Institution Archives, (2) Manuscript Division, Library of Congress, (3) State Archives, State Libraries, and State Historical Societies, and (4) Academic and Research Libraries and Other Repositories. Each part is a self-contained publication with its own index. The index is a listing of subjects and names that refers to the titles of finding aids published by libraries, archives, etc., that describe the contents of collections, including the contents of folders and even documents. This collection allows one to find specific manuscript collections, which one could then visit or request photocopies from. The first part of the collection, Federal Records, includes the records of Congress in the National Archives. But as the manuscripts of former members of Congress or government records could be in a variety of different libraries, all four parts of the collection can be used to find archival material.

# DIRECTORIES

A variety of research centers, both federal and private, disseminate information about the Congress and the federal government. There are several directories useful not only for finding addresses, telephone numbers, etc., but for determining what an organization or agency does and what kinds of services it provides. In the course of research on the Congress, you often run across the name of a particular institution that is advocating a change in policy, seeking reform, or merely publishing information about federal activities as a public service. In order to find out more about an organization or institution, you can consult a directory. A selected list of research centers, including addresses and phone numbers, can be found in Appendix 2 (see pp. 271–75).

The following is a descriptive list of the major directories. At the end of the list are citations to a number of secondary directories.

Congressional Quarterly. *Washington Information Directory.* Washington, DC: Congressional Quarterly, 1975– .

This is a thoroughly indexed guide to over 5,000 information sources in Congress, the executive branch, and nongovernmental organizations. This annual directory helps the researcher make some sense out of the maze of agencies, institutes, associations, and foundations in the Washington area. In addition to the standard organizational information, a concise statement spells out the committee's, organization's, or agency's activities. Besides identifying all of the major offices in Congress, the directory also discusses hundreds of organizations and public interest groups like Ralph Nader's Public Citizen, Inc., Americans for Democratic Action, and the National Committee for an Effective Congress. These organizations seek to bring about change in governmental procedures and regulations, monitor legislative proposals, and assess and evaluate federal programs. Many public interest groups distribute newsletters and other materials free of charge or for a nominal fee. It is certainly worthwhile to write to organizations asking about their activities and what publications are available to the public. The directory is indexed by subject and agency.

*Washington 86.* New York: Columbia Books, 1986.

This is a comprehensive directory to 3,400 public and private institutions in the Washington area. It is arranged by subject into seventeen chapters, providing information on governmental, business, labor, educational, political, religious, cultural, and social organizations. It also includes a composite index of organizations and individuals.

Kruzas, Anthony T., and Kay Gill, eds. *Government Research Centers Directory*. 3rd ed. Detroit, MI: Gale Research Company, 1983.

This directory identifies and describes all research facilities funded by the federal government. It provides a wealth of information about research centers, bureaus, and institutes, both in regard to the kinds of analysis they conduct and the collection of data. The directory has a name index, subject key word index, agency index, and geographical index.

Dresser, Peter D. *Research Centers Directory: A Guide to Over 9,700 University-related and Other Nonprofit Research Organizations*. 2 vols. 12th ed. Detroit, MI: Gale Research Company, 1988.

This directory is the best guide for identifying and finding out information about university-related and other nonprofit research organizations throughout the United States and Canada. The book is arranged in sixteen broad categories, listing research institutes, centers, foundations, laboratories, and bureaus. The directory is very easy to use and includes a subject index, alphabetical index, and institutional index and is updated periodically by the supplement *New Research Centers,* also published by Gale. This supplement lists new research centers as well as those being formed.

Jennings, Margaret, comp. *Library and Reference Facilities in the Area of the District of Columbia*. 11th ed. White Plains, NY: Knowledge Industry Publications, 1983.

This directory includes profiles on more than 450 libraries and reference centers in the District of Columbia area. It includes federal libraries as well as public, academic, and special libraries. It is extremely useful for identifying smaller reading rooms and information and referral centers. Each entry provides information on services, collections, hours, and any restrictions on use. The address, telephone number, and name of the individual in charge are also listed. This directory is especially useful for anyone who is going to do research in Washington and wants to find out in advance which libraries have certain resources, what services they provide, and whether one can use the library.

U.S. Congress. House. Commission on Information and Facilities. *Inventory of Information Resources and Services Available to the U.S. House of Representatives, Parts I–IV*. Westport, CT: Greenwood Press, 1977.

This is an excellent guide to internal sources of congressional information on the legislative process, managing of congressional offices, and the organization and operation of Congress. It also describes the resources of the Congressional Budget Office, General Accounting Office, Government Printing Office, Library of Congress, and Office of Technology Assessment.

*United States Senate Telephone Directory.* Washington, DC: U.S. Government Printing Office, 1986.

*Telephone Directory: United States House of Representatives.* Washington, DC: U.S. Government Printing Office, 1986.

These two directories provide a name and location list of all House and Senate employees, including members, their Washington and field office staffs, committee and subcommittee members and staff, and support office staff.

*Washington Pocket Directory: A Citizen's Guide to Major Government Offices and Information Services.* Washington, DC: Want Publishing, 1986.

Nagel, Stuart, and Marian Neef. *Policy Research Centers Directory.* Urbana, IL: Policy Studies Organization, 1978.

Nagel, Stuart, and Marian Neef. *The Political Science Utilization Directory.* Urbana, IL: Policy Studies Organization, 1975.

*Who Knows: Researchers' Guide to Washington.* 8th ed. Washington, DC: Washington Researchers Publishing, 1986.

# BIOGRAPHICAL SOURCES

Sources for biographies fall into two categories: biographical collections and directories and biographical indexes. The sources to be covered include directories focusing on Congress as well as general political directories and collections. In addition to all the sources listed in the following section, most general encyclopedias, yearbooks, and even some almanacs are good sources for short biographical sketches.

## Directories and Collections

Biographical collections and directories can direct a researcher to information about members of the Congress. Most directories and collections provide information about an individual's family, educational background, and achievements as well as standard biographical data such as birth and death dates, etc.

## Congress

Biographical Directory of the American Congress, 1774–1971. Rev. ed. U.S. Congress, Washington, DC: U.S. Government Printing Office, 1972.

This directory provides short biographies, arranged alphabetically, of senators and representatives who served in Congress from 1774 to 1971. Also included is a chronological list of executive officers of administrations from 1789 to 1971, a listing of delegates to the Continental Congress, and a listing of Congresses by date and session.

Ehrenhalt, Alan, ed. *Politics in America: Members of Congress in Washington and at Home.* Washington, DC: Congressional Quarterly, 1980– .

This directory provides a description of each congressman's performance, legislative influence, political power, personal style, election data, campaign finances, voting records, and interest group rating. Each member's birth date, education, military career, election returns, family members, religion, political career, and address is given. The directory provides profiles and maps of each congressional district. Also included is the membership of Senate and House committees and subcommittees. The directory is issued every two years.

U.S. Congress. *Congressional Directory.* Washington, DC: U.S. Government Printing Office, 1809– .

Published annually, this directory contains biographical, organizational, and statistical information about members and administrative units of the government. The directory is a who's who of the Congress and all government departments. It includes (1) biographical sketches of congressmen, (2) state delegations, (3) terms of service, (4) committees, (5) congressional sessions, (6) governors of states, (7) votes cast for congressmen, (8) biographical sketches of cabinet members and Supreme Court justices, (9) officials of independent agencies, (10) press galleries, (11) maps of congressional districts, and (12) an index by names of individuals. Material about individual members is submitted by the members themselves. Political party membership, birth date and place, education, military career, religion, memberships, occupations, political careers, family, and committee membership are listed for most. Maps of congressional districts are included. In 1978, a supplement to the directory was issued for the first time.

Brownson, Charles B., ed. *Congressional Staff Directory.* Alexandria, VA: 1959– .

This yearly publication is a companion to the official *Congressional Directory.* It lists the staffs of all congressmen as well as the committees and subcommittees of both houses, and gives short biographical sketches of key staff personnel. Included are the committee and subcommittee assignments, key federal officials and their liaison staffs, and an index of personal names. An alphabetical listing of cities with a population of over 1,500 provides the latest census figures, number of the congressional district, and the names of the congressmen. Prior to the publication of the *Congressional Staff Directory* every April, a *C.S.D. Advance Locator* is issued at the beginning of the year. The *Locator* helps to fill the information gap until the complete *Directory* is published. Before each congressional election an advance *C.S.D. Election Index* is published in September, previewing candidates, providing past election statistics, and listing the cities and towns in each district.

Barone, Michael, and Grant Ujifusa. *The Almanac of American Politics, 1988.* Washington, DC: National Journal, 1987.

This work was first published in 1972. It is an extensive guide to legislators and their districts. Background material contained within this volume is invaluable. The work is arranged alphabetically by state. An introductory description of the state's political background precedes a section covering legislators, giving a sketch of their background, ideology, and record. More importantly, it provides a short outline of their career, the committees they serve on, their record on key votes, and their electoral history. Also included are ratings on congressmen by interest groups such as the AFL-CIO's Committee on Political Education (which rates members of Congress on their voting related to labor issues). Finally, there is a profile of each district within a state. Included within this section is the political background of the district, census data, federal outlays, tax burdens, and characteristics of the voters. The work is revised and updated biennially.

Congressional Quarterly. *Members of Congress since 1789.* 3d ed. Washington, DC: Congressional Quarterly, 1985.

This work gives a historical profile of Congress, noting age, occupation, sex, religion, and race of the members of Congress. There is an alphabetical list of all those who served in Congress from March 4, 1789, through January 1985. The following material is given for each entry: name; party; state (of service); date of birth; date of death; congressional service; service as president, vice president, member of the cabinet or Supreme Court, governor, or party office. A table giving the leaders of the Senate and House is also given.

Buhler, Michaela, and Dorothy Lee Jackson, eds. *Congressional Yellow Book: A Directory of Members of Congress, Including Their Committees, and*

*Key Staff Aides*. Washington, DC: Washington Monitor, 1977– .
This annual directory gives addresses and other office information for senators and representatives. It provides information for Senate and House committees, including jurisdiction, membership, and staff aides. It also gives membership and phone numbers for House and Senate leadership, party-related organizations, informal groups, and congressional support agencies.

Christopher, Maurine. *Black Americans in Congress*. Rev. ed. New York: Thomas Y. Crowell, 1976.
Contains biographical essays of past and contemporary black American legislators. The book spans the period from 1870 to 1970 and has sketches on forty-six individuals. Included are a chronological list of members of Congress, an extensive bibliography, and a subject index.

Englebarts, Rudolf. *Women in the United States Congress, 1917–1972: Their Accomplishments, with Bibliographies*. Littleton, CO: Libraries Unlimited, 1974.
The best reference work on women in Congress, this book has a lengthy introductory essay on the history and role of women in Congress. Descriptive information on congresswomen is given in chronological order and arranged in two lists, one for the House of Representatives and the other for the Senate. Each biographical entry includes party affiliation, state elected from, period of service, précis of congressional career, and a bibliography. There is a bibliography on subjects related to the study of women and politics. The work is indexed by individual's name and subject. For current information about women in Congress, the National Women's Political Caucus publishes a newsletter and *Women's Political Times*. There are two other guides to women in Congress which can be used to supplement the Englebarts volume:

Tolchin, Susan. *Women in Congress: 1917–1976*. Washington, DC: U.S. Government Printing Office, 1976.

Chamberlin, Hope. *A Minority of Members: Women in the U.S. Congress*. New York: Praeger, 1973.

One further guide is

Ralph Nader Congress Project. *Citizens Look at Congress*. Washington, DC: Grossman Publishers, 1972–1976.

This series provides detailed profiles, including biographies, voting records, interest group ratings, and the personal financial and legislative interests of legislators elected in the 1972 election. The set has the distinction of being interesting and lively reading. The Congress Project has started to publish similar works focusing on House and Senate committees, revenue committees, commerce committees, environmental committees, and money committees. *Ruling Congress: A Study of How the House and Senate Rules Govern the Legislative Process* (Washington, DC: Grossman Publishers, 1975), also by the Congress Project, relates directly to legislative tracing.

## General Political Directories

Listed below are several directories that can be used to find information on politicians, both at the federal level and the state and local level. They also include party leaders and other important political leaders. As governors, state legislators, and party leaders across the country often play a role in congressional elections and politics, these directories can be quite useful. Following the annotated entries is a list of other directories, some of which are more specialized or historical in nature. Depending on a researcher's need, they can be invaluable reference tools.

*American Leaders 1789–1987.* Washington, DC: Congressional Quarterly, 1987.
The biographical directory provides information for presidents, vice presidents, senators, representatives, Supreme Court justices, and state governors. It includes dates of birth and death, political affiliation, and dates and places of service.

*Who's Who in American Politics: A Biographical Directory of United States Political Leaders.* New York: Bowker, 1967– .
This directory presents biographical data for about 12,500 political figures from presidents down to the local level, including federal government employees, national party leaders, state legislators, local officials of large cities, county chairmen of parties, and minority party leaders. Information includes address, party affiliation, education, family data, political and business background, and achievements. The directory is revised biennially.

*Who's Who in Government.* 3 vols. Indianapolis, IN: Marquis Who's Who, 1972–1977.
This directory provides biographical information on political leaders on the federal and state level. It presents basically the same information as the

directory listed above. The value of this directory lies in the format of its indexes: One arranges political figures according to office within the government structure; the other arranges politicians according to type of responsibilities.

*Black Elected Officials, 1986: A National Roster.* 15th ed. Washington, DC: Joint Center for Political Studies, 1985.
   This work lists black elected officials at all levels of government, providing the mailing address and office held. There is an analysis of changes by region, state, and level of office. The Joint Center also publishes a monthly newsletter entitled *Focus* that regularly contains articles concerning congressional affairs affecting blacks.

*Taylor's Encyclopedia of Government Officials: Federal and State.* Dallas, TX: Political Research, 1969– .
   This work is not really an encyclopedia at all, but a directory of members of federal and state government departments and agencies. While no biographical information is given for officials, this series is valuable because it issues quarterly supplements listing changes, additions, and corrections; thus it records changes far in advance of the annual directories.

Center for the American Women and Politics. *Women in Public Office: A Biographical Directory and Statistical Analysis.* 2d ed. New York: Bowker, 1978.
   A comprehensive directory of women in public office at all levels of government.

Other directories include the following:

Morris, Dan, and Inez Morris, eds. *Who Was Who in American Politics. A Bibliographical Dictionary of Over 4,000 Men and Women Who Contributed to the United States Political Scene from the Colonial Days Up To and Including the Immediate Past.* New York: Hawthorn Books, 1974.

Preston, Wheeler. *American Biographies.* New York: Harper and Brothers Publishers, 1940.

Wilson, James Grant, and John Fiske. *Appleton's Cyclopaedia of American Biography.* 6 vols. New York: D. Appleton and Co., 1888–1894.

Wilson, James Grant, ed. *Appleton's Cyclopaedia of American Biography.* 2 vols. New York: D. Appleton and Co., 1901.

Dearborn, L.E., ed. *A Supplement to Appleton's Cyclopaedia of American Biography*. 6 vols. New York: Press Association Compilers, 1918–1931.

*Current Biography Yearbook*. New York: H. W. Wilson, 1940–1985.

*Dictionary of American Biography*. New York: Charles Scribner's Sons, 1928.

Garraty, John A., ed. *Encyclopedia of American Biography*. New York: Harper and Row, 1974.

*The National Cyclopaedia of American Biography*. New York: James T. White and Co., 1892.

Johnson, Rossiter, ed. *The Twentieth Century Biographical Dictionary of Notable Americans*. 10 vols. Boston: The Biographical Society, 1904.

Van Doren, Charles, ed. *Webster's American Biographies*. Springfield, MA: G & C Merriam Co., 1984.

*Who Was Who in America. Historical Volume, 1607–1896. A Companion Volume of Who's Who in American History*. Rev. ed. Chicago: Marquis Who's Who, 1967.

*Who Was Who in America. Volume One, 1897–1942. A Companion Volume of Who's Who in American History*. Chicago, Marquis, 1943.

*Who Was Who in America. Volume Two, 1943–1950. A Companion Biographical Reference Work to Who's Who in America*. Chicago, Marquis, 1963.

*Who Was Who in America. Volume Three, 1951–1960. A Companion Biographical Reference Work to Who's Who in America*. Chicago, Marquis, 1963.

*Who Was Who in America. Volume Four, 1961–1968. A Companion Biographical Reference Work to Who's Who in America*. Chicago, Marquis, 1968.

*Who Was Who in America. Volume Five, 1969–1973. A Companion Biographical Reference Work to Who's Who in America*. Chicago, Marquis, 1973.

*Who Was Who in America. Volume Six, 1974–1976. A Companion Biographical Reference Work to Who's Who in America.* Chicago, Marquis, 1976.

*Who Was Who in America. Volume Seven, 1977–1981. A Companion Biographical Reference Work to Who's Who in America.* Chicago, Marquis, 1981.

*Who Was Who in America. Volume Eight, 1982–1985. A Companion Biographical Reference Work to Who's Who in America.* Chicago, Marquis, 1985.

## Biographical Indexes

Biographical indexes provide references to more complete information in periodicals, books, or biographical encyclopedias. While it is possible to identify biographical information through newspapers and general indexes, it is time-consuming and haphazard. Biographical indexes can be especially useful in finding information about emerging politicians.

*Biography Index.* New York: H. W. Wilson, 1946– .
This quarterly index identifies biographical materials in books and magazines. It includes references to obituaries, diaries, collections of letters, and memoirs. The entries are arranged by the name of the biographee, and the profession/occupation index makes it possible to identify various kinds of political figures. There is also a *Current Biography Cumulated Index, 1940–1979,* which was published by Wilson in 1973.

*Biographical Dictionaries Master Index.* Detroit, MI: Gale Research Company, 1975–76.
This volume, along with its 1979 and 1980 supplements, is a guide to biographical listings in over fifty current biographical reference works. This is a valuable tool for finding information about recent political actors.

*Biography and Genealogy Master Index.* 8 vols. Detroit, MI: Gale Research Company, 1980.
This guide provides citations to information in all of the major biographical dictionaries in political science and history. By using this guide to identify information about political figures both living and dead, it is possible to find several and sometimes dozens of references to information about a single person. In 1982, a three-volume supplement to the *Index* was published.

*Bio-Base*. 2nd ed. Detroit, MI: Gale Research Company, 1981– .
This index is a microfiche reference service that provides citations to biographical sketches in more than 375 biographical indexes. In part, some of the citations come from the hardcover edition of the two Gale indexes listed above. But as it includes thousands of other citations, this is the most complete single index to biographical materials.

## Databases

There is essentially only one on-line biographical database, BIOG-RAPHY MASTER INDEX, produced by Gale Research Company. Basically, it is an expanded on-line version of *Bio-Base*. It is an index to biographical information contained in more than 600 source publications, including *Who's Who*s, dictionaries, handbooks, and encyclopedias. Records include the name of the individual, birth and death dates, and the names and dates of biographical sources.

In addition to BIOGRAPHY MASTER INDEX, it is possible to use a variety of other databases to identify information about political figures as well as materials written by them. As most databases can be searched by author and key words in the title, it is possible to search a database to see what a particular congressman has written. Likewise, the titles of entries can be searched to gather citations about individuals. This strategy could be applied to advantage using a number of databases, including AMERICA: HISTORY AND LIFE, PSYCINFO, SOCIOLOGICAL ABSTRACTS, PAIS INTERNATIONAL, U.S. POLITICAL SCIENCE DOCUMENTS, SOCIAL SCISEARCH, and COMPREHENSIVE DISSERTATION INDEX. As political biographies have long been a traditional form of research for dissertations written in the fields of history and political science, a subject search for dissertations written about a congressman can yield hundreds of citations.

# 8. Campaigns and Elections

This chapter covers the enormous number of reference tools dealing with campaigns and elections. Campaigning and elections have long been areas of intensive research for political scientists and historians. With the increase in data and its availability that has taken place in the last forty years, the growth of research has increased significantly. Data are now available on almost every aspect of campaigning and elections, including public opinion polls, election returns, and financial data. The tools cited in this section are not only sources for data but can be used for generating one's own data.

This field of research is also a rapidly changing one. There are now more primaries than ever before, and the cost of campaigning is constantly increasing. Campaigns start much earlier than they did before, and the role of political action committees has changed the way candidates raise funds and even their campaign strategies. In addition to the resources discussed in the following section, many of the tools described in previous sections can be used for researching campaigns and elections. Almanacs, newspapers, newsmagazines, and indexes are vital tools for studying campaigns and elections. Many of the bibliographies and resources, such as the publications of Congressional Quarterly, also contain a considerable amount of material relevant to this field.

## CAMPAIGNS

### Finances

One area of election statistics that has been badly neglected is campaign contributions. It is only within the past twenty-five years that a systematic

173

174 Campaigns and Elections

collection of data on campaign contributions has been undertaken. As the issue of money in elections has always been prominent, the massive volumes of campaign contribution statistics should lead to many new and fascinating studies. In accordance with the Federal Election Campaign Act of 1971 (Public Law 92-225), the General Accounting Office, the clerk of the House, and the secretary of the Senate were responsible for making public statistics on contributions to presidential and congressional candidates. Unfortunately, the act was amended by P.L. 93-443, whereby the data are not required to be made public. Even so, it is now possible to do extensive research on campaign expenditures. The amount of statistics now published provide researchers with considerable raw data for extended analyses.

Alexander, Herbert E., and Caroline D. Jones, eds. *CRF Listing of Contributors of National Level Political Committees to Incumbents and Candidates for Public Office.* Princeton, NJ: Citizens' Research Foundation, 1968–1972.

This work provides data on contributions given to candidates by national-level political committees of the Republican and Democratic parties, as well as committees representing labor, business, and professional interests.

Alexander, Herbert E., and Caroline D. Jones, eds. *CRF Listing of Political Contributors of $500 or More.* Princeton, NJ: Citizens' Research Foundation, 1968–1974.

This volume provides a listing of contributors, arranged alphabetically, who gave to candidates both at the national and state levels. The address of the contributor, the amount of the contribution, and the candidate and party to which it was given are provided.

Paul, Barbara D., et al., eds. *CRF Listing of Contributors and Lenders of $10,000 or More in 1972.* Princeton, NJ: Citizens' Research Foundation, 1975.

This work is a compilation of campaign contributions to presidential, congressional, state, and local committees and candidates. More than 1,300 contributors are included, arranged alphabetically. The home and business addresses, profession, and business affiliation are given. CRF has gathered data on individuals who made contributions of more than $10,000 in presidential election years since 1960. These data have been published in Herbert E. Alexander's quadrennial series, *Financing the . . . Election.* Six volumes in all have been published, covering the 1960, 1964, 1968, 1972, 1976, 1980, and 1984 elections.

*Studies in Political Finance.* No. 1, 1960– .

These studies tend to be very specific, usually examining a single state or election contest. As research studies they serve as examples of what directions an analysis of political contributions can take. The first twenty-one studies have also been published in a three-volume series by Citizens' Research Foundation, *Studies in Money in Politics* (1975), edited by Herbert E. Alexander.

Common Cause. The Campaign Finance Monitoring Project. 10 vols. *1972 Federal Campaign Finances*. Washington, DC: Common Cause, 1974.

This work provides a summary of the campaign finances of every major candidate for Congress in the 1972 general election. The study is organized into ten volumes divided by regional area: (1) New England states, (2) Mid-Atlantic states, (3) Border states, (4) Southeastern states, (5) Southern states, (6) Southwestern states, (7) West Coast states, (8) Mountain states, (9) Plains states, and (10) Great Lakes states. Each volume contains data on three areas of a candidate's campaign finances: (1) a summary of campaign financial data, (2) listing of registered special-interest and national political party committees and their contributions, and (3) a list of large contributions from individuals. A five-volume set, *1974 Congressional Campaign Finances*, has also been published by Common Cause.

Common Cause. The Campaign Finance Monitoring Project. 3 vols. *1972 Federal Campaign Finances: Interest Groups and Political Parties*. Washington, DC: Common Cause, 1974.

This work provides the finances of all nationally registered political committees that contributed $5,000 or more to federal candidates in 1972. The lists of political committees have been arranged into three volumes: (1) Business, Agriculture and Dairy, Health, (2) Labor, and (3) Miscellaneous, Democratic, Republican. Each of the volumes contains (1) a detailed table of contents, covering the interest groups for that volume, (2) a financial summary for each interest committee, including a brief description of the group or interest that the committee represents and its activities in the 1972 elections, (3) a complete listing of every individual and group that received contributions from the committee and the amount received, and (4) an index listing the name and affiliation of all political committees registered during 1972.

U.S. Congress. House. *The Annual Statistical Report of Contributions and Expenditures Made During the 1972 Election Campaigns for the U.S. House of Representatives*, W. Pat Jennings, comp. Doc. No. 93-284. Washington, DC: U.S. Government Printing Office, 1974.

This volume contains three main sections and two appendixes: (1) receipts and expenditures for candidates and political committees supporting a single candidate, arranged alphabetically by state and by district number; (2) receipts and expenditures for political committees supporting two or more candidates, arranged alphabetically by committee; (3) individual contributions in excess of $100, arranged alphabetically by contributor or committee, including the address of the contributor and date of the contribution. Appendix A is an alphabetical list of candidates and their supporting political committees. Appendix B is an alphabetical list of political committees and the candidates they supported.

U.S. Congress. Senate. *The Annual Statistical Report of Receipts and Expenditures Made in Connection with Elections for the U.S. Senate in 1972.* Washington, DC: U.S. Government Printing Office, 1975.

This report is divided into five sections. The first section, arranged by state, includes amounts reported by all Senate candidates and associated committees that support one candidate. Within-state breakdowns are listed according to party and candidate. The next section records amounts reported by all political committees supporting more than one candidate. This section is arranged alphabetically by committee. (The list of candidates supported is found in Appendix B.) The third section, arranged alphabetically by contributor, presents itemized receipts over $100 received by committees and candidates as reported to the secretary of the Senate for 1972. Receipts are coded according to (1) individual contributions, (2) sales and collections, (3) loans received, (4) other receipts, and (5) transfers. Appendix A is the committee-to-candidate cross-index; Appendix B is the candidate-to-committee cross-index. The last two sections provide cross-indexing of sections I, II, and III. Provided also is a cross-index by state and party. The House and Senate volumes use the same format, which makes it easy to use the two together for comparative purposes.

The Federal Election Commission, using information based on financial disclosure provisions of the 1977 House and Senate ethics codes, has a series, the *FEC Disclosure Series.* The commission also publishes *Reports on Financial Activity.* Congressional Quarterly and the *National Journal* also publish various studies based on Common Cause and federal data, as well as research conducted by their own staff. The series *Vital Statistics on Congress* has an excellent section on campaign finance, including information on expenditures and political action committees. Newspapers can also be an important source for information about campaign finances. In addition to the various sources of data on campaign financing, there is now a looseleaf service that serves as a guide to all aspects of campaign finance.

Schwarz, Thomas J., and Alan G. Straus. *Federal Regulation of Campaign Finance and Political Activity.* Albany, NY: Matthew Bender, 1981– .
This basic two-volume set is to be updated with periodic looseleaf additions and an annual supplement. The guide provides a detailed description of the history and development of laws governing campaign finance and lobbying. It includes the amended statutes and regulations of the Federal Election Campaign Act, Presidential Primary Matching Account Act, Lobbying Act, Hatch Act, and Federal Communications Act. The two volumes provide a discussion of what constitutes contributions and expenditures as well as what parties, corporations, labor unions, and other groups must do to comply with the law. There are sections also covering the statutes regulating lobbying and broadcasting activities. Though this guide is designed as a sourcebook for candidates, accountants, lawyers, and party officials involved in campaigns, it is an excellent reference source for students and researchers.

## Interest Groups

This section will discuss some of the directories that identify and provide information on lobbyists, political action committees, and other associations and organizations involved in the political process. While the directories listed below will provide a considerable amount of information about interest groups, some of the sources cited earlier are extremely useful. Both *Congressional Quarterly Weekly Report* and *National Journal* give extensive coverage to interest groups. *CQ Weekly Report* regularly lists new lobbyists as well as publishes the ratings of members of Congress by various interest groups, such as the AFL-CIO Committee on Political Education. The newsletters cited earlier are an invaluable source for learning about the activities of interest groups. Newspaper and magazine literature are other important sources of information, as their coverage goes behind the scenes to detail the efforts of political groups. As trade, industrial, and professional journals have regular volumes or sections on national politics, there are several indexes that should be consulted. These are *Business Periodicals Index* (New York: H.W. Wilson, 1958– ; monthly with annual cumulations), *Applied Science and Technology Index* (New York: H.W. Wilson, 1958– ; monthly with annual cumulations), and *Public Affairs Information Service Bulletin* (New York: Public Affairs Information Service, 1915– ; semimonthly with quarterly cumulations). The first two of these are also available on CD-ROM. Finally, one particularly useful newsletter is *Political Finance/Lobby Reporter.* This newsletter, which is published 48 times a year by Amward Publications, provides short stories on current issues and developments in regard to financing as well as new lobby registration.

*Lobbyists*

*Directory of Washington Representatives of American Associations and Industry.* Washington, DC: Columbia Books, 1977– .

This directory includes lobbyists, legal advisors, information collectors, and consultants representing public interest groups, corporations, labor unions, trade and professional associations, state and local governments, political action committees, and foreign governments. The information is gathered from the lobby registration filed with the clerk of the House of Representatives, the foreign agent registrations of the Department of Justice, dockets of regulatory agencies, commissions, and department and other federal records. The information is arranged in two alphabetically cross-referenced lists. The first is a list of representatives giving their names, addresses, and data of registration. The second is a list of organizations represented, including the addresses, names, and titles of their representatives and a brief description of their activities. There are also subject and country indexes.

*Directory of Registered Lobbyists and Lobbyist Legislation.* 2d ed. Chicago: Marquis Academic Media, 1975.

This is a comprehensive sourcebook of all registered lobbyists in Washington and the forty-eight states requiring registration. The directory is arranged by state, with lobbyists listed alphabetically. The name, address, phone number, and organizational ties are given for each lobbyist. For easy reference use there is a lobbyist index and organizational index. The complete texts of all federal and state laws relating to lobbying are reprinted.

Zuckerman, Ed, ed. *The Washington Lobbyists/Lawyers Directory.* 5th ed. Washington, DC: Amward Publications, 1982.

This directory lists lobbyists in an alphabetical name index and then cross-indexes them according to their business or organizational affiliation. A third part of the guide indexes the political action committees of corporations, unions, and professional associations.

Close, Arthur C., and Laurie Evens, eds. *Washington Representatives 1987: Who Does What for Whom in the Nation's Capitol.* 11th ed. Washington, DC: Columbia Books, 1987.

This annual directory is organized much like the prior two volumes. It contains a list of representatives, a list of organizations, a subject index, and a country index. This directory does include a list of the congressional committees and their membership, and regulatory agencies that are the focus of lobbying efforts.

## Informal Congressional Groups

In addition to formal party groups, a number of informal congressional groups exist on Capitol Hill. Informal groups are those for which membership is optional or a membership fee is required. These groups normally form around common issues, interests, or geographic concerns. Some number of them are bipartisan. They have increased in recent years and continue to grow, particularly in the House. The informal organizations can assist members in gathering information about or developing support for proposed legislation. Some of the major informal congressional groups are listed below.

*Congressional Black Caucus.* Founded in 1971, it attempts to present a
    single voice for blacks and to serve as a federal and legislative informa-
    tion clearinghouse for elected minority officials. It has become increas-
    ingly concerned with legislative matters and frequently holds its own
    informational hearings.
*Congressional Rural Caucus.* Founded in 1973, it attempts to coordinate
    legislative activity on issues relating to agriculture, finance, housing,
    and other issues. It is bipartisan and includes more than 100 members in
    the House.
*Democratic Study Group.* Founded in 1959, it was formed as a reform
    group, but it has become a moderate-liberal political force within the
    House. It publishes studies, position papers, and weekly legislative
    reports and maintains its own whip organization. Its primary publica-
    tion is the weekly *Legislative Report,* which provides summaries and
    analyses of legislation scheduled for the House floor in upcoming
    weeks.
*Environmental Study Conference.* Founded in 1975, it is a bipartisan and
    bicameral group of more than 200 members sharing an interest in the
    environmental impact of legislation. It publishes the *Weekly Bulletin,*
    analyzing environmental legislation coming up for floor action and
    committee consideration. Analyses include basic issues, amendments,
    and views of congressmen, the administration, and major lobbying
    groups. The *Weekly Bulletin* is available by subscription.
*State delegations.* State delegations of representatives and senators from a
    state comprise another type of informal group in Congress. These
    delegations vary widely in organization and operation. Some are parti-
    san, others not. Some meet weekly; others do not meet as a group at all.
    For a complete listing of these state delegations consult Section VII of
    the *Congressional Yellow Book.*

Other informal groups include:

Coalition for Peace through Strength (House)
Conference of Great Lakes Congressmen (House)
Congressional Balanced Budget Caucus (House)
Congressional Clearinghouse on the Future (bicameral)
Congressional Coal Group (House)
Congressional Hispanic Caucus (House)
Congressional Metropolitan Area Caucus (House)
Congressional Steel Caucus (House)
Congressional Suburban Caucus (House)
Congressional Sunbelt Caucus (bicameral)
Congressional Textile Caucus (House)
Export Task Force (House)
Freshman Senators' Caucus
House Democratic Research Organization
House Fair Employment Practices Committee
House Republican Study Committee
House Wednesday Group (Republican)
Members of Congress for Peace through Law (bicameral)
Mid-West Conference of Democratic Senators
New England Congressional Caucus (House)
Northeast-Midwest Coalition (Senate)
Northeast-Midwest Congressional Coalition (House)
Senate Coal Caucus
Senate Export Caucus
Senate Steel Caucus
Senate Wednesday Group (Republican)
United Democrats of Congress (bicameral)
Vietnam Veterans in Congress (bicameral)
Western State Coalition

## Political Action Committees

The following volumes are directories to political action committees providing a listing of PACs and their interests. As the number of political action committees grows with each election, keeping up with the number and affiliation of PACs is difficult. Consequently, for current research one should always be sure to use *CQ Weekly Report* and the *National Journal*.

Fraser, Edith, ed. *The PAC Handbook: Political Action for Business*. Cambridge, MA: Ballinger, 1982.

This volume, while intended more as a handbook for groups forming PACs or for already established PACs, contains much useful information. It can be used to research the organization, funding, and business management of PACs.

*Political Action Register*. Orlando, FL: Interstate Bureau of Regulations, 1982– .

This looseleaf service is the best comprehensive authority on the laws and regulations governing the organization of PACs. It details the rights, responsibilities, and legal requirements of PACs as well as how the states deal with the reporting requirements, responsibilities, and penalties relating to PACs. It also includes information regarding the role of PACs in campaign fundraising.

Roeder, Edward. *PACs Americana: A Directory of Political Action Committees and Their Interests*. 2d ed. Washington, DC: Sunshine Services Corporation, 1987.

Schapsmeier, Edward L., and Frederick H. Schapsmeier. *Political Parties and Civic Action Groups*. Westport, CT: Greenwood Press, 1981.

*State Political Action Legislation and Regulations: Index and Directory of Organizations*. Orlando, FL: Interstate Bureau of Regulation, 1984.

*Tyke's Register of Political Action Committees*. Washington, DC: Tyke Research Associates, 1978.

Weinberger, Marvin I., David U. Greevy, and Chadwick R. Gore, comps. *PAC Directory*. Cambridge, MA: Ballinger, 1984– .

## Other Directories

The directories listed below were not designed to identify lobbyists and interest groups per se, but if one wants to acquire additional information about a particular association, organization, or group that is represented by registered lobbyists, one can go to these directories for more detailed information.

*Encyclopedia of Associations.* Detroit, MI: Gale Research Company, 1956– .

*Greenwood Encyclopedia of American Institutions.* Westport, CT: Greenwood Press, 1977– .

*National Directory of Corporate Public Affairs.* Washington, DC: Columbia Books, 1987– .

*National Trade and Professional Associations of the United States and Canada.* Washington, DC: Columbia Books, 1975– .

*Research Services Directory: A Descriptive Guide to Approximately 3,400 Firms, Laboratories, Individuals, and Other Facilities in the Private Sector that Provide Contract or Fee-Based Research Services.* 3rd ed. Detroit, MI: Gale Research Company, 1987.

## Communications

In the age of electronic media, image-makers are becoming perhaps more important than the candidates themselves. Sophisticated public relations firms work extremely hard to package and sell their candidates. There is an obvious connection between a candidate's financial funds and his ability to maximize television exposure. While there is not an abundance of statistical information on communications, there are some important sources of data.

Federal Communications Commission. *Survey of Political Broadcasting.* Washington, DC: The Commission, 1960– .
This series contains data on primary and general elections obtained through questionnaires sent to broadcast stations, including AM and FM radio stations and TV stations. The information covers several major areas of interest: (1) overall political broadcast activity, (2) charges for political broadcasts, (3) political broadcast activity with respect to specified offices, and (4) editorializing. For additional information regarding rulings by the FCC on political broadcasting, one should check the following: *Decisions and Reports, 1st series* (1934–1965) and *Decisions and Reports, 2nd series* (1965– ), and *Decisions Interpreting the Communications Act of 1934* (1978). These volumes contain reports, decisions, memoranda, orders, and policy statements regarding the regulation of political broadcasting. Also, the *Federal Communications Law Journal* contains numerous articles relating to political communication.

Rosenbloom, David, ed. *The Political Marketplace*. New York: Quadrangle Books, 1972.

This directory is intended as a guide to campaign information for political candidates, but the book also serves as an excellent reference work. Even though it was written solely for the 1972 elections, it continues to be a valuable source of information. The book is a large compendium of campaign services. It includes a directory to: (1) campaign management and counseling firms, (2) political advertising and public relations firms, (3) computer-list and direct-mail houses, (4) TV and radio time buyers, (5) media outlets and film producers, (6) telephone consultants, (7) demographic and audience research firms, and (8) numerous other aspects of campaign management.

# Bibliographies

Listed below are several bibliographies that focus on campaigning and the activities of political parties. Most of the bibliographies cited in other sections of this guide also have sections on campaigning.

Agranoff, Robert. *Political Campaigns: A Bibliography*. De Kalb: Center for Government Studies, Northern Illinois University, 1972.

This is a bibliography of about 200 unannotated citations. The bibliography is of a general nature, focusing on three areas: (1) campaign strategies, electioneering, and party activities, (2) campaign techniques, media advertising, and polls, and (3) campaigns and election finance.

*The Democratic and Republican Parties in America: A Historical Bibliography*. Santa Barbara, CA: ABC-Clio, 1984.

This bibliography includes over 1,000 abstracts summarizing journal articles published between 1973 and 1982. It covers such topics as the origin and growth of parties, candidates and campaign platforms, and lobbying. The entries are arranged by chapter, and there is a detailed multiterm subject index.

Rockwood, D. Stephen, Cecelia Brown, Kenneth Eshleman, and Deborah Shaffer. *American Third Parties since the Civil War*. New York: Garland, 1985.

This bibliography of over 1,200 annotated citations is organized into chapters by party. Each chapter includes an introductory summary of the party's history. The bibliography primarily includes citations to books and journal articles. It includes an author and title index.

Kaid, Lynda Lee, Keith R. Sanders, and Robert O. Hirsch. *Political Campaign Communication: A Bibliography and Guide to the Literature.* Metuchen, NJ: Scarecrow Press, 1974.

This is a general bibliography on the communication process in political campaigns. Covering the period from 1950 to 1972, it contains over 1,500 entries, the majority of which are unannotated. Included in the bibliography are books, articles, government documents, pamphlets, and dissertations, covering analysis and evaluation, public opinion polling, media use and expenditures, and all aspects of the communication process. The volume has a subject index.

Kaid, Lynda Lee, and Anne Wadsworth. *Political Campaign Communication: A Bibliography and Guide to the Literature, 1973–1982.* Metuchen, NJ: Scarecrow Press, 1985.

This bibliography is a continuation of the above work. Together the two bibliographies cover from 1950 to 1982.

Hansen, Donald A., and J. Herschel Parsons. *Mass Communications: A Research Bibliography.* Berkeley, CA: Glendessavy Press, 1968.

This bibliography identifies almost 3,000 books and articles on mass communication. While its scope is much broader than just the political aspects of mass communication, it does contain many useful citations. It is also useful for finding theoretical and empirical studies of a general nature that can be applied to research on the Congress.

Another source of information on political communication is the literature in the fields of communication and journalism. Journals such as *Journalism Quarterly, Quarterly Journal of Speech, Public Opinion Quarterly, Columbia Journalism Quarterly,* and *Journal of Communication* are a rich source for information dealing with politics and the media. The best way to identify materials in this area of research is to use *Communication Abstracts* and *Journalism Abstracts*. These two tools can also be used to research other topics, such as the role of the media in covering campaigns, elections, and congressional politics, or the use of public relations techniques employed in campaigning or by a congressman in office. In general, these abstracting services can be used to research any aspect of the Congress that is related to the media or mass communication.

# ELECTIONS

In this section we will focus on major sources of statistics available for the study of congressional elections. While we have limited it to only a single aspect of the electoral system, we have attempted to make this section as complete as possible. Thus, although the primary focus is on congressional elections, sources that simultaneously cover other federal elections have been described in full. Our chief aim was to identify sources of election returns, but the section covers other areas involved with the study of elections. In order to assist the reader in finding more obscure sources of data, we have listed all the major reference works that serve as guides to additional statistical sources. We have also included any significant bibliography relating to congressional elections. In evaluating each source we have indicated the extent, usefulness, and content of the data.

## Electoral Systems

As the laws regulating campaign finances and electoral procedures have an impact on party competition and the nature of the electoral process, it is important to know where to find information on legislation governing elections and party activities. The three Senate publications listed below also provide an introduction to and analysis of the statutes governing elections.

Young, Michael L. *The American Dictionary of Campaigns and Elections.* New York: Hamilton Press, 1987.

This dictionary includes over 725 entries divided into seven chapters, which represent major subject areas. They are (1) campaign process, (2) media and politics, (3) polling and public opinion, (4) electoral strategies and tactics, (5) parties and PACs, (6) voting and political behaviors, and (7) money and politics. There is also a complete index of all the entries at the end of the volume.

U.S. Congress. Senate. *Factual Campaign Information.* Compiled by the Senate Library. Washington, DC: U.S. Government Printing Office, 1939– .

This series is compiled to serve senators in their campaigns and is the best source for information on the American electoral system. It contains limited statistical data, with the accent on senatorial elections, but includes information about minor parties and presidential and congressional primaries. There is a lengthy section on the major statutory provisions governing federal elections as well as other miscellaneous laws. There is a section dealing with party organizations, both Republican and Democratic. Members of national committees, senatorial campaign committees, national congressional committees, and chairmen of state committees are listed.

U.S. Congress. Senate. Select Committee on Presidential Activities. *Election Reform: Basic References*. 93d Congress, 1st Sess., Washington, DC: U.S. Government Printing Office, 1973.

The main body of this work is composed of a collection of eighteen essays and reports on the issue of campaign spending. The articles have been well chosen and provide a good discussion on the issue. The work includes a short history of the major events in the movement for federal campaign reform. There is an annotated bibliography of selected references on financing political campaigns. The bibliography covers the period from 1967 to 1973. The text of the Federal Election Campaign Act of 1971 is reprinted.

U.S. Congress. Senate. Committee on Rules and Administration. Subcommittee on Privileges and Elections. *Federal Election Campaign Laws*. Washington, DC: U.S. Government Printing Office, 1975.

This is a compilation of all federal laws affecting federal elections and campaign practices. Included are the Federal Election Campaign Act of 1971, the Federal Election Act Amendments of 1974, and the Hatch Act. These laws, as well as commentaries on them, can also be found reprinted in various Congressional Quarterly publications.

There are also several excellent reference guides that contain information on the electoral system and political parties of the United States, as well as other countries of the world. All of the tools can be used to find concise information about the American electoral and party system. As cross-national research is especially prevalent in the areas of election and campaign research, these tools are very useful for comparative research as well. They can be used as fact books to find information and as sources of data and tools for generating one's own data.

Day, Alan J., and Henry W. Degenhardt. *Political Parties of the World: A Keesing's Reference Publication*. Detroit, MI: Gale Research Company, 1984.

Delury, George. *World Encyclopedia of Political Systems and Parties*. 2d ed. New York: Facts on File, 1987.

*Political Handbook and Atlas of the World.* New York: Harper and Row, 1927– .

*Statesman's Yearbook.* New York: St. Martin's Press, 1864– .

*Worldmark Encyclopedia of the Nations.* 7th ed. New York: Worldmark Press, 1988.

## Data Compilations

When studying elections it is crucial to know something about the voters themselves. Factors such as age, sex, race, education, and income can be used in explanations of why the electorate voted a certain way. On an individual basis this kind of information is generally available only from public opinion surveys. The largest producer of aggregate data is the U.S. Bureau of the Census. Virtually hundreds of political, economic, and social variables can be drawn from census data. There are data on hundreds of subject categories and they are often broken down geographically by congressional districts, counties, standard metropolitan statistical areas, unincorporated places, and city blocks. With some patience the researcher can find what he is seeking.

### District Data

While the *Congressional District Data Book* is the standard source for finding social, economic, and political data about districts, the other works listed below are best for finding data about industries and roll-call votes.

U.S. Bureau of the Census. *Congressional District Data Book: A Statistical Abstract Supplement.* Washington, DC: U.S. Government Printing Office, 1963– .

The *Congressional District Data Book* presents a wide range of data from census and recent election statistics for congressional districts. Socioeconomic data, such as population, sex, residency, race, age, households and families, marital status, industry, occupation, migration, and housing are reported. Maps for each state show counties and congressional districts. Appendices give data on apportionment, redistricting, and the population of the districts. As the data are based on the decennial census, new editions and supplements of the *Data Book* are irregularly issued. Maps and data of congressional districts are also irregularly published by the Census Bureau in its *Congressional District Atlas* (Washington, DC: Bureau of the Census, 1964– ). Congressional Quarterly has published *Congressional Districts in the 1980's* (Washington, DC: Congressional Quarterly, 1983), which contains all essential demographic and political information on all 435 congressional districts. This is the most up-to-date guide, providing demographic, economic, and business data and maps for the new districts. While the Congressional Quarterly volume is not as encompassing as the Census Bureau series, it is easier to use.

*Congressional District Business Patterns.* 2 vols. New York: Economic Information Systems, 1981.

This directory identifies industries and businesses within congressional districts. It will identify how many establishments there are within an industry, the number of employees, the volume of sales, and the industry's share of state and national employment and sales volume. The two-volume set also provides a cross-reference table of industrial activity within districts. Consequently, this guide can be used to determine the economic basis, employment, and sales for any district as well as make comparisons with other districts. It can also be used to identify which districts have a particular industry and determine which districts would be affected by legislation, regulatory action, and administrative law.

Martis, Kenneth C. *The Historical Atlas of United States Congressional Districts, 1789–1983.* New York: Free Press, 1983.

This atlas is the only volume that illustrates all congressional districts for the ninety-seven Congresses. It identifies all representatives and locates their districts on maps. Also included is a complete legal history of redistricting for every state. Thus, the atlas provides an easy way to illustrate voting data and map voting patterns. By mapping the geographical patterns of any roll-call vote, one can quickly analyze regional and sectional politics. The atlas can also be used to map the geographical distribution of committee memberships, party membership, and the margin of electoral victory; consequently, it can be used for studying congressional elections and illustrating geographical roll-call voting patterns.

Parsons, Stanley B., William W. Beach, and Dan Herman. *United States Congressional Districts, 1788–1841.* Westport, CT: Greenwood, 1978.

Parsons, Stanley B., William W. Beach, and Michael J. Dubin. *United States Congressional Districts, 1843–1883.* New York: Greenwood Press, 1986.

Both of these volumes provide population data for both districts and counties. Along with districts and county maps is included information about the creation of the counties. Also given are the names and party affiliation of representatives for each district by Congress.

Finally, if the kind of data or information one is seeking about a district is of a general nature, two of the almanacs cited earlier can be used as ready reference guides. Both the *Almanac of American Politics* and *Politics in America: Members of Congress in Washington and at Home* include data and information for congressional districts. They both provide short profiles of districts, including their social and economic structure, political history, and constituent concerns. The *County and City Data Book* (Washington, DC: U.S. Government Printing Office, 1952– ) presents a wide range of statistical information for counties, standard metropolitan statistical areas, cities, urbanized areas, and unincorporated places. It includes data on agriculture, birth and death rates, business firms, crime, education, employment, government revenue and expenditures, housing, income, and congressional voting. The data presented are taken from various censuses, including the census of governments; census of business, manufacturers, and mineral industries; and census of population and housing.

### Population Data

The U.S. Census Bureau publishes two series within their Current Population Reports that provide information on various aspects of the voting population. The *Population Estimates, P-25 Series* includes regular reports on the estimates and projections of population of voting age. The *Population Characteristics, P-20 Series* provides information about the demographic characteristics of the voting population and the degree of participation in general elections by those eligible to vote. These reports, as well as others published by the Census Bureau, are indexed in the *Bureau of the Census Catalog* (Washington, DC: U.S. Government Printing Office, 1964–1984) and the *American Statistical Index: A Comprehensive Index to the Statistical Publications of the U.S. Government* (Washington, DC: Congressional Information Service, 1974– ). The *American Statistical Index,* as noted earlier, is the most inclusive index to statistics published by the federal government. It provides abstracts of the documents it indexes. The index covers the publication of all major statistical agencies as well as statistics reported in committee hearings and prints. Without this index it would be impossible to systematically search for statistics published in hearings and prints.

Listed below are all the P-20 and P-25 *Current Population Reports* published to date that focus on voting and registration. Some of the P-20 series, the *Voting Participation in Elections,* are available from the Census Bureau in machine-readable form. They are also in the archival holdings of the Inter-University Consortium for Political and Social Research (see the section on data archives, pp. 199–206). The *County and City Data Book* and the *Congressional District Data Book* are also available from the Census Bureau in machine-readable form and are in the archival holdings of the Inter-University Consortium for Political and Social Research.

## P-20 Series, Population Characteristics

No. 143, October 1965. *Voter Participation in the National Election, Nov. 1964*
No. 172, May 1968. *Characteristics of Persons of Voting Age, 1964–1968*
No. 174, August 1968. *Voting and Registration in the Election of Nov. 1966*
No. 177, December 1968. *Voter Participation in Nov. 1968*
No. 192, December 1969. *Voting and Registration in the Election of Nov. 1968*
No. 208, December 1970. *Voter Participation in Nov. 1970*
No. 230, December 1971. *Characteristics of New Voters: 1972*
No. 244, December 1972. *Voter Participation in Nov. 1972*
No. 253, October 1973. *Voting and Registration in the Election of Nov. 1972*
No. 275, January 1975. *Voter Participation in Nov. 1974*
No. 293, April 1976. *Voting and Registration in the Election of Nov. 1974*
No. 304, December 1976. *Voter Participation in November 1976*
No. 322, March 1978. *Voting and Registration in the Election of Nov. 1976*
No. 332, December 1978. *Voting and Registration in the Election of Nov. 1978*
No. 344, September 1979. *Voting and Registration in the Election of Nov. 1978*
No. 359, January 1981. *Voting and Registration in the Election of Nov. 1980*
No. 370, April 1982. *Voting and Registration in the Election of Nov. 1980*
No. 383, November 1983. *Voting and Registration in the Election of Nov. 1982*
No. 405, March 1986. *Voting and Registration in the Election of Nov. 1984*

## P-25 Series, Population Estimates

No. 15, October 1948. *Estimates of the Population of Voting Age, by States: 1948*
No. 90, March 1954. *Estimates of the Population of the United States and Components of Population Change: 1950–1954*

No. 143, October 1956. *Estimates of the Civilian Population of Voting Ages, for States: Nov. 1952 and 1956*

No. 185, October 1960. *Estimates of the Civilian Population of Voting Age, for States: Nov. 1958*

No. 221, October 1960. *Estimates of the Civilian Population of Voting Age, for States: Nov. 1960*

No. 225, October 1962. *Estimates of the Civilian Population of Voting Age, for States: Nov. 1962*

No. 315, August 1965. *Estimates of the Population of Voting in General Elections, 1920–1964*

No. 325, January 1966. *Projections of the Population of Voting Age: Nov. 1966 and 1968*

No. 342, June 1966. *Projections of the Population of Voting Age, for States: Nov. 1966 and 1968*

No. 406, October 1968. *Estimates of the Population of Voting Age, for States: Nov. 1968*

No. 479, March 1972. *Projections of the Population of Voting Age, for States: Nov. 1972*

No. 526, September 1974. *Projections of the Population of Voting Age, for States: Nov. 1974*

No. 626, May 1976. *Projections of the Population of Voting Age, for States: Nov. 1976*

No. 627, June 1976. *Language Minority, Illiteracy, and Voting Data Used in Making Determinations for the Voting Rights Act Amendments of 1975 (Public Law 94-73)*

No. 732, September 1978. *Projections of the Population of Voting Age for States: Nov. 1978*

No. 879, March 1980. *Projections of the Population of Voting Age for States: Nov. 1980*

No. 916, July 1982. *Projections of the Population of Voting Age for States: Nov. 1982*

No. 984, April 1984. *Projections of the Population of Voting Age for States: Nov. 1984*

## Election Returns

The collection and dissemination of election statistics is a meticulous and time-consuming activity that all democratic nations undertake. In the case of the United States the evolution of systematically recording election statistics has been intertwined with the political process itself. The availability of election data makes it theoretically possible for every citizen to scrutinize and question campaign practices and outcomes. For this kind of statistical inspection, the scholar requires data that permit comparability over long periods of time. Two factors also allow for more convenient examination of election statistics. The greater the breakdown of tabulations, the more useful the data will be to the researcher. Secondly, to engage in a rigorous study of elections the scholar needs to check his data against several sources. The following guides are the best sources for election returns.

Congressional Quarterly. *Guide to U.S. Elections*. 2nd ed. Washington, DC: Congressional Quarterly, 1985.

This work is the most definitive source of statistical data on national elections. Included are the complete voting records of elections for the presidency, Congress, and governorships. This volume is an excellent reference guide to all aspects of elections, including extensive background material on the history of political parties, convention ballots and platforms, preference primaries, demographic data, the electoral college, and redistricting. Accompanying each major section of the work is a topical bibliography. The format makes this an especially useful reference work. There are three ways by which to locate information. A detailed table of contents provides an overall view of the scope and coverage of the work. There are candidate indexes for presidential, gubernatorial, Senate, and House candidates. By using the candidate indexes the reader can pinpoint voting returns for over 60,000 candidates. Finally, there is a general index, which covers all subjects discussed in the work. For researchers interested in congressional elections this guide should be the single most useful source.

Government Affairs Institute, Washington, DC. *America Votes: A Handbook of Contemporary American Election Statistics*. Washington, DC: Congressional Quarterly, 1955– .

This biennial work includes presidential, congressional, and gubernatorial returns. The total vote (Republican and Democratic), pluralities, and percentages per county and congressional district are reported. Sections on each of the states include the following: (1) a profile of the state, giving the population, electoral vote, incumbent senators, representatives, and governors, and composition of the state legislature by party and the postwar vote for governor and senator; (2) a map of the state, depicting counties and congressional districts; (3) a geographical breakdown by county and districts for presidential, senatorial, and gubernatorial returns; and (4) tables of the congressional returns. Every volume is virtually an almanac for each election year.

Government Affairs Institute, Election Research Center. *America at the Polls: A Handbook of American Presidental Election Statistics, 1920–1962.* Pittsburgh, PA: University of Pittsburgh Press, 1965.

This work provides statistics for twelve elections from Harding through Johnson. The data in this study are organized along two lines. National presidential voting figures by state are given, and a detailed county-by-county breakdown of the data for each state is provided. Both the state and county data include total vote, Republican, Democrat, and other breakdowns, and pluralities. The work is distinguished by the inclusion of percentages of the total vote and the major vote for Republican and Democratic candidates. Tables relating to national data are followed by notes listing candidates, their national vote, and any special characteristics in the state vote. Every state data section is followed by notes providing the composition of the "other" vote and any special characteristics of the state vote. The excellent layout makes this volume especially easy and enjoyable to use.

Scammon, Richard M., and Alice V. McGillivray. *America at the Polls 2: A Handbook of American Presidential Election Statistics, 1968–1984.* Washington, DC: Congressional Quarterly, 1988.

This work provides state-by-state tables summarizing the results of presidential elections from 1968 to 1984. A detailed breakdown of the vote by counties is given. Primary election results are also included.

*Statistical Abstract of the United States.* Washington, DC: Department of Commerce, U.S. Bureau of Census, 1878– .

This annual document is the basic statistical abstract for data on social, economic, and political affairs in the United States. Dating back to 1878, the coverage on elections varies considerably over the years. Recent volumes include information on votes cast for presidential, congressional, and gubernatorial elections; voter registration and participation; voting age population; and campaign expenditures. The work is useful for locating other sources of data through its bibliographic citations. As an abstract, the series includes a wealth of additional background information that can be used in conjunction with the study of elections. There are statistics on education, employment, income, housing, communications, etc. As a general statistical compendium the series is recognized by scholars and researchers alike as a standard source of statistical data on almost every aspect of society. For retrospective coverage of colonial times, volumes of the *Statistical Abstracts* should be used in conjunction with the *Historical Statistics of the United States, Colonial Times to 1970, Bicentennial Edition.*

Austin, Eric W. *Political Facts of the United States since 1789.* New York: Columbia University Press, 1986.
This general statistical compendium has a section on elections. It provides the popular vote for president, senators, and representatives. It also contains data on apportionment and campaign spending.

The *National Journal* also publishes the results of the elections in a special issue a week or two following an election. The *National Journal* and *CQ Weekly Report* also publish several preelection issues on the candidates and campaign developments. For a week-by-week analysis of a campaign and election, these two journals are indispensible. The *New York Times* and the *Washington Post,* as well as most major newspapers, publish the unofficial election results the day after the election. Local newspapers can be very useful as well for the returns and an analysis of voting within a state and its major cities.

There are individual compilations of congressional election statistics for almost every state. These compendiums are published by state historical societies, legislative research bureaus, and university institutes. An example of such a publication is *Minnesota Votes: Election Returns by County for Presidents, Senators, Congressmen, and Governors, 1857–1977* (St. Paul, MN: Minnesota Historical Society, 1977).

Finally, if one is not interested in finding detailed statistical summaries of election statistics, the almanacs mentioned before contain election results. The *World Almanac and Book of Facts* (New York: Newspaper Enterprise Association, 1868– ), *Information Please Almanac* (Boston: Houghton Mifflin, 1947– ), and *Official Associated Press Almanac* (New York: New York Times Book and Educational Division, 1974– ) are all useful ready reference sources, published annually. While each of the almanacs uses a different format, they all contain essentially the same information. Election returns since 1789 are given on a national basis, including the electoral vote, popular vote, and sometimes percentages or pluralities. For the most recent elections, the election results are broken down by state. All of these almanacs often vary from year to year in regard to the data given. Usually almanacs published following an election year will include somewhat more detailed statistics, such as election results by county. For quick and easy checking on congressional elections, almanacs should not be forgotten or bypassed in the search for statistics. The series *Vital Statistics on Congress* (Washington, DC: Congressional Quarterly) also has election statistics and includes tables on shifts in House and Senate seats, incumbents reelected, and ticket-splitting. Yet for more scholarly research these sources should only be regarded as the initial step.

## Party Strength

Voting returns by themselves do not convey the entire story of an election. Students of elections can learn considerably more about elections by developing their own statistical measures. Today, political scientists are employing statistical data in highly sophisticated ways. By using data in different configurations the researcher can bring to light new perspectives on elections. The following works are the major studies that have sought to examine concepts of party strength, competitiveness, and voting behavior.

Miller, Warren E., Arthur H. Miller, and Edward J. Schneider. *American National Election Studies Data Sourcebook, 1952–1978.* Cambridge, MA: Harvard University Press, 1980.

The data compendium is the printed version of fourteen data archives available at the Inter-University Consortium for Political and Social Research. The studies are surveys conducted by the Survey Research Center and Center for Political Studies. Each of the studies contains information from 1,000 to 2,000 interviews with voters for elections from 1952 to 1978. Areas covered include the respondents' (1) expectations about the outcome of the election, (2) party identification, (3) interest in politics, (4) issue positions, (5) perception of interest groups, (6) assessment of major problems facing the country, (7) financial and class identity, (8) source of political information, (9) measures of political efficacy, (10) personal data, and (11) postelection voting behavior.

Cox, Edward F. *State and National Voting in Federal Elections, 1910–1970.* Hamden, CT: Archon Books, 1972.

This work uses the national elective format as the organization for the data. Tables are by nation and state, including the total vote and percentages of all votes. Voting information covers presidential and congressional elections. Data on the election of representatives are compiled on a statewide aggregate basis. Election data for representatives are not broken down by congressional district, which is a serious drawback. The aggregate elective format provides a useful method for comparing the vote of the three national elective positions. With this kind of format it is simple to measure the voting strength of each party for president, senators, and representatives in each election. The compendium suffers from a poor layout, making interpretation of the tables difficult and tedious.

Cox, Edward F. *Voting in Postwar Federal Elections: A Statistical Analysis of Party Strengths Since 1945.* Rev. ed. Dayton, OH: Wright State University, 1968.

As an interpretation of the significance of American voting in federal elections from 1946 to 1966, the book presents measures of party performance, strength, competitiveness, and individual candidate performance. Geographical analyses are by district and state. The author delineates major trends and future directions for party competition. The book includes two chapters on methodological issues related to the statistical analyses employed in the study. The analyses of the eleven federal elections examined are presented in 251 tables. One failing is the lack of an index.

Cox, Edward F. *The Representative Vote in the Twentieth Century*. Bloomington: Institute of Public Administration, Department of Political Science, Indiana University, 1981.

This volume extends and complements Cox's two previous works. It provides data for all congressional elections, regular as well as special, from 1900 to 1972. What makes this statistical compendium special is that it provides complete data for all candidates and parties for elections to the U.S. House of Representatives. Congressional Quarterly's *Guide to U.S. Elections* provides only the data for leading candidates, i.e., those with percentages in excess of 5 percent. Consequently, this volume is an important statistical compendium for anyone researching minor parties and party performance. It can also be used as a companion work to the other data sources on election returns.

Cummings, Milton C. *Congressmen and the Electorate: Elections for the U.S. House and President, 1920–1964*. New York: Free Press, 1966.

This work provides an extensive analysis of the interrelationships between the vote for congressmen and president in presidential election years. The central thrust of the book is the examination of the degree of similarities and differences between presidential and congressional support polled by the major parties. Other issues covered in the book are ticket-splitting, party strength, the role of minor parties, and the impact of the electoral system on presidential and congressional elections. The work includes fifty-one statistical tables relating to the topics discussed.

David, Paul T. *Party Strength in the United States, 1872–1970*. Charlottesville: University Press of Virginia, 1972.

The aim of this book is to provide index numbers for party strength that extend over a period from 1872 to 1970. The study contains the percentages of the vote won by Democratic, Republican, and other parties and candidates in presidential, gubernatorial, and congressional elections. The text provides the statistical and technical background to the formulation of the index numbers. Additional data covering the later elections can be found in

"Party Strength in the United States: Changes in 1972." *Journal of Politics*
36 (August 1974): 785–796.
"Party Strength in the United States: Some Corrections." *Journal of Politics*
37 (May 1975): 641–642.
"Party Strength in the United States: Changes in 1976." *Journal of Politics*
40 (August 1978): 770–780.

Janda, Kenneth. *Political Parties: A Cross-National Survey.* New York: Free
Press, 1982.
   This is the most systematic and comprehensive empirical study of political
parties throughout the world. Included in the volume are surveys of 153
parties in fifty-eight countries from 1950 to 1978. The first part of the volume
describes the conceptual framework, using twelve basic concepts: (1) insti-
tutionalization, (2) government status, (3) social attraction, concentration,
and reflection, (4) issue orientation, (5) goal orientation, (6) autonomy,
(7) degree of organization, (8) centralization of power, (9) coherence,
(10) involvement, (11) electoral data, and (12) validating the framework. The
concepts are measured by clusters of more than 100 variables to illustrate
party characteristics. The second part of the volume provides the findings for
each country, chapter by chapter. Along with the data and analysis for each
country are included a party history and electoral trends. The volume is
useful not only for studying American political parties but for comparing
parties cross-nationally. In addition to providing data on party strength, it is
an unmatched compendium of data on party characteristics. The data are also
available as a file from the ICPSR.

## Public Opinion Polls

   Public opinion surveys are a rather recent development in social science
research. There are several ways to find information dealing with polls
focusing on the Congress and congressional elections.

*American Public Opinion Index.* Louisville, KY: Opinion Research Service,
1981– .
   This is the only index to public opinion polls. There is a topical index to
questions and listing of the polls at the back of the volume, giving the name
and address of the organization that took the poll. The actual polls are not
reproduced, but the polls are sold on microfiche by Opinion Research
Service. The index covers over fifty-five national, state, and local polls and
includes over 7,500 entries.

Gallup, George Horace. *The Gallup Poll: Public Opinion, 1935–1971*. 3 vols. New York: Random House, 1972.

This is a complete collection of the Gallup Polls from 1935 to 1971. An index in the third volume provides easy subject access to the polls.

Supplementary volumes have also been published:

*The Gallup Poll: Public Opinion, 1972–1977*. Wilmington, DE: Scholarly Resources, 1978.

*The Gallup Poll: Public Opinion, 1978*. Wilmington, DE: Scholarly Resources, 1979.

*The Gallup Poll: Public Opinion, 1979*. Wilmington, DE: Scholarly Resources, 1980.

*The Gallup Poll: Public Opinion, 1980*. Wilmington, DE: Scholarly Resources, 1981.

*The Gallup Poll: Public Opinion, 1981*. Wilmington, DE: Scholarly Resources, 1982.

*The Gallup Poll: Public Opinion, 1982*. Wilmington, DE: Scholarly Books, 1983.

*The Gallup Poll: Public Opinion, 1984*. Wilmington, DE: Scholarly Books, 1985.

*The Gallup Poll: Public Opinion, 1985*. Wilmington, DE: Scholarly Books, 1986.

*The Gallup Poll: Public Opinion, 1986*. Wilmington, DE: Scholarly Books, 1987.

*Gallup Opinion Index Report: Political, Social and Economic Trends*. Princeton, NJ: Gallup International, 1965– .

This series publishes data generated by the American Institute of Public Opinion and Gallup affiliates. The report is published monthly, with special issues occurring from time to time. The surveys, based on a population of at least 1,500 scientifically chosen respondents, include findings on congressional popularity, congressional performance, and a variety of campaign and election issues.

*Public Opinion.* Washington, DC: American Enterprise Institute for Public Policy Research, 1978– .

This journal includes a section providing the results of surveys conducted by numerous public opinion research organizations throughout the country. The journal also publishes several research articles on the results of surveys and public opinion studies in each issue. Its predecessor, *Current Opinion*, was published from 1973 to 1977.

Finally, many of the ABC/*Washington Post*, CBS/*New York Times*, and Harris surveys are available as a data set. The Inter-University Consortium for Political and Social Research has many of these in its archival holdings. See the following section for a listing of what is available.

## Data Archives

There are many data archives throughout the country whose holdings include quantitative data on congressional elections. The major social science data archive is the Inter-University Consortium for Political and Social Research at the University of Michigan. One of the major files of data available from the consortium is the *Historical Election Returns, 1824–1972*. This collection of election data contains county-level returns for presidential, gubernatorial, and congressional elections. For more information about the archive's holdings one should consult the consortium's *Guide to Resources and Services, 1987–1988* (Ann Arbor: University of Michigan, 1987).

In addition to the election data cited above, the consortium also holds many other data files relevant to congressional elections. Many of the statistical sources mentioned throughout the guide, such as Census Bureau publications and public opinion polls, are available on tape. For example, the *Congressional District Data Book* and *County and City Data Book* are available, as well as CBS/*New York Times* and ABC/*Washington Post* polls.

The *Guide to Resources and Services* also includes information about training programs, classes, remote access computer assistance, and information on how to obtain data and codebooks from the consortium. The listing of archival holdings provides the name of the data collector, the title and detailed description of the data file, and related publications that have used the data. Listed below are a selected number of data files dealing with conventions, candidates, elections, ecological data, and public opinion polls. Also, included at the end of the list are data sets on the Congress, such as roll-call voting.

## Congressional Data

Congressional Quarterly, Inc.: *Voting Scores for Members of the United States Congress, 1945–1982.*

Inter-University Consortium for Political and Social Research (ICPSR): *Roster of United States Congressional Officeholders and Biographical Characteristics of Members of the United States Congress, 1789–1985: Merged Data.*

ICPSR: *United States Congressional Biographical Data, 1789–1985.*

ICPSR: *United States Congressional Roll Call Voting Records, 1789–1986* [House of Representatives].

ICPSR: *United States Congressional Roll Call Voting Records, 1789–1986* [Senate].

McKibbin, Carroll L.: *Biographical Characteristics of Members of the United States Congress, 1789–1979.*

O'Leary, Michael, David Kovenock, and Roger Davidson: *Congressional Attitudes Toward Congressional Organization.*

United Nations Association of the United States of America: *United States Congressional Survey, 1975.*

## Primaries, Conventions, and Candidates

CBS News/*New York Times: CBS News/New York Times Election Surveys, 1978.*

CBS News/*New York Times: CBS News Election Surveys, 1978.*

CBS News/*New York Times: CBS News Election Surveys, 1982.*

CBS News: *CBS News Election Day Surveys, 1984: State Surveys.*

CBS News/*New York Times: CBS News/New York Times National Surveys, 1982.*

CBS News/*New York Times* Election Survey, 1984: *Election Day National Survey.*

Goldenberg, Edie N., and Michael W. Traugott. *Congressional Campaign Study, 1978.*

Federal Election Commission: *Survey of United States Congressional Candidates, 1976.*

*Detroit News: Michigan Survey of Voter Attitudes, October 1980.*

*Detroit News: National Survey of Voter Attitudes, June 1980.*

Federal Election Commission: *Campaign Expenditures by Party and Non-Party Political Committees, 1977–1978 and 1979–1980.*

Federal Election Commission: *Campaign Expenditures in the United States, 1981–1982.*

Federal Election Commission: *Campaign Expenditures in the United States, 1983–1984.*

## Election Studies

Campbell, Angus, and Robert L. Kahn: *American National Election Study, 1948.*

Campbell, Angus, et al.: *American National Election Study, 1952.*

Campbell, Angus, et al.: *American National Election Study, 1956.*

Campbell, Angus, et al.: *American National Election Study, 1958.*

Survey Research Center: *Minor American National Election Study, 1960.*

Political Behavior Program, Survey Research Center: *American National Election Study, 1962.*

Political Behavior Program, Survey Research Center: *American National Election Study, 1964.*

Political Behavior Program, Survey Research Center: *American National Election Study, 1966.*

Political Behavior Program, Survey Research Center: *American National Election Study, 1968.*

Center for Political Studies: *American National Election Study, 1970.*

Miller, Warren, et al.: *American National Election Study, 1972.*

Miller, Warren, et al.: *American National Election Study, 1974.*

Miller, Warren, and Arthur Miller: *American National Election Study, 1976.*

Center for Political Studies: *American National Election Series: 1972, 1974, 1976.*

Miller, Warren E., and National Election Studies/Center for Political Studies (NES/CPS): *American National Election Study, 1978.*

Miller, Warren E., Arthur H. Miller, and Edward J. Schneider: *American National Election Studies Data Sourcebook, 1952–1978.*

Miller, Warren E., and National Election Studies/Center for Political Studies (NES/CPS): *American National Election Pilot Study, Spring 1979.*

Miller, Warren E., and NES/CPS: *American National Election Study, 1980.*

Miller, Warren E., and NES/CPS: *American National Election Study, 1982: Post-Election Survey File.*

Survey Research Center: *American Panel Study: 1956, 1958, 1960.*

Shanks, Merrill, Maria Sanchez, Betsy Morton, Giovanna Morchio, Alice Hayes, and Southward Swede: *National Election Studies Method Comparison Project, 1982.*

Miller, Warren E., and NES/CPS: *American National Election Study 1984: 1983 Pilot Study.*

Miller, Warren E., and NES/CPS: *American National Election Study, 1984.*

Miller, Warren E., and NES/CPS: *American National Election Study: 1985 Pilot Study.*

Miller, Warren E., and NES/CPS: *American National Election Study: 1986 Pilot Study.*

Jackson, John E.: *Media Predictions and Voter Turnout in the United States, Election Day 1980.*

Kovenock, David M., and James W. Prothro: *Comparative State Elections Project, 1968.*

Lazarsfeld, Paul F., Bernard R. Berelson, and Hazel Gaudet: *Erie County Study, 1940.*

Lazarsfeld, Paul F., Bernard R. Berelson, and William N. McPhee: *Elmira Community Study, 1948.*

National Opinion Research Center: *National Election Study, 1944.*

National Opinion Research Center: *National Election Study, 1948.*

U.S. Dept. of Commerce, Bureau of the Census: *Current Population Survey: Voter Supplement File, 1972.*

U.S. Dept. of Commerce, Bureau of the Census: *Current Population Survey: Voter Supplement File, 1974.*

U.S. Dept. of Commerce, Bureau of the Census: *Current Population Survey: Voter Supplement File, 1976.*

U.S. Dept. of Commerce, Bureau of the Census: *Current Population Survey: Voter Supplement File, 1978.*

U.S. Dept. of Commerce, Bureau of the Census: *Current Population Survey: Voter Supplement File, 1980.*

U.S. Dept. of Commerce, Bureau of the Census: *Current Population Survey: Voter Supplement File, 1982.*

U.S. Dept. of Commerce, Bureau of the Census: *Current Population Survey: Voter Supplement File, 1984.*

## Election Returns

Bartley, Numan V., and Hugh D. Graham: *Southern Primary and General Election Data, 1946–1972.*

Burnham, W. Dean, Jerome M. Clubb, and William Flanigan: *State-Level Congressional, Gubernatorial and Senate Election Data for the United States, 1824–1972.*

Clubb, Jerome M., William H. Flanigan, and Nancy H. Zingale: *Electoral Data for Counties in the United States: Presidential and Congressional Races, 1840–1972.*

Heard, Alexander, and Donald S. Strong: *Southern Primary and General Election Data, 1920–1949.*

Inter-University Consortium for Political and Social Research (ICPSR): *Candidate and Constituency Statistics of Elections in the United States, 1788–1985.*

ICPSR: *Candidate Name and Constituency Totals, 1788–1985.*

ICPSR: *General Election Data for the United States, 1968–1985.*

ICPSR: *Referenda and Primary Election Materials, 1968–1984.*

ICPSR: *Southern Primary Candidate Name and Constituency Totals, 1920–1972.*

ICPSR: *United States Historical Election Returns, 1788–1823.*

ICPSR: *United States Historical Election Returns, 1788–1985.*

Michigan Department of State: *Michigan Election Returns, 1972: Precinct-Level.*

Michigan Department of State: *Michigan Election Returns, 1974: Precinct-Level.*

Michigan Department of State: *Michigan Election Returns, 1978: Precinct-Level Data from the August Primary Election.*

Michigan Department of State: *Michigan Election Returns, 1978: Precinct-Level Primary Election Data from the November Primary Election.*

## Ecological Data

ICPSR: *Data Confrontation Seminar, 1969: United States Data.*

U.S. Department of Commerce, Bureau of the Census: *County and City Data Books: 1952, 1956, 1962, 1967, 1972, 1977, 1983.*

U.S. Department of Commerce, Bureau of the Census: *County and City Data Book Consolidated File: City Data, 1944–1977.*

U.S. Department of Commerce, Bureau of the Census: *County and City Data Book Consolidated File: City Data, 1947–1977.*

U.S. Department of Commerce, Bureau of the Census: *United States Congressional District Data Books, 1961–1965.*

U.S. Department of Commerce, Bureau of the Census: *United States Congressional District Book for the Ninety-Third Congress, 1973.*

## Public Opinion

ABC News: *General Election Exit Survey, 1984.*

ABC News/*Washington Post: ABC News/Washington Post Polls, 1981, 1982, 1983.*

CBS News/*New York Times: CBS News/New York Times Polls, 1976–1978.*

Davis, James A., James S. Coleman, Norman H. Nie, John Riley, and Christopher Jencks: *NORC Amalgam Survey, December 1973.*

Louis Harris and Associates, Inc.: *Harris 1973 Confidence in Government Survey.*

Holm, John D: *Watergate Hearings Panel Survey.*

Miscellaneous

Janda, Kenneth: *Comparative Political Parties Data, 1950–1982.*

Milbrath, Lester: *Washington Lobbyists Survey, 1956–1957.*

Miller, Warren E., and Donald E. Stokes: *American Representation Study, 1958.*

Verba, Sidney, and Norman Nie: *Political Participation in America, 1967.*

Commission on the Operation of the Senate: *Daily Operation of the United States Senate, 1975.*

## Directories

A number of institutions other than ICPSR also have data archives with files on congressional elections and activities. To locate other institutions and their holdings, the following sources should be consulted:

Sessions, Vivian S., ed. *Directory of Data Bases in the Social and Behavioral Sciences.* New York: Science Associates International, Inc., 1974.
This directory gives an extensive listing of 685 databases and centers in the United States. For each database, the following information is provided: (1) address, (2) director and principal staff, (3) data holdings, (4) storage media, and (5) avenue of access. Over fifteen institutions are identified that have data holdings relating to election returns and electoral behavior. The work includes a subject index, institutional index, and geographical index. The subject index contains several relevant entries: Election Data, Election Returns, Election Studies, Electoral Data, and Electoral Studies.

*S S Data: Newsletter of Social Science Archival Acquisitions.* Iowa City: Laboratory for Political Research, University of Iowa, 1971– .
This newsletter provides information on data acquired by archives throughout the United States and Canada. The data set descriptions are provided by the participating archives. The descriptions usually include (1) the original data collection agency and principal investigator and (2) the time period of the data, the population, and a descriptive paragraph explaining the nature of the study.

There are also several journals that regularly contain articles using data files as well as notes on new data sets available and research in progress.

These are *Social Science Information, Historical Methods Newsletter,* and *Review of Public Data Use*. The last journal is especially useful for keeping up to date on Census Bureau developments and its distribution of data files. A second set of journals that are useful to anyone planning to use data files are those that focus on mathematical applications and quantitative research. They contain articles on statistical techniques as well as research findings based on the use of data files. These journals are *Social Science Research, Sociological Methods and Research, Political Methodology, Mathematical Social Sciences, Quality and Quantity, Journal of Mathematical Sociology,* and *Multivariate Behavioral Research.*

## Data Source Books

This section identifies a variety of secondary sources that can be used to find additional data compilations. Other important sources of statistics are provided by numerous state agencies. Within each state there are various departments and organizations that collect data relating to many different aspects of campaigning and electioneering. The guides listed below identify where to find state election results, demographic data, and socioeconomic information.

Council of State Governments. *State Blue Books and Reference Publications: A Selected Bibliography.* Rev. ed. Lexington, KY: Council of State Governments, 1983.
    This is a listing, arranged alphabetically by states, of reference materials on the states and territories. Each state includes reference materials on legislative and general state government digests or summaries of legislative action, and guides, statistics, etc. Included with each entry is the source and place of publication, the date and frequency of publication, and the cost. An important addition to the revised edition is a table indicating the types of material included in the State Blue Books. An appendix contains a number of tables of comparative information. There is directory information, both current and historical, on the state level for the executive, judicial, and legislative branches as well as for the federal government. There is also a table covering election returns, both current and historical. This reference work can be used to identify state sources of election statistics.

U.S. Department of Commerce. Bureau of the Census. *Directory of Non-Federal Statistics for States and Local Areas: A Guide of Sources, 1969.* Washington, DC: U.S. Government Printing Office, 1970.
    This is a comprehensive listing of statistics covering all areas of study. The work is arranged by state, then by a topical breakdown within each state.

Within each state there is a listing of material dealing with elections and voting. Each document is described according to its (1) tabular detail, (2) areas to which data apply, (3) frequency of data, and (4) source document. There is also a *Directory of Federal Statistics for Local Areas: A Guide to Sources, 1976,* published by the Census Bureau.

Burnham, Walter D. *Sources of Historical Election Data: A Preliminary Bibliography.* East Lansing: Institute for Community Development and Services, Michigan State University, 1963.
   This is a short annotated bibliography on election data. The bibliography includes four sections: (1) general sources of election returns, (2) state publication of election returns, (3) elections reported below the county level, and (4) demographic material. It is particularly useful for its bibliography of nonofficially published compilations of election returns by state, e.g., Riker, Dorothy L., *Indiana Election Returns, 1816–1851* (Indianapolis: Indiana State Historical Society, 1960).

Press, Charles, and Oliver Williams. *State Manuals, Blue Books, and Election Results.* Berkeley: Institute of Governmental Studies, University of California, 1962.
   This is a listing by states of source materials for official election results, legislative manuals, directories of state officials, and related information. Corresponding with each entry is an outline of the kind of information contained within each source. The place and frequency of publication are also noted.

## Bibliographies

When studying congressional elections it is always useful to get as much background information as possible. Ever since the first election, people have been analyzing the results and writing commentaries. A good way to begin a search for literature is to use the following bibliographies.

*The American Electorate: A Historical Bibliography.* Santa Barbara, CA: ABC-Clio, 1983.
   This bibliography contains over 1,300 abstracts of articles on electoral history and politics, voting patterns, and individual elections. The bibliography includes periodical literature published since 1963. It is organized by chapter according to a major subject, with entries arranged by author. There is also a subject index.

Mauer, David J. *United States Politics and Elections: Guide to Information Sources*. Detroit, MI: Gale Research Company, 1978.

This lengthy annotated bibliography includes citations to articles and books on electoral politics in general, congressional elections, and congressional candidates. It is arranged by chapter according to historical periods and contains a wealth of biographical materials on members of Congress and candidates. It also includes citations to important political issues and trends for each historical period.

Wynar, Lubomyr R., comp. *American Political Parties: A Selective Guide to Parties and Movements of the 20th Century*. Littleton, CO: Libraries Unlimited, 1969.

This work is a compilation of over 3,000 books, monographs, and unpublished dissertations on significant twentieth-century American parties and movements. The arrangement is by subject and party. The book is helpful in providing general background material related to elections, public opinion, parties, and political behavior.

Agranoff, Robert. *Elections and Electoral Behavior: A Bibliography*. De Kalb: Center for Governmental Studies, Northern Illinois University, 1972.

This bibliography is a listing of over 300 items dealing with theoretical and practical issues of elections. The bibliography is divided into four sections: (1) electoral system and voting rights, (2) candidate selection, nominations and party conventions, (3) voting behavior, and (4) electoral interpretation. Entries are not annotated, nor is the pagination given for either articles or books.

Smith, Dwight L., and Lloyd W. Garrison, eds. *The American Political Process: Selected Abstracts of Periodical Literature (1954–1971)*. Santa Barbara, CA: ABC-Clio, 1974.

This work contains a lengthy section on American elections, including a subsection on presidential elections and campaigns. The abstracts in the work were taken from *Historical Abstracts* (Santa Barbara, CA: ABC-Clio, 1955– ; published quarterly) and *America: History and Life* (Santa Barbara, CA: ABC-Clio, 1974– ; published triennially).

The following bibliographies, while shorter and more broad in scope, also contain many citations relating to election and voting research.

Goehlert, Robert. *Federal Elections: A Select Bibliography*. Monticello, IL: Vance Bibliographies, 1982.

————— . *Reapportionment and Redistricting: A Selected Bibliography.*
Monticello, IL: Vance Bibliographies, 1981.
————— . *Voting Research and Modeling: A Bibliography.* Monticello, IL:
Vance Bibliographies, 1981.

Steward, Alva W. *Congressional Reapportionment and Redistricting in the 1980's: A Preliminary Bibliography.* Monticello, IL: Vance Bibliographies, 1982.

Lutes, Terry. *Voting Behavior, 1968–1980.* Monticello, IL: Vance Bibliographies, 1981.

# 9. Library Collections

Large academic libraries and research institutions will probably have most of the reference works discussed in this guide. Smaller libraries usually cannot afford to purchase all the guides to congressional research. Most libraries will have *CIS/Index* and its *Annual,* but not all will subscribe to the *Congressional Monitor* or *Congressional Index.* Large university libraries will usually have all the journals, statistical sources, directories, and other works cited earlier.

The size of a library's government document collection can range from limited vertical files to vast holdings. The Depository Library Act of 1962 represented a major step in establishing a national system of federal documents authorized for distribution under the program, while selective depositories receive only what they decide to collect. Thousands of libraries not part of the depository system have government document collections, but their holdings may not be sufficient in all instances to do extensive legislative research. The depository system also makes it possible to acquire government documents through interlibrary loan. A selected list of depository libraries for United States documents can be found in Appendix 1 (see pp. 267–70). In addition to the depository libraries, there are numerous library collections housed in various federal agencies in Washington and around the country. Mildred Benton's *Federal Library Resources: A User's Guide to Research Collections* (New York: Science Associates International, 1973) provides valuable information about many federal libraries. The Government Documents Round Table of the American Library Association has compiled a *Directory of Government Document Collections and Librarians,* 5th ed., edited by Barbara Kile (Washington, DC: Congressional Information Service, 1987), which is especially useful for obtaining the names and addresses of librarians who administer federal document collections.

Large libraries often have segregated government document collections, whereas smaller institutions tend to incorporate government documents into the library's holdings. In the latter case, government publications are classified in the same fashion as the entire collection. Consequently, government documents are distributed throughout the library. Since separate government document collections can be administered in various ways, it is not uncommon for libraries to catalog and classify government publications according to their own distinctive schemes.

## CITING DOCUMENTS

When students use government documents in their research, they are often unsure of how to cite them. Cited below are the publications relating to the Privacy Act of 1974 as they would appear in a bibliography. Footnotes would also provide the specific page cited. There are various formats for citing government publications in bibliographies and footnotes, but regardless of stylistic variations, all citations should include the basic information. For congressional publications, it is necessary to record the chamber, committee, title, Congress and session, date, and type of document (i.e., report, committee print, etc.) and its identification number. When citing executive branch publications, include the department, agency or office, title, personal author if applicable, publisher, and date.

### Bills

U.S. Congress. House. *A Bill to Safeguard Individual Privacy from the Misuse of Federal Records and* . . . 93d Cong., 2d sess., 1974. H.R. 16373.

U.S. Congress. Senate. *A Bill to Establish a Federal Privacy Board* . . . 93d Cong., 2d sess., 1974. S. 3418.

### Hearings and Prints

U.S. Congress. Senate. Committee on Government Operations. Ad Hoc Subcommittee on Privacy and Information Systems. Committee on the Judiciary. Subcommittee on Constitutional Rights. *Privacy: The Collection, Use and Computerization of Personal Data.* Joint Hearing on S. 3418 . . . 93d Cong., 2d sess. Washington, DC: U.S. Government Printing Office, 1974.

U.S. Congress. Senate. Committee on Government Operations. *Materials Pertaining to S. 3418 and Protecting Individual Privacy in Federal Gathering, Use, and Disclosure of Information*. 93d Cong., 2d sess. Washington, DC: Government Printing Office, 1974. Committee Print.

## Reports

U.S. Congress. House. Committee on Government Operations. *Privacy Act of 1974*. 93d Cong., 2d sess., 1974. H. Rept. 93-1416.

U.S. Congress. Senate. Committee on Government Operations. *Preservation, Protection, and Public Access with Respect to Certain Tape Recordings and Other Materials*. 93d Cong., 2d sess., 1974. S. Rept. 93-1416.

## Senate Vote

Note that citations to the vote differ.

*Congressional Record*, 93d Cong., 2d sess., Nov. 21, 1974, 120, S19858. [Daily edition.]

*Congressional Record*, 93d Cong., 2d sess., 1974, 120 36917. [Bound volume.]

*Journal of the Senate*, 93d Cong., 2d sess., 1974, 1475. [Bound volume.]

## Presidential Statement

Note that citations to the same statement in the *Weekly Compilation of Presidential Documents* and *Public Papers of the President* differ.

U.S. President. "Right of Privacy Legislation [Oct. 9, 1974]," *Weekly Compilation of Presidential Documents 10*, no. 41 (Oct. 14, 1974): 1250.

U.S. President. "Statement on Privacy Legislation [Oct. 9, 1974]," *Public Papers of the Presidents of the United States: Gerald R. Ford (1974)*. U.S. National Archives and Records Administration. Washington, DC: U.S. Government Printing Office, 1975, pp. 243-244.

## Law

Pub. L. 93-579 (Dec. 31, 1974), *Privacy Act of 1974*, 88 Stat. 1896.

## Executive Publications

U.S. Department of Health, Education and Welfare. Secretary's Advisory Committee on Automated Personal Data Systems. *Records, Computers and the Rights of Citizens*. DHEW Pub. No. (05)73-94. Washington, DC: U.S. Government Printing Office, 1973.

U.S. President's Domestic Council. Committee on the Right of Privacy. *Privacy, A Public Concern: A Resource Document*. Kent S. Larsen, ed. Washington, DC: U.S. Government Printing Office, 1975.

Presidential materials are located in the *Federal Register*, the *Code of Federal Regulations*, and the *Weekly Compilation of Presidential Documents*. Materials include proclamations, executive orders, memos, letters, veto and other messages, and a variety of other publications.

## Series Citations

### Executive Orders

E.O. number (date)

### Proclamations

Proc. number (date)

## Source Citations

### Weekly Compilation of Presidential Documents

*Weekly Compilation of Presidential Documents* volume number, issue number (date of issue), page(s).

### United States Statutes at Large

Pub. L. number (date approved), *Title*. Volume number of *Statutes at Large* stat. Page number.

### United States Code

Title number *U.S.C.* Section number (edition year).

## United States Treaties and Other International Agreements

Volume number, part, TIAS number, date of signature.

## Constitution of the United States

U.S. Constitution, article or amendment, section.

## Federal Register

Volume number *F.R.* page(s) (year).

## Code of Federal Regulations

Title number (always 3 or 3A) *C.F.R.* (years of compilation), page(s).

## Federal Register (Regulations)

Volume number *F.R.,* page number.

## Code of Federal Regulations (Regulations)

Title number *C.F.R.,* section number (edition year).

While there are abbreviated formats for citing government publications, it is always best to provide as complete a bibliographic entry as possible. When footnoting, using abbreviations can save considerable space and be an effective shorthand, but it is important to be consistent in one's use of abbreviations. The best guides to the use of abbreviations are *Effective Legal Research* and *A Uniform System of Citation* (sold by the Harvard Law Review Association, Gannett House, Cambridge, MA 02138) and *The Complete Guide to Citing Government Documents,* by Diane L. Garner and Diane H. Smith (Congressional Information Service, 1984).

For additional information on citing government publications, consult Kate L. Turabian's *A Manual for Writers of Term Papers, Theses, and Dissertations,* 5th ed. (Chicago IL: University of Chicago Press, 1987), *The Chicago Manual of Style,* 13th ed. (Chicago IL: University of Chicago Press, 1982), or George D. Brightbill and Wayne C. Maxson's *Citation Manual for United States Publications,* Study Guide and Teaching Aids, Paper no. 10 (Philadelphia: Center for Study of Federalism, Temple University, 1974). No matter what style you use in citing government publications, be consistent. Supply the same information in the same order and format.

# Figures

**Figure 1.**
**House Bill**

93D CONGRESS
2D SESSION

# H. R. 16373

IN THE HOUSE OF REPRESENTATIVES

AUGUST 12, 1974

Mr. MOORHEAD of Pennsylvania (for himself, Ms. ABZUG, Mr. ALEXANDER, Mr. BROOMFIELD, Mr. ERLENBORN, Mr. FASCELL, Mr. GOLDWATER, Mr. GUDE, Mr. KOCH, Mr. LITTON, Mr. McCLOSKEY, Mr. MOSS, Mr. THONE, and Mr. WRIGHT) introduced the following bill; which was referred to the Committee on Government Operations

# A BILL

To amend title 5, United States Code, by adding a section 552a to safeguard individual privacy from the misuse of Federal records and to provide that individuals be granted access to records concerning them which are maintained by Federal agencies.

1    *Be it enacted by the Senate and House of Representa-*

2    *tives of the United States of America in Congress assembled,*

3    That this Act may be cited as the "Privacy Act of 1974".

4    SEC. 2. (a) The Congress finds that—

5        (1) the privacy of an individual is directly affected

6        by the collection, maintenance, use, and dissemination

7        of personal information by Federal agencies;

I

**Figure 2.**
**Senate Bill**

93D CONGRESS
2D SESSION

# S. 3418

---

## IN THE SENATE OF THE UNITED STATES

### MAY 1, 1974

Mr. ERWIN (for himself, Mr. PERCY, and Mr. MUSKIE) introduced the following bill; which was read twice and referred to the Committee on Government Operations

---

# A BILL

To establish a Federal Privacy Board to oversee the gathering and disclosure of information concerning individuals, to provide management systems in Federal agencies, State, and local governments, and other organizations regarding such information, and for other purposes.

1     *Be it enacted by the Senate and House of Representa-*

2 *tives of the United States of America in Congress assembled,*

3         TITLE I—FEDERAL PRIVACY BOARD

4             ESTABLISHMENT OF BOARD

5     SEC. 101. (a) There is established in the executive

6 branch of the Government the Federal Privacy Board which

7 shall be composed of five members who shall be appointed

8 by the President by and with the advice and consent of the

II

Figure 3.
Senate Committee Hearing

# PRIVACY
## THE COLLECTION, USE, AND COMPUTERIZATION
## OF PERSONAL DATA

# JOINT HEARINGS
BEFORE THE

## AD HOC SUBCOMMITTEE ON PRIVACY AND
## INFORMATION SYSTEMS

OF THE

## COMMITTEE ON
## GOVERNMENT OPERATIONS

AND THE

## SUBCOMMITTEE ON CONSTITUTIONAL RIGHTS

OF THE

## COMMITTEE ON THE JUDICIARY
## UNITED STATES SENATE

NINETY-THIRD CONGRESS

SECOND SESSION

ON

## S. 3418, S. 3633, S. 3116, S. 2810, S. 2542

JUNE 18, 19, AND 20, 1974

PART 1

Printed for the use of the Committee on Government Operations and the
Committee on the Judiciary

U.S. GOVERNMENT PRINTING OFFICE

37–583 O          WASHINGTON : 1974

**Figure 4.**
Senate Committee Print

| 93d Congress ⎫<br>2d Session ⎭ | COMMITTEE PRINT |
| --- | --- |

MATERIALS PERTAINING TO S. 3418 AND
PROTECTING INDIVIDUAL PRIVACY IN
FEDERAL GATHERING, USE AND
DISCLOSURE OF INFORMATION

---

COMPILED BY STAFF

OF THE

COMMITTEE ON GOVERNMENT OPERATIONS
UNITED STATES SENATE

NOVEMBER 12, 1974

---

U.S. GOVERNMENT PRINTING OFFICE

41-950 O                         WASHINGTON : 1974

# Figure 5.
## House Committee Report

| 93D CONGRESS<br>*2d Session* | HOUSE OF REPRESENTATIVES | REPORT<br>No. 93–1416 |
|---|---|---|

## PRIVACY ACT OF 1974

OCTOBER 2, 1974.—Committed to the Committee of the Whole House on the State
of the Union and ordered to be printed

Mr. MOORHEAD of Pennsylvania, from the Committee on Government
Operations, submitted the following

# REPORT

together with

## ADDITIONAL VIEWS

[To accompany H.R. 16373]

The Committee on Government Operations, to whom was referred
the bill (H.R. 16373) to amend title 5, United States Code, by adding
a section 552a to safeguard individual privacy from the misuse of
Federal records and to provide that individuals be granted access to
records concerning which are maintained by Federal agencies,
having considered the same, report favorably thereon with an amendment and recommend that the bill as amended do pass.

The amendment to the text of the bill strikes out all after the enacting clause and inserts a substitute text which appears in italic type in
the reported bill.

DIVISIONS OF THE REPORT

Summary and purpose.
Background.
Committee action and vote.
Discussion:
    Definitions.
    Conditions of disclosure.
    Accounting of certain disclosures.
    Access to records.
    Agency requirements.
    Agency rules.
    Civil remedies.
    Rights of legal guardians.
    Criminal penalties.
    General exemptions.

Figure 6.
Senate Committee Report

# Calendar No. 1125

| 93D CONGRESS | SENATE | REPORT |
|---|---|---|
| 2d Session | | No. 93–1181 |

PRESERVATION, PROTECTION, AND PUBLIC ACCESS
WITH RESPECT TO CERTAIN TAPE RECORDINGS AND
OTHER MATERIALS

SEPTEMBER 26, 1974.—Ordered to be printed

Mr. ERVIN, from the Committee on Government Operations,
submitted the following

## REPORT

[To accompany S. 4016]

The Committee on Government Operations, to which was referred
the bill (S. 4016) to protect and preserve recordings of conversations
involving former President Richard M. Nixon and made during his
tenure as President, and for other purposes, having considered the
same, reports favorably thereon with an amendment and recommends
that the bill as amended do pass.
The amendment is in the nature of a substitute.

### PURPOSE AND PROVISIONS

The purpose of S. 4016, as amended, is to (1) protect and preserve
tape recordings of conversations, and other materials, recorded or prepared in the White House, the Executive Office Building, and certain
other specified places, between January 20, 1969 and August 9, 1974;
(2) make them available for use by the Special Watergate Prosecution
Force and for access by the public, under regulations promulgated by
the Administrator of General Services who would be required to retain
custody and control of such tapes and other materials; and (3) make
them available to Richard M. Nixon, or his designees, for copying, or
any other purpose, consistent with the Administrator's regulations.
In order to accomplish these objectives, the Committee amendment
directs the Administrator of General Services, notwithstanding the
agreement or understanding he entered into with former President

38–010

Figure 7.
*Congressional Record*

# Congressional Record

United States
of America

PROCEEDINGS AND DEBATES OF THE $100^{tb}$ CONGRESS, SECOND SESSION

| Vol. 134 | WASHINGTON, WEDNESDAY, JULY 6, 1988 | No. 100 |

## House of Representatives

The House met at 12 noon and was called to order by the Speaker pro tempore [Mr. FOLEY].

### DESIGNATION OF SPEAKER PRO TEMPORE

The SPEAKER pro tempore laid before the House the following communication from the Speaker:

WASHINGTON, DC,
*June 30, 1988.*

### MESSAGE FROM THE SENATE

A message from the Senate by Mr. Hallen, one of its clerks, announced that the Senate had passed with amendments in which the concurrence of the House is requested, a bill of the following title:

H.R. 4775. An act making appropriations for the Treasury Department, the U.S. Postal Service, the Executive Office of the President, and certain independent agencies, for the fiscal year ending September 30, 1989, and for other purposes.

best ones to investigate because they would be investigating people close to themselves. That seemed in 1978 and again in 1982 to be overwhelmingly clear. The last time we considered this the Reagan administration raised a series of constitutional issues which many of us felt to be specious.

The Supreme Court has just spoken 7 to 1. Chief Justice Rehnquist, who was elevated by President Reagan, wrote a firm opinion rejecting every single one of the administration's

# Figure 8.
## Slip Law

Public Law 93-579
93rd Congress, S. 3418
December 31, 1974

## An Act

To amend title 5, United States Code, by adding a section 552a to safeguard
individual privacy from the misuse of Federal records, to provide that
individuals be granted access to records concerning them which are maintained
by Federal agencies, to establish a Privacy Protection Study Commission, and
for other purposes.

*Be it enacted by the Senate and House of Representatives of the
United States of America in Congress assembled,* That this Act may
be cited as the "Privacy Act of 1974".

SEC. 2. (a) The Congress finds that—
    (1) the privacy of an individual is directly affected by the
collection, maintenance, use, and dissemination of personal information by Federal agencies;
    (2) the increasing use of computers and sophisticated infor-
mation technology, while essential to the efficient operations of
the Government, has greatly magnified the harm to individual
privacy that can occur from any collection, maintenance, use, or
dissemination of personal information;
    (3) the opportunities for an individual to secure employment,
insurance, and credit, and his right to due process, and other legal
protections are endangered by the misuse of certain information
systems;
    (4) the right to privacy is a personal and fundamental right
protected by the Constitution of the United States; and
    (5) in order to protect the privacy of individuals identified in
information systems maintained by Federal agencies, it is necessary and proper for the Congress to regulate the collection, maintenance, use, and dissemination of information by such agencies.
    (b) The purpose of this Act is to provide certain safeguards for an
individual against an invasion of personal privacy by requiring
Federal agencies, except as otherwise provided by law, to—
    (1) permit an individual to determine what records pertaining
to him are collected, maintained, used, or disseminated by such
agencies;
    (2) permit an individual to prevent records pertaining to him
obtained by such agencies for a particular purpose from being
used or made available for another purpose without his consent;
    (3) permit an individual to gain access to information pertain-
ing to him in Federal agency records, to have a copy made of all
or any portion thereof, and to correct or amend such records;
    (4) collect, maintain, use, or disseminate any record of identi-
fiable personal information in a manner that assures that such
action is for a necessary and lawful purpose, that the information is current and accurate for its intended use, and that
adequate safeguards are provided to prevent misuse of such
information;
    (5) permit exemptions from the requirements with respect to
records provided in this Act only in those cases where there is an
important public policy need for such exemption as has been
determined by specific statutory authority; and
    (6) be subject to civil suit for any damages which occur as a
result of willful or intentional action which violates any individual's rights under this Act.
    SEC. 3. Title 5, United States Code, is amended by adding after
section 552 the following new section:

Privacy Act
of 1974.
5 USC 552a
note.
Congressional
findings.
5 USC 552a
note.

Statement of
purpose.

88 STAT. 1896
88 STAT. 1897

# UNITED STATES
# STATUTES AT LARGE

CONTAINING THE

LAWS AND CONCURRENT RESOLUTIONS
ENACTED DURING THE SECOND SESSION OF THE
NINETY-THIRD CONGRESS
OF THE UNITED STATES OF AMERICA

# 1974

AND

PROCLAMATIONS

## VOLUME 88

IN TWO PARTS

## PART 2

PUBLIC LAWS 93–447 THROUGH 93–649,
PRIVATE LAWS, CONCURRENT RESOLUTIONS
AND PROCLAMATIONS

UNITED STATES
GOVERNMENT PRINTING OFFICE
WASHINGTON : 1976

**Figure 10.**
*Weekly Compilation of Presidential Documents*

*Weekly Compilation of*

# PRESIDENTIAL
# DOCUMENTS

Monday, January 6, 1975

Volume 11 · Number 1

Pages 1-15

## Figure 11.
*CIS/Annual*: Legislative History of Privacy Act of 1974

### PL93-579 PRIVACY ACT OF 1974.
Dec. 31, 1974. 93-2. 15 p.
* ●Item 575.
88 STAT. 1896.

"To amend title 5, United States Code, by adding a section 552a to safeguard individual privacy from the misuse of Federal records, to provide that individuals be granted access to records concerning them which are maintained by Federal agencies, to establish a Privacy Protection Study Commission, and for other purposes."

Legislative history: (S. 3418 and related bills):

**1970 CIS/Annual:**
House Hearings: H621-15.

**1972 CIS/Annual:**
House Document: H920-1.
Senate Hearings: S521-13; S521-14.

**1973 CIS/Annual:**
House Hearings: H401-7; H401-9; H401-33.
House Report: H403-11 (No. 93-598).

**1974 CIS/Annual:**
House Hearings: H401-20; H401-40.
Senate Committee Prints: S402-29; S522-10; S522-12; S522-13; S522-17; S522-18; S522-19; S522-21.
House Report: H403-27 (No. 93-1416, accompanying H.R. 16373).
Senate Report: S403-18 (No. 93-1183).

**Congressional Record Vol. 120 (1974):**
Nov. 21, considered and passed Senate.
Dec. 11, considered and passed House, amended, in lieu of H.R. 16373.
Dec. 17, Senate concurred in House amendment with amendments.
Dec. 18, House concurred in Senate amendments.

**Weekly Compilation of Presidential Documents Vol. 11, No. 1:**
Jan. 1, Presidential statement.

# Figure 12.
## Congressional Record, Daily Digest: Legislative History of Privacy Act of 1974

| Title | Bill No. | Date introduced | Committee | | Date reported | | Report No. | | Page of Congressional Record of passage | | Date of passage | | Public Law | |
|---|---|---|---|---|---|---|---|---|---|---|---|---|---|---|
| | | | House | Senate | House | Senate | House | Senate | House | Senate | House | Senate | Date approved | No. |
| To authorize and request the President to call a White House Conference on Library and Information Sciences in 1976. | S.J. Res. 40 | Jan. 26 1973 | EdL | Com | May 22 | Nov. 16 1973 | 93-1056 | 93-521 | H 11774 | S 20847 | Dec. 12 | Nov. 20 1973 | Dec. 31 | 93-568 |
| To improve veterans' home loan programs............ | H.R. 15912 (S. 3883) | July 16 | VA | VA | July 29 | Dec. 11 | 93-1213 | 93-1334 | H 7669 | S 21396 | Aug. 5 | Dec. 13 | Dec. 31 | 93-569 |
| Making further continuing appropriations for fiscal year 1975 through Feb. 28, 1975. | H.J. Res. 1178 | Dec. 17 | App | App | Dec. 17 | Dec. 18 | 93-1614 | 93-1405 | H 12226 | S 22142 | Dec. 18 | Dec. 19 | Dec. 31 | 93-570 |
| Providing authority for military bands to make recordings and tapes for commercial sale in connection with the Bicentennial celebration. | H.R. 14401 | Apr. 25 | AS | AS | Sept. 19 | Dec. 12 | 93-1364 | 93-1344 | H 9950 | S 21835 | Oct. 7 | Dec. 17 | Dec. 31 | 93-571 |
| To provide a program of emergency unemployment compensation for up to an additional 13 weeks. | H.R. 17597 | Dec. 10 | WM | ......... | Dec. 10 | ......... | 93-1549 | ......... | H 11698 | S 21676 | Dec. 12 | Dec. 16 | Dec. 31 | 93-572 |
| To extend certain copyright laws, and to establish a National Commission on New Technological Uses of Copyrighted Workers. | S. 3976 | Sept. 9 | Jud | ......... | Dec. 12 | ......... | 93-1581 | ......... | H 12360 | S 16185 | Dec. 19 | Sept. 9 | Dec. 31 | 93-573 |
| Granting certain land to the city of Albuquerque for public purposes. | S. 2125 | July 9 1973 | IIA | IIA | Dec. 13 | July 22 | 93-1592 | 93-1025 | H 12077 | S 13391 | Dec. 17 | July 24 | Dec. 31 | 93-574 |
| Authorizing transfer of certain Colorado lands to the Secretary of Agriculture for purpose of their inclusion in the Arapaho National Forest. | S. 3615 | June 10 | IIA | IIA | Dec. 13 | Aug. 19 | 93-1596 | 93-1105 | H 12078 | S 15407 | Dec. 17 | Aug. 21 | Dec. 31 | 93-575 |
| Authorizing supplementary funds for the Atomic Energy Commission for fiscal year 1975. | H.R. 16609 (S. 4035) | Sept. 11 | AE | AE | Oct. 7 | Oct. 8 | 93-1434 | 93-1246 | H 11015 | S 20955 | Nov. 25 | Dec. 10 | Dec. 31 | 93-576 |
| Providing Federal support for programs of research and development of fuels and energy. | S. 1283 (H.R. 13565) | Mar. 19 1973 | IIA | IIA | June 26 | Dec. 1 1973 | 93-1157 | 93-589 | H 9139 | S 22246 | Sept. 11 | Dec. 7 1973 | Dec. 31 | 93-577 |
| Authorizing conveyance of certain lands in Yuma County, Ariz., to Wide River Farms, Inc., as a result of change in the course of the Colorado River. | S. 3574 | June 4 | IIA | IIA | Dec. 13 | Oct. 10 | 93-1595 | 93-1274 | H 12078 | S 19663 | Dec. 17 | Nov. 20 | Dec. 31 | 93-578 |
| → To protect individual privacy in Federal gathering, use, and disclosure of information. | S. 3418 (H.R. 16373) | May 1 | GO | GO | Oct. 2 | Sept. 26 | 93-1416 | 93-1183 | H 11666 | S 19858 | Dec. 11 | Nov. 21 | Dec. 31 | 93-579 |
| Providing for the establishment of an American Indian Policy Review Commission. | S.J. Res. 133 (H.J. Res. 1117) | July 16 1973 | IIA | IIA | Oct. 3 | Dec. 3 1973 | 93-1420 | 93-594 | H 10782 | S 21879 | Nov. 19 | Dec. 5 1973 | Jan. 2 1975 | 93-580 |

# Figure 13.
## U.S. Code Congressional and Administrative News: Legislative History of Privacy Act of 1974

| No.93- | Date App. | 88 Stat. Page | Bill No. | Report No. 93- House | Report No. 93- Senate | Comm. Reporting House | Comm. Reporting Senate | Cong.Rec.Vol.120 (1974) Dates of Consideration and Passage House | Cong.Rec.Vol.120 (1974) Dates of Consideration and Passage Senate |
|---|---|---|---|---|---|---|---|---|---|
| 558 | Dec. 30 | 1793 | S. 3191 | 1544 | 1229 | AS | AS | Dec. 16 | Oct. 8 |
| 559 | Dec. 30 | 1795 | S. 3394 | 1471 1610 | 1134 1299 | FA Conf (H.R. 17234) | FR FR | Dec. 11, 18 | Dec. 4, 17 |
| 560 | Dec. 30 | 1820 | H.R. 7978 | 1354 | 1359 | IIA | IIA | Oct. 7 | Dec. 16 |
| 561 | Dec. 30 | 1821 | S.J.Res. 224 | none | 1294 | none | J | Dec. 16 | Nov. 21 |
| 562 | Dec. 30 | 1821 | S. 939 | 1519 | 744 | IIA | IIA | Dec. 16 | Mar. 26 |
| 563 | Dec. 31 | 1822 | H.R. 16901 | 1379 1561 | 1296 | App Conf | App | Oct. 9 Dec. 12 | Nov. 25 Dec. 17 |
| 564 | Dec. 31 | 1843 | S. 3489 | 1593 | 1054 | IIA | AgrF | Dec. 17 | Aug. 5 |
| 565 | Dec. 31 | 1843 | S. 3518 | 1594 | 1108 | IIA | IIA | Dec. 17 | Aug. 21 |
| 566 | Dec. 31 | 1844 | S. 191 | 1591 | 679 | IIA | IIA | Dec. 17 | Feb. 7 |
| 567 | Dec. 31 | 1845 | H.R. 16596 | 1528 1621 | 1327 | EL Conf | LPW (S. 4079) | Dec. 12, 18 | Dec. 13, 18 |
| 568 | Dec. 31 | 1855 | S.J.Res. 40 | 1056 1619 | 521 1409 | EL Conf | C Conf | Dec. 12, 19 | Nov. 20 * Dec. 13, 16, 19 |
| 569 | Dec. 31 | 1863 | H.R. 15912 | 1232 | 1334 | VA | VA (S. 3883) | Aug. 5 Dec. 17 | Dec. 13 |
| 570 | Dec. 31 | 1867 | H.J.Res. 1178 | 1614 | 1405 | App | App | Dec. 18, 19 | Dec. 19 |
| 571 | Dec. 31 | 1868 | H.R. 14401 | 1364 | 1344 | AS | AS | Oct. 7 | Dec. 17 |
| 572 | Dec. 31 | 1869 | H.R. 17597 | 1549 | none | WM | none | Dec. 12, 19 | Dec. 16 |
| 573 | Dec. 31 | 1873 | S. 3976 | 1581 | none | J | none | Dec. 19 | Sept. 9 Dec. 19 |
| 574 | Dec. 31 | 1875 | S. 2125 | 1592 | 1025 | IIA | IIA | Dec. 17 | July 24 |
| 575 | Dec. 31 | 1878 | S. 3615 | 1596 | 1105 | IIA | IIA | Dec. 17 | Aug. 21 |
| 576 | Dec. 31 | 1878 | H.R. 16609 | 1434 | 1246 | AE | AE (S. 4033) | Nov. 25 Dec. 17 | Dec. 10 |
| 577 | Dec. 31 | 1878 | S. 1283 | 1157 1563 | 589 | IIA (H.R. 13565) Conf. | IIA | Sept. 11 Dec. 16 | Dec. 7 * Dec. 17 |
| 578 | Dec. 31 | 1895 | S. 3574 | 1595 | 1274 | IIA | IIA | Dec. 17 | Nov. 20 |
| → 579 | Dec. 31 | 1896 | S. 3418 | 1416 | 1183 | GO (H.R. 16373) | GO | Dec. 11, 18 | Nov. 21 Dec. 17, 18 |

# Figure 14.
## U.S. Statutes at Large: Legislative History of Privacy Act of 1974

A20                                                GUIDE TO LEGISLATIVE HISTORY OF

| Public Law | | 88 Stat. | Bill No. | House | |
| No. | Date approved | | | Report No. | Committee reporting |
|---|---|---|---|---|---|
| | 1974 | | | | |
| 93-540 | Dec. 22 | 1738 | H.R. 6925 | 93-376 | Interior and Insular Affairs |
| 93-541 | Dec. 26 | 1739 | S.J. Res. 263 | | |
| 93-542 | Dec. 26 | 1740 | S.J. Res. 234 | | |
| 93-543 | Dec. 26 | 1740 | S. 2343 | 93-1520 | Interior and Insular Affairs |
| 93-544 | Dec. 26 | 1741 | H.R. 10834 | 93-800 | Interior and Insular Affairs |
| 93-545 | Dec. 26 | 1741 | H.R. 5056 | 93-1386 | Armed Services |
| 93-546 | Dec. 26 | 1742 | H.R. 1355 | 93-1336 | Government Operations |
| 93-547 | Dec. 26 | 1742 | H.R. 14349 | 93-1366 | Armed Services |
| 93-548 | Dec. 26 | 1743 | H.R. 16006 | 93-1224 | Armed Services |
| 93-549 | Dec. 26 | 1743 | H.R. 15067 | 93-1384 | Post Office and Civil Service |
| 93-550 | Dec. 26 | 1744 | H.R. 11013 | 93-968 | Interior and Insular Affairs |
| 93-551 | Dec. 26 | 1744 | H.R. 8864 | 93-1409 | Judiciary |
| 93-552 | Dec. 27 | 1745 | H.R. 16136 | 93-1244 | Armed Services |
| | | | | 93-1545 | [Conference] |
| 93-553 | Dec. 27 | 1770 | S. J. Res. 260 | | |
| 93-554 | Dec. 27 | 1771 | H.R. 16900 | 93-1378 | Appropriations |
| | | | | 93-1503 | [Conference] |
| 93-555 | Dec. 27 | 1784 | H.R. 7077 | 93-1511 | Interior and Insular Affairs |
| 93-556 | Dec. 27 | 1789 | H.R. 16424 | 93-1395 | Government Operations |
| 93-557 | Dec. 27 | 1792 | S. 4013 | 93-1558 | Judiciary |
| 93-558 | Dec. 30 | 1793 | S. 3191 | 93-1544 | Armed Services |
| 93-559 | Dec. 30 | 1795 | S. 3394 (H.R. 17234) | 93-1471 | Foreign Affairs |
| | | | | 93-1610 | [Conference] |
| 93-560 | Dec. 30 | 1820 | H.R. 7978 | 93-1354 | Interior and Insular Affairs |
| 93-561 | Dec. 30 | 1821 | S.J. Res. 224 | | |
| 93-562 | Dec. 30 | 1821 | S. 939 | 93-1519 | Interior and Insular Affairs |
| 93-563 | Dec. 31 | 1822 | H.R. 16901 | 93-1379 | Appropriations |
| | | | | 93-1561 | [Conference] |
| 93-564 | Dec. 31 | 1843 | S. 3489 | 93-1593 | Interior and Insular Affairs |
| 93-565 | Dec. 31 | 1843 | S. 3518 | 93-1594 | Interior and Insular Affairs |
| 93-566 | Dec. 31 | 1844 | S. 194 | 93-1591 | Interior and Insular Affairs |
| 93-567 | Dec. 31 | 1845 | H.R. 16596 (S. 4079) | 93-1528 | Education and Labor |
| | | | | 93-1621 | [Conference] |
| 93-568 | Dec. 31 | 1855 | S.J. Res. 40 | 93-1056 | Education and Labor |
| | | | | 93-1619 | [Conference] |
| 93-569 | Dec. 31 | 1863 | H.R. 15912 (S. 3883) | 93-1232 | Veterans' Affairs |
| 93-570 | Dec. 31 | 1867 | H.J. Res. 1178 | 93-1614 | Appropriations |
| 93-571 | Dec. 31 | 1868 | H.R. 14401 | 93-1364 | Armed Services |
| 93-572 | Dec. 31 | 1869 | H.R. 17597 | 93-1549 | Ways and Means |
| 93-573 | Dec. 31 | 1873 | S. 3976 | 93-1581 | Judiciary |
| 93-574 | Dec. 31 | 1875 | S. 2125 | 93-1592 | Interior and Insular Affairs |
| 93-575 | Dec. 31 | 1878 | S. 3615 | 93-1596 | Interior and Insular Affairs |
| 93-576 | Dec. 31 | 1878 | H.R. 16609 (S. 4033) | 93-1434 | Joint Committee on Atomic Energy. |
| 93-577 | Dec. 31 | 1878 | S. 1283 (H.R. 13565) | 93-1157 | Interior and Insular Affairs |
| | | | | 93-1563 | [Conference] |
| 93-578 | Dec. 31 | 1895 | S. 3574 | 93-1595 | Interior and Insular Affairs |
| → 93-579 | Dec. 31 | 1896 | S. 3418 (H.R. 16373) | 93-1416 | Government Operations |

BILLS ENACTED INTO PUBLIC LAW

| Senate | | Dates of consideration and passage: Congressional Record, Vol. 119 (1973); Vol. 120 (1974) | | Presidential statement: Public Papers of the Presidents |
|---|---|---|---|---|
| Report No. | Committee reporting | House | Senate | |
| 93-1308 | Interior and Insular Affairs_____ | Sept. 17, 1973___ | Dec. 9, 1974____ | Ford: 1974 |
| 93-1322 | Banking, Housing and Urban Affairs. | Dec. 13, 1974___ | Dec. 11, 1974___ | |
| 93-1180 | Government Operations_____ | Dec. 17, 1974___ | Oct. 1, 1974____ | |
| 93-684 | Interior and Insular Affairs_____ | Dec. 16, 1974___ | Feb. 27, 1974___ | |
| 93-1186 | Interior and Insular Affairs_____ | Feb. 19, Dec. 12, 1974. | Oct. 1, Dec. 14, 1974. | |
| 93-1341 | Armed Services_____ | Oct. 7, 1974____ | Dec. 14, 1974___ | |
| 93-1329 | Government Operations_____ | Oct. 7, 1974____ | Dec. 12, 1974___ | |
| 93-1343 | Armed Services_____ | Nov. 18, 1974___ | Dec. 13, 1974___ | |
| 93-1337 | Armed Services_____ | Aug. 5, 1974____ | Dec. 13, 1974___ | |
| 93-1339 | Post Office and Civil Service_____ | Oct. 7, 1974____ | Dec. 13, 1974___ | |
| 93-1221 | Interior and Insular Affairs_____ | May 7, Dec. 11, 1974. | Oct. 4, 1974____ | |
| 93-1352 | Judiciary_____ | Nov. 18, 1974___ | Dec. 16, 1974___ | |
| 93-1136 | Armed Services_____ | Aug. 9, Dec. 12, 1974. | Sept. 11, Dec. 14, 1974. | |
| 93-1255 | Appropriations_____ | Dec. 16, 1974___ Sept. 30, Oct. 1, 2, Dec. 4, 16, 1974. | Nov. 26, 1974___ Oct. 10, Nov. 18-20, Dec. 9-11, 14, 1974. | |
| 93-1328 | Interior and Insular Affairs_____ | Dec. 9, 1974____ | Dec. 12, 1974___ | Dec. 28. |
| 93-1323 | Government Operations_____ | Oct. 7, 1974____ | Dec. 12, 1974___ | Dec. 27. |
| 93-1215 | Judiciary_____ | Dec. 16, 1974___ | Oct. 4, 1974____ | |
| 93-1229 | Armed Services_____ | Dec. 16, 1974___ | Oct. 8, 1974____ | |
| 93-1134, 93-1299 | Foreign Relations_____ | Dec. 10, 11, 18, 1974. | Sept. 24, Oct. 1, 2, Dec. 3, 4, 17, 1974. | Dec. 30. |
| 93-1359 | Interior and Insular Affairs_____ | Oct. 7, 1974____ | Dec. 16, 1974___ | |
| 93-1294 | Judiciary_____ | Dec. 16, 1974___ | Nov. 21, 1974___ | |
| 93-744 | Interior and Insular Affairs_____ | Dec. 16, 1974___ | Mar. 26, 1974___ | |
| 93-1296 | Appropriations_____ | Oct. 9, Dec. 12, 1974. | Nov. 25, Dec. 17, 1974. | |
| 93-1054 | Agriculture and Forestry_____ | Dec. 17, 1974___ | Aug. 5, 1974____ | |
| 93-1108 | Interior and Insular Affairs_____ | Dec. 17, 1974___ | Aug. 21, 1974___ | |
| 93-679 | Interior and Insular Affairs_____ | Dec. 17, 1974___ | Feb. 7, 1974____ | |
| 93-1327 | Labor and Public Welfare_____ | Dec. 12, 18, 1974. | Dec. 13, 18, 1974. | Dec. 31. |
| 93-521 | Labor and Public Welfare_____ | Dec. 12, 19, 1974. | Nov. 20, 1973; Dec. 13, 16, 19, 1974. | |
| 93-1409 | [Conference] | | | |
| 93-1334 | Veterans' Affairs_____ | Aug. 5, Dec. 17, 1974. | Dec. 12, 13, 1974. | |
| 93-1405 | Appropriations_____ | Dec. 18, 19, 1974. | Dec. 19, 1974___ | |
| 93-1344 | Armed Services_____ | Oct. 7, 1974____ | Dec. 17, 1974___ | |
| | | Dec. 12, 17, 1974. | Dec. 16, 1974___ | Dec. 31. |
| | | Dec. 19, 1974___ | Sept. 9, Dec. 19, 1974. | |
| 93-1025 | Interior and Insular Affairs_____ | Dec. 17, 1974___ | July 24, 1974___ | |
| 93-1105 | Interior and Insular Affairs_____ | Dec. 17, 1974___ | Aug. 21, 1974___ | |
| 93-1246 | Joint Committee on Atomic Energy. | Nov. 25, Dec. 17, 1974. | Dec. 10, 17, 1974. | |
| 93-589 | Interior and Insular Affairs_____ | Aug. 22, Sept. 11, Dec. 16, 1974. | Dec. 5-7, 1973; Dec. 17, 1974. | |
| 93-1274 | Interior and Insular Affairs_____ | Dec. 17, 1974___ | Nov. 20, 1974___ | Ford: 1975 |
| 93-1183 | Government Operations_____ | Dec. 11, 18, 1974. | Nov. 21, Dec. 17, 1974. | Jan. 1. |

# Figure 15.
## Digest of Public General Bills and Resolutions: Legislative History of Privacy Act of 1974

Pub. L. 93-579. Approved 12/31/74:  S. 3418.

Privacy Act - Prohibits disclosure by Federal agencies of any record contained in a system of records, except pursuant to a written request by or with the prior written consent of the individual to whom the record pertains.  Makes exceptions to this prohibition for use of such records by the individual involved, the Congress, the courts, officers of the agency maintaining the record, the Bureau of the Census, and for criminal and civil law enforcement purposes.

Requires agencies which keep records systems to keep account of disclosures of records, and to inform the subjects of such disclosures.

Allows subjects of records to have access and copying rights to such records.  Establishes a procedure for amendment of such records, and of judicial appeal of agency refusal to amend.

Requires relevancy of records to official purposes;  accuracy;  disclosure of purposes to informants;  publication annually of the existence, character, and accessibility of records systems;  and appropriate safeguards to maintain confidentiality of such records.  Prohibits maintenance of records describing individuals' exercise of first amendment rights, with specified exceptions.  Requires recordkeeping agencies to establish rules relating to notice, access, and amendment.

Permits civil suits against agencies by individuals adversely affected by agency actions not in compliance with this Act.  Describes remedies available in such actions.

Sets forth criminal penalties for noncompliance with this Act.

Provides for exemptions from this Act, such as for specified records of the Central Intelligence Agency and records of investigations compiled for law enforcement purposes.

Prohibits an agency from selling or renting an individual's name and address.

Requires agencies to notify the Congress and Office of Management and Budget in advance of any proposal to establish or alter records systems.

Requires the President to report to the Congress annually on the number of records which were exempted from the coverage of this Act.

Establishes the Privacy Protection Study Commission to study government and private data systems and make recommendations for protecting privacy by the application of this Act or additional legislation.

Lists suggestive and required areas of study for the Commission.

Grants subpena power to the Commission.

Makes it unlawful for Federal, State, or local agencies to deny legal rights, benefits, or privileges to individuals because of such individuals' refusal to disclose their social security account number.

5-01-74   Referred to Senate Committee on Government Operations
9-26-74   Reported to Senate, amended, S. Rept. 93-1183
11-21-74  Measure called up by unanimous consent in Senate
11-21-74  Measure considered in Senate
11-21-74  Measure passed Senate, amended, roll call #496 (74-9)
11-22-74  Provisions as passed Senate 11/21/74 inserted in H.R. 16373
12-11-74  Measure called up by unanimous consent in House
12-11-74  Measure considered in House
12-11-74  Measure passed House, amended (provisions of H.R. 16373 inserted as
          passed House)
12-17-74  Senate agreed to House amendments with an amendment, roll call #567
          (77-8)
12-18-74  House agreed to Senate amendments with an amendment
12-18-74  Senate agreed to House amendments to the Senate amendments
12-31-74  Public law 93-579

Figure 16.
Slip Law: Legislative History of Privacy Act of 1974

LEGISLATIVE HISTORY:

HOUSE REPORT No. 93-1416 accompanying H.R. 16373 (Comm. on Government
    Operations).

SENATE REPORT No. 93-1183 (Comm. on Government Operations).
CONGRESSIONAL RECORD, Vol. 120, (1974):

    Nov. 21, considered and passed Senate.
    Dec. 11, considered and passed House, amended, in lieu of
        H.R. 16373

    Dec. 17, Senate concurred in House amendment with amendments.
    Dec. 18, House concurred in Senate amendments.
WEEKLY COMPILATION OF PRESIDENTIAL DOCUMENTS, Vol. 11, No. 1:
    Jan. 1, Presidential statement.

# Tables

## Table 1.
## The Legislative Process and Congressional Publications

| Legislative Process | Publications |
|---|---|
| Bill is Introduced and Referred to Committee | Bills<br>Resolutions |
| Committee Holds Hearings | Hearings<br>Prints |
| Committee Recommends Passage | House Reports<br>Senate Reports |
| Chamber Debates and Votes | *Congressional Record*<br>House/Senate *Journals* |
| Bill Sent to Conference | Conference Reports |
| Law | Slip Law<br>*Statutes at Large*<br>*U.S. Code* |
| Veto | Veto Message |
| Overriding a Veto | *Congressional Record*<br>House/Senate *Journals* |
| Presidential Statements | *Weekly Compilation of Presidential Documents* |

**Table 2.**
**A Legislative History of the Privacy Act of 1974**

| History | House | Senate |
|---|---|---|
| Bill Number | H.R. 16373 | S. 3418 |
| Introduced by | William S. Moorhead Dem., Pa. | Sam J. Ervin, Jr. Dem., N.C. |
| Date Introduced | Aug. 12, 1974 | May 1, 1974 |
| Committee Referred to | Government Operations Committee | Government Operations Committee |
| Committee Hearings | —— | Y4.G74/6:P93/2 |
| Committee Print | —— | Y4.G74/6:P93/4 |
| Date Reported | Oct. 2, 1974 | Sept. 26, 1974 |
| Report Number | H. Rept. 93-1416 | S. Rept. 93-1183 |
| Date of Passage | Dec. 11, 1974 | Nov. 21, 1974 |
| Vote in *Congressional Record* | Vol. 120, No. 172, p. H11666 | Vol. 120, No. 162, p. S19858 |
| Presidential Statements | *Weekly Compilation of Presidential Documents* Feb. 23, 1974, Vol. 10, No. 8, pp. 245–47 Oct. 9, 1974, Vol. 10, No. 41, p. 1250 Jan. 1, 1975, Vol. 11, No. 1, pp. 7–8 Sept. 29, 1975, Vol. 11, No. 40, pp. 1083–84 | |
| Date Approved | Dec. 31, 1974 | |
| Title of Law | Privacy Act of 1974 | |
| Public Law Number | PL 93-579 | |
| *Statutes at Large* | 88 *Stat.* 1896 | |
| *U.S. Code* | 5 *U.S.C.* 552 | |
| Related Congressional Publications | Y4.G74/6:L52/3; Y4.J89/2:C76/20 Y4.G74/7:R24/7; Y4.G74/7:P93/5 | |
| Related Executive Publications | HE1.2:R24/3; PrEx15.2:P93; Y3.P93/5:2T19 GS4.107/a:P939; Pr37.8:St2/R29 | |
| Background Information | *CQ Almanac* Vol. 30 (1974), pp. 292–94 *CQ Weekly Report,* Vol. 32, No. 39 (Sept. 28, 1974), pp. 2611–14 *National Journal,* Vol. 6, No. 41 (Oct. 12, 1974), pp. 1521–30 | |

**Table 3.**
**Legislative Tracing Form**

**HOUSE INTRODUCTION**

| Title | Bill number | Date of bill | Sponsor |
|-------|-------------|--------------|---------|
| | | | |

Bill _____

Related bills _____

**Table 3—*Continued*.**
**Legislative Tracing Form**

| | | HOUSE ACTION | | | | |
|---|---|---|---|---|---|---|
| | Committee | Subcommittee | Report number | Date reported | Page of *Congressional Record* on which passage is recorded | Vote | Date of passage |

Bill

Related bills

## SENATE INTRODUCTION

Title     Bill number     Date of bill     Sponsor

Bill

Related bills

**Table 3—*Continued*.**
**Legislative Tracing Form**

## SENATE ACTION

| | | | Committee | Subcommittee | Report number | Date reported | Page of *Congressional Record* on which passage is recorded | Vote | Date of passage |
|---|---|---|---|---|---|---|---|---|---|

Bill

Related bills

| Report number | Date reported | Date House considers conference report | Date Senate considers conference report | PL number | Date | Veto: overridden, upheld |
|---|---|---|---|---|---|---|
| | | | | | | |

Bill

Related bills

**Table 4.**
**Information Checklist**

   I. Prior history
       1.   Prior bills
       2.   Prior hearings
  II. Introduction of bill
       1.   Origins of bill
       2.   Date
       3.   Number
       4.   Substance
       5.   Chief sponsors (name, party, and state)
       6.   Similar bills
 III. House committee action
       1.   Type of referral
           a.  Exclusive
           b.  Joint
           c.  Split
           d.  Sequential
       2.   Referred to
           a.  Portion of bill
           b.  Committee (chairman and members)
           c.  Subcommittee (chairman and members)
       3.   Agents' comments
           a.  Date
           b.  Substance
       4.   Subcommittee hearings
           a.  Hearings (SuDocs number)
           b.  Location
           c.  Dates
           d.  Major witnesses
                 i.  Administration officials
                ii.  State and local officials
              iii.  Members of Congress
              iv.  Experts
               v.  Interest groups
              vi.  Citizens
       5.   Subcommittee mark-up
           a.  Drafts
           b.  Dates
           c.  Amendments
                 i.  Sponsor

        ii. Subject

       iii. Vote and date

6. Reported to full committee
   a. Vote and date
   b. Clean bill number
7. Full committee hearings
   a. Hearings (Sudocs number)
   b. Location
   c. Dates
   d. Major witnesses
      i. Administration officials
      ii. State and local officials
      iii. Members of Congress
      iv. Experts
      v. Interest groups
      vi. Citizens
8. Full committee mark-up
   a. Drafts
   b. Dates
   c. Amendments
      i. Sponsor
      ii. Subject
      iii. Vote and date
9. Ordered reported/tabled
   a. Vote
   b. Clean bill number
   c. Report number
   d. Date filed
   e. Summary of report

IV. Senate committee action
   1. Type of referral
      a. Exclusive
      b. Joint
      c. Split
      d. Sequential
   2. Referred to
      a. Portion of bill
      b. Committee (chairman and members)
   3. Agency comments

**Table 4—*Continued.***
**Information Checklist**

      a. Date
      b. Substance
4. Subcommittee hearings
      a. Hearings (SuDocs number)
      b. Location
      c. Dates
      d. Major witnesses
          i. Administration officials
          ii. State and local officials
          iii. Members of Congress
          iv. Experts
          v. Interest groups
          vi. Citizens
5. Subcommittee mark-up
      a. Drafts
      b. Dates
      c. Amendments
          i. Sponsor
          ii. Subject
          iii. Vote and date
6. Reported to full committee
      a. Vote and date
      b. Clean bill number
7. Full committee hearings
      a. Hearings (SuDocs number)
      b. Location
      c. Dates
      d. Major witnesses
          i. Administration officials
          ii. State and local officials
          iii. Members
          iv. Experts
          v. Interest groups
          vi. Citizens
8. Full committee mark-up
      a. Drafts
      b. Dates
      c. Amendments
          i. Sponsor

**Table 4—*Continued.***
**Information Checklist**

          a.  Sponsor
          b.  Subject
          c.  Vote and date
     8.  Floor Action
          a.  Method of consideration
          b.  Suspension of the rules
          c.  Unanimous consent
          d.  Dates of consideration
          e.  Date and vote of final action
VII.  In Senate
     1.  Concurred in same language
          a.  Vote
          b.  Date
     2.  Agreed after further amendments
          a.  Vote
          b.  Date
     3.  Rejected and requested conference
          a.  Vote
          b.  Date
     4.  Agreed to go to conference
          a.  Vote
          b.  Date
     5.  Unanimous-consent time control agreement
          a.  Provisions
          b.  Date
          c.  Floor managers
          d.  General debate
          e.  Amendments eligible
     6.  Senate final action
          a.  Date
          b.  Vote
     7.  Passage in lieu
          a.  Bill number
          b.  Date
VIII.  Conference committee action
     1.  Conferees appointed
     2.  Dates of conference meetings
     3.  Major conference amendments
     4.  Conference reports filed

        a.  H.Rept. number and date
        b.  S.Rept. number and date
    5.  Report adopted/rejected
        a.  House vote and date
        b.  Senate vote and date
    6.  Further conference requested
    7.  Report adopted/rejected
        a.  House vote and date
        b.  Senate vote and date
IX.  Presidential action
    1.  Date sent to White House
    2.  President's decision
        a.  Signed
        b.  Vetoed
        c.  Pocket vetoed
        d.  Date
        e.  Page in *Weekly Compilation*
X.  Congressional reaction
    1.  First chamber (House or Senate)
    2.  Override attempt date
    3.  Vote
    4.  Page in *Congressional Record*
XI.  Public Law
    1.  Title
    2.  PL number
    3.  Date signed
    4.  Effective date
    5.  *United States Statutes at Large*
    6.  *United States Code*
XII.  Background material
    1.  *Congressional Quarterly Weekly Report*
    2.  *National Journal*
    3.  Newspaper articles
    4.  Journal articles
    5.  Books
    6.  Other information

**Table 4—*Continued.***
**Information Checklist**

### Sample State Delegation Tally Sheet

### Alabama

### House of Representatives

| Name | Yea | Nay |
|------|-----|-----|
| 1. _____ | _____ | _____ |
| 2. _____ | _____ | _____ |
| 3. _____ | _____ | _____ |
| 4. _____ | _____ | _____ |
| 5. _____ | _____ | _____ |
| 6. _____ | _____ | _____ |
| 7. _____ | _____ | _____ |

### Senate

| Name | Yea | Nay |
|------|-----|-----|
| 1. _____ | _____ | _____ |
| 2. _____ | _____ | _____ |

## Table 5.
## Bill Status Table

| Reference Tool | Section/Index |
|---|---|
| *CIS/Index* | Bill Numbers |
| *Congressional Record* | History of Bills and Resolutions |
| *Congressional Record, Daily Digest* | Subject index of bills acted upon |
| *Congressional Index* | Bill Status Tables |
| *Digest of Public General Bills* | Synopsis of bills |
| *Federal Index* | Calendar of Legislation |
| *House of Representatives Calendars* | Numerical order of bills and resolutions which have passed either or both houses, and bills now pending on the calendar |

*Source:* Robert U. Goehlert and Fenton S. Martin, *The Presidency: A Research Guide* (Santa Barbara, CA: ABC-Clio, 1985), p. 237. Copyright 1985, Robert U. Goehlert and Fenton S. Martin.

## Table 6.
## Locating Legislative Histories

| REFERENCE TOOL | TABLE/INDEX |
|---|---|
| *Calendars of the House and History of Legislation* | Index Key and History of Bill |
| *CIS/Annual* | Index of Bill, Report and Document Number |
| *CIS Legislative History Annotated Directories* | Table of Contents |
| *CIS Legislative History Annual**\** | Subject or Title Index |
| *Congressional Index* | Bill Status Tables |
| *Congressional Record, Daily Digest* | History of Bills Enacted into Law |
| *CQ Almanac* | Subject Index |
| *Digest of Public General Bills and Resolutions* | Public Law Listing |
| *Federal Index* | Calendar of Legislation |
| *House Journal* | History of Bills and Resolutions |
| *Senate Journal* | History of Bills and Resolutions |
| Slip Law | Legislative History |
| *Statutes at Large* | Guide to Legislative History of Bills Enacted into Public Law |
| *U.S. Code Annotated* | Annotations and Legislative History |
| *U.S. Code Congressional and Administrative News* | Table of Legislative History |
| *U.S. Code Service* | Annotations and Legislative History |

---

*Published as a third volume of *CIS/Index* starting with the 1984 edition.

*Source:* Robert U. Goehlert and Fenton S. Martin, *The Presidency: A Research Guide* (Santa Barbara, CA: ABC-Clio, 1985), p. 238. Copyright 1985, Robert U. Goehlert and Fenton S. Martin.

**Table 7.**
**Research Chart for *Statutes at Large* and *U.S. Code*** *

| REFERENCE | U.S. STATUTES AT LARGE | U.S. CODE | U.S. CODE SUPPLEMENT | ADDITIONAL FINDING AIDS |
|---|---|---|---|---|
| 1. Revised Statutes Section (e.g., Rev. Stat. 56) | Revised Statutes, 1873, were published as pt. 1, vol. 18, U.S. Statutes at Large 2d ed. published in 1878 | Use tables in U.S.C. Popular Names and Tables volume to find U.S.C. section; verify text; then— | Check latest U.S.C. Supplement for recent changes; verify text. | Check Table 3 in latest U.S.C.C.A.N. for changes during current period; if Code section is included, verify text in same publication or in slip law. |
| 2. a. For the date of a law any year up to and through year of last edition of U.S.C. | Use Stat. volume for that year to check the List of Laws; get law number and verify page number from list; then— | Use tables in U.S.C. Popular Names and Tables volume to find U.S.C. section; verify text; then— | Check latest U.S.C. Supplement for recent changes; verify text. | Check Table 3 in latest U.S.C.C.A.N. for changes during current period; if Code section is included, verify text in same publication or in slip law. |
| 2. b. For any year after year of last edition of U.S.C. and through year of latest Supplement | Use Stat. volume for that year to check the list of Public Laws; get law number and verify page number from List; then— | | Use tables in latest U.S.C. Supplement to find U.S.C. section; verify text. | Check Table 3 in latest U.S.C.C.A.N. for changes during current period; if Code section is included, verify text in same publication or in slip law. |

*Continued on next page*

**Table 7—Continued.**
**Research Chart for Statutes at Large and U.S. Code**

| REFERENCE | U.S. STATUTES AT LARGE | U.S. CODE | U.S. CODE SUPPLEMENT | ADDITIONAL FINDING AIDS |
|---|---|---|---|---|
| 2. c. For current year | | | | Use slip law or U.S.C.C.A.N. text to get law number, Stat. citation, and to verify subject matter; also use Table 2, U.S.C.C.A.N. to find U.S.C. classification |
| 3. a. For name of Law: any year up to and through year of last edition of U.S.C. (e.g. | | Use Acts Cited by Popular Name index (in U.S.C. Popular Names and Tables volume) to obtain Stat. and U.S.C. citations; verify both; then— | Check latest U.S.C. Supplement for recent changes; verify text. | Check Table 3 in latest U.S.C.C.A.N. for changes during current period; verify any changes in same publication or in slip law. Other sources: Index of Popular Name Acts Affected in U.S. Statutes at Large Laws Affected Tables, 1956–1970 and 1971–1975; Table of Federal Statutes by Popular Names in U.S. Supreme Court Reports; Shepard's Acts and Cases by Popular Name; U.S.C.A. |

| | | Popular Name Table; U.S.C.S. tables volume. |
|---|---|---|
| 3. b. For any year after year of last edition of U.S.C. and through year of latest Supplement | Use Acts Cited by Popular Name Index preceding Tables in U.S.C. Supplement to obtain Stat. and U.S.C. citation; verify both; then— | Check Table 3 in latest U.S.C.C.A.N. for changes during current period; verify any changes in same publication or in slip law. Other sources: Index of Popular Name Acts Affected in U.S. Statutes at Large Laws Affected Tables, 1956–1970 and 1971–1975; Table of Federal Statutes by Popular Names in U.S. Supreme Court Reports; Shepard's Acts and Cases by Popular Name; U.S.C.A. Popular Name Table; U.S.C.S. tables volume. |
| 3. c. For current year | | Use House Calendar index and numerical list to get bill number, then law number if assigned; or U.S.C.C.A.N. Index or Table 10; use slip law or U.S.C.C.A.N. text to get Stat. Citation and U.S.C. classification, and to verify |

*Continued on next page*

## Table 7—Continued.
### Research Chart for *Statutes at Large* and *U.S. Code*

| REFERENCE | U.S. STATUTES AT LARGE | U.S. CODE | U.S. CODE SUPPLEMENT | ADDITIONAL FINDING AIDS |
|---|---|---|---|---|
| | | | | date and subject matter; also, with law number, use Table 2, U.S.C.C.A.N. to find U.S.C. classification. |
| 4. a. For the number of a law any year up to and through year of last edition of U.S.C. and the law— does not have a numerical prefix | You will need additional information, such as the Congress, the year, or the Stat. volume— year used then use the Stat. volume to check the List of Public Laws; get and verify page number from List; then— | Use tables in U.S.C. Popular Names and Tables section to find U.S.C. section, verify text; then— | Check latest U.S.C. Supplement for recent changes; verify text. | Check Table 3 in latest U.S.C. for changes during current period; if Code section is included, verify text in same publication or in slip law. |
| 4. b. For a number of a law for any year up to and through year of last edition of U.S.C. and the law— does have a numerical prefix | Use Stat. volume for the Congress indicated by the numerical prefix; check the list of Public Laws; get and verify page number from List; then— | Use tables in U.S.C. Popular Names and Tables volume to find U.S.C. section; verify text; then— | Check latest U.S.C. Supplement for recent changes; verify text. | Check Table 3 in latest U.S.C.C.A.N. for changes during current period; if Code section is included, verify text in same publication or in slip law. |
| 4. c. For any year after last edition of U.S.C. and | Use Stat. volume for the Congress indicated by the | | Use tables in latest U.S.C. Supplement to find U.S.C. | Check Table 3 in latest U.S.C.C.A.N. for changes |

| Situation | Step 1 | Step 2 | Step 3 | Step 4 |
|---|---|---|---|---|
| through year of latest Supplement | numerical prefix; check the List of Public Laws; get and verify page number from List; then— | | | during current period; if Code section is included, verify text in same publication or in slip law. |
| 4. d. For current year | | | | Use slip law or U.S.C.C.A.N. text to get Stat. citation, U.S.C. classification, and to verify date and subject matter; also, with law number, use Table 2, U.S.C.C.A.N. to find U.S.C. classification. |
| 5. a. For Stat. Citation any year up to and through year of last edition of U.S.C. | Use Stat. volume to get date and law number; verify subject matter; then— | Use tables in U.S.C. Popular Names and Tables volume to find U.S.C. section; verify text; then— | Check latest U.S.C. Supplement for recent changes; verify text; then— | Check Table 3 in latest U.S.C.C.A.N. for changes during current period; if Code section is included, verify text in same publication or in slip law. |
| 5. b. For any year after year of last edition of U.S.C. and through year of latest Supplement | Use Stat. volume to get date and law number; verify subject matter; then— | Use tables in latest U.S.C. Supplement to find U.S.C. | | Check Table 3 in latest U.S.C.C.A.N. for changes during current period; if Code section is included, verify text in same publication or in slip law. |

*Continued on next page*

**Table 7—Continued.**
**Research Chart for Statutes at Large and U.S. Code**

| REFERENCE | U.S. STATUTES AT LARGE | U.S. CODE | U.S. CODE SUPPLEMENT | ADDITIONAL FINDING AIDS |
|---|---|---|---|---|
| 5. c. For current year | | | | Use slip law or U.S.C.C.A.N. text to verify subject matter, date, U.S.C. classification and law number. Table 2, U.S.C.C.A.N. also may be used to find U.S.C. classification. |
| 6. a. For the U.S.C. Citation for any year up to and through year of last edition of U.S.C. | | Check section in U.S.C. to verify subject matter and determine appropriate Stat. citation; verify text against Stat. volume; then— | Check latest U.S.C. Supplement for recent changes; verify text; then— | Check Table 3 in latest U.S.C.C.A.N. for changes during current period; if Code section is included, verify text in same publication or in slip law. |
| 6. b. For any year after year of last edition of U.S.C. and through year of latest Supplement | | | Check section in latest U.S.C. Supplement to verify subject matter and determine appropriate Stat. citation; verify text against Stat. volume; then— | Check Table 3 in latest U.S.C.C.A.N. for changes during current period; if Code section is included, verify text in same publication or in slip law. |

6. c. For current year

Check Table 3 in latest
U.S.C.C.A.N.; if Code
section is included, get page
number on which text of law
appears and get law number
from that page (Code citation
should appear as a marginal
note), then verify Stat.
citation and subject matter
from slip law.

---

*Source:* Robert U. Goehlert and Fenton S. Martin, *The Presidency: A Research Guide* (Santa Barbara, CA: ABC-Clio, 1985), pp. 231–236. Copyright 1985, Robert U. Goehlert and Fenton S. Martin.

**Table 8.**
**Sources of Treaty Information**

| ACTION | SOURCE |
|---|---|
| Initial Negotiations | *Department of State Bulletin* |
| | *Federal Index* |
| | *Public Affairs Information Service Bulletin* |
| | *Weekly Compilation of Presidential Documents* |
| Presidential Approval | *Department of State Bulletin* |
| | *Federal Index* |
| | *Public Affairs Information Service Bulletin* |
| Transmittal to Senate | *Congressional Record* |
| | *CQ Weekly Report* |
| | *Federal Index* |
| | *Senate Executive Journal* |
| | *Weekly Compilation of Presidential Documents* |
| Senate Foreign Relations Committee Action | *CIS/Index* |
| | *Congressional Index* |
| | *Congressional Record* |
| | *Congressional Record, Daily Digest* |
| | *CQ Weekly Report* |
| | *Monthly Catalog* |
| | *Senate Executive Journal* |

| ACTION | SOURCE |
|---|---|
| Senate Action | *Congressional Index* |
| | *Congressional Record* |
| | *CQ Weekly Report* |
| | *Federal Index* |
| | *Senate Executive Journal* |
| Withdrawal | *Congressional Record, Daily Digest* |
| | *Federal Index* |
| | *Senate Executive Journal* |
| | *Weekly Compilation of Presidential Documents* |
| Ratification | *Department of State Bulletin* |
| | *Federal Index* |
| | *Public Affairs Information Service Bulletin* |
| | *Weekly Compilation of Presidential Documents* |
| Promulgation | *Department of State Bulletin* |
| | *Federal Index* |
| | *Statutes at Large* |
| | *Shepard's United States Citations* |
| | *Treaties in Force* |
| | *United States Code Annotated* |

*Continued on next page*

**Table 8—*Continued*.**
**Sources of Treaty Information**

| ACTION | SOURCE |
|---|---|
| | *United States Code Congressional and Administrative News* |
| | *United States Treaties and other International Agreements* |
| | *Weekly Compilation of Presidential Documents* |

---

*Source:* Robert U. Goehlert and Fenton S. Martin, *The Presidency: A Research Guide* (Santa Barbara, CA: ABC-Clio, 1985), pp. 240–242. Copyright 1985, Robert U. Goehlert and Fenton S. Martin.

# Appendixes

# APPENDIX 1
## SELECTED DEPOSITORY LIBRARIES

Certain libraries are designated depositories for government publications. Through them federal documents are made available to residents of every state. Distribution of publications to the libraries is made by the superintendent of documents at the Government Printing Office. Not every government publication is available at all depository libraries. Designated regional depositories are required to receive and retain one copy of all government publications made available to depository libraries, either in printed or microfacsimile form. All other libraries are allowed to select the classes of publications best suited to the interests of their particular clientele.

A complete list of depository libraries is available free upon request by writing to the U.S. Government Printing Office, North Capitol and H Streets N.W., Washington, DC 20401. The following is a list of the regional depository libraries.

**ALABAMA**
University      University of Alabama Library

**ARIZONA**
Phoenix      Department of Library Archives and Public Records
Phoenix Public Library
Tucson      University of Arizona Library

**CALIFORNIA**
Sacramento      California State Library

**COLORADO**
Boulder      University of Colorado Libraries
Denver      Denver Public Library

**CONNECTICUT**
Hartford      Connecticut State Library

**FLORIDA**
Gainesville      University of Florida Libraries

**GEORGIA**
Athens      University of Georgia Libraries

HAWAII
Honolulu                          University of Hawaii Library

IDAHO
Moscow                            University of Idaho Library

ILLINOIS
Springfield                       Illinois State Library

INDIANA
Indianapolis                      Indiana State Library

IOWA
Iowa City                         University of Iowa Library

KANSAS
Lawrence                          University of Kansas Library

KENTUCKY
Lexington                         University of Kentucky Libraries

LOUISIANA
Baton Rouge                       Louisiana State University Library
Ruston                            Louisiana Technical University Library

MAINE
Orono                             University of Maine Library

MARYLAND
College Park                      University of Maryland Library

MASSACHUSETTS
Boston                            Boston Public Library

MICHIGAN
Detroit                           Detroit Public Library
Lansing                           Michigan State Library

MINNESOTA
Minneapolis                       University of Minnesota Library

MISSISSIPPI
University                    University of Mississippi Library

MONTANA
Missoula                     University of Montana Library

NEBRASKA
Lincoln                      Nebraska Publications Clearinghouse

NEVADA
Reno                         University of Nevada Library

NEW JERSEY
Newark                       Newark Public Library

NEW MEXICO
Albuquerque                  University of New Mexico Library
Santa Fe                     New Mexico State Library

NEW YORK
Albany                       New York State Library

NORTH CAROLINA
Chapel Hill                  University of North Carolina Library

NORTH DAKOTA
Fargo                        North Dakota State University Library

OHIO
Columbus                     Ohio State Library

OKLAHOMA
Oklahoma City                Oklahoma Department of Libraries
Stillwater                   Oklahoma State University Library

OREGON
Portland                     Portland State University Library

PENNSYLVANIA
Harrisburg                   State Library of Pennsylvania

TEXAS
Austin                          Texas State Library
Lubbock                         Texas Tech University Library

UTAH
Logan                           Utah State University Library

VIRGINIA
Charlottesville                 University of Virginia Library

WASHINGTON
Olympia                         Washington State Library

WEST VIRGINIA
Morgantown                      West Virginia University Library

WISCONSIN
Madison                         State Historical Society Library
Milwaukee                       Milwaukee Public Library

WYOMING
Cheyenne                        Wyoming State Library

# APPENDIX 2
## SELECTED RESEARCH CENTERS

A number of research centers, foundations, and private institutions study congressional activities. The following list represents the major institutions whose work includes the Congress. Addresses are also given for the agencies or organizations whose publications have been referred to throughout this book.

American Enterprise Institute for Public Policy Research
1150 17th Street, N.W.
Washington, DC 20036
Tel: (202) 296-5616

American Institute for Political Communication
402 Prudential Building
Washington, DC 20005
Tel: (202) 783-6373

American Institute of Public Opinion
53 Bank Street
Princeton, NJ 08541
Tel: (609) 924-9600

Americans for Democratic Action
1424 16th Street, N.W.
Washington, DC 20036
Tel: (202) 265-5771

Bill Status Office
2401A Rayburn House Office Building
Washington, DC 20515
Tel: (202) 225-1772

Brookings Institution
1775 Massachusetts Avenue, N.W.
Washington, DC 20036
Tel: (202) 483-8919

Center for Congressional and Presidential Studies
College of Public and International Affairs
American University
Massachusetts and Nebraska Avenues, N.W.
Washington, DC 20016
Tel: (202) 686-2378

Center for Public Financing of Elections
201 Massachusetts Avenue, N.W.
Washington, DC 20002
Tel: (202) 546-5511
Citizen's Research Foundation
245 Nassau Street
Princeton, NJ 08540
Tel: (609) 924-0246
Clerk of the House of Representatives
H-105 Capitol Building
Washington, DC 20515
Tel: (202) 225-7000
Commerce Department
Census Bureau
Population Division
Washington, DC 20233
Tel: (202) 763-5161
Common Cause
2030 M Street, N.W.
Washington, DC 20036
Tel: (202) 833-1200
Congressional Budget Office
Second and D Street, S.W.
Washington, DC 20515
Tel: (202) 225-4416
Congressional Information Service
7101 Wisconsin Avenue
Washington, DC 20014
Tel: (301) 654-1550
Congressional Quarterly Inc.
1414 22nd Street, N.W.
Washington, DC 20037
Tel: (202) 887-8500
Congressional Record Office
H-112 Capitol Building
Washington, DC 20515
Tel: (202) 225-2100
Democratic National Committee
1625 Massachusetts Avenue, N.W.
Washington, DC 20036
Tel: (202) 797-5900

Elections Research Center
1619 Massachusetts Avenue, N.W.
Washington, DC 20036
Tel: (202) 387-6066
Everett McKinley Dirksen Congressional Leadership Research Center
Broadway and Fourth Streets
Pekin, IL 61554
Tel: (309) 347-7113
Fair Campaign Practices Committee
613 Pennsylvania Avenue, S.E.
Washington, DC 20003
Tel: (202) 544-5656
Federal Communications Commission
1919 M Street, N.W.
Washington, DC 20554
Tel: (202) 655-4000
Federal Election Commission
1325 K Street, N.W.
Washington, DC 20005
Tel: (202) 382-5162
Free Congress and Education Foundation
721 2nd Street, N.E.
Washington, DC 20002
Tel: (202) 546-3004
General Accounting Office
441 G Street, N.W.
Washington, DC 20548
Tel: (202) 386-4949
Government Printing Office
Congressional Desk
North Capitol and H Streets, N.W.
Washington, DC 20401
Tel: (202) 376-2030
Heritage Foundation
513 C Street, N.E.
Washington, DC 20002
Tel: (202) 546-4400
Institute for Contemporary Studies
260 California Street
Suite 811
San Francisco, CA 94111
Tel: (415) 398-3010

Institute of Election Administration
American University
Washington, DC 20016
Tel: (202) 676-2350
Inter-University Consortium for Political and Social Research
P.O. Box 1248
Ann Arbor, MI 48106
Tel: (313) 764-2570
Joint Center for Political Studies
1426 H Street, N.W.
Washington, DC 20005
Tel: (202) 638-4477
Louis Harris and Associates
1270 Avenue of the Americas
New York, NY 10020
Tel: (212) 245-7414
National Committee for an Effective Congress
201 Massachusetts Avenue, N.E.
Washington, DC 20002
Tel: (202) 833-4000
National Opinion Research Center
University of Chicago
6036 South Ellis Avenue
Chicago, IL 60637
Tel: (312) 752-6444
Public Citizen, Inc.
1346 Connecticut Avenue
Washington, DC 20036
Tel: (202) 293-9142
Republican National Committee
310 1st Street, S.E.
Washington, DC 20003
Tel: (202) 484-6500
Robert Maynard Hutchins Center for the Study of Democratic Institutions
Box 4068
Santa Barbara, CA 93103
Tel: (805) 961-2611
Roper Public Opinion Research Center
Williams College
Williamstown, MA 01267
Tel: (413) 458-7131

Secretary of the Senate
  S-221 Capitol Building
  Washington, DC 20501
  Tel: (202) 224-2115
Senate Historical Office
  United States Senate
  Washington, DC 20510
  Tel: (202) 224-6900
Twentieth Century Fund
  41 East 70th Street
  New York, NY 10021
  Tel: (212) 535-4441
White Burkett Miller Center of Public Affairs
  University of Virginia
  Box 5707
  Charlottesville, VA 22905
  Tel: (804) 924-7236

For information concerning current activities of these organizations one
should write directly to the organization. Most of them are listed in one of the
directories listed on pp. 181–82.

# Glossary

**Act.** Legislation that has been passed by both the House and Senate, signed by the president (or passed by Congress over a presidential veto), and thus has become law.

**Ad hoc committee.** A temporary committee formed by the House Speaker to consider bills that overlap the jurisdictions of more than one standing committee.

**Amendment.** Change or addition to a bill proposed by a member of Congress.

**Appropriations bill.** Legislation that provides the actual money for spending already authorized.

**Authorization.** Legislation that establishes or continues a substantive program and indicates the amount of money needed to implement it. An authorization usually precedes actual appropriation of funds.

**Backdoor spending.** Spending authority provided outside of the usual appropriations process.

**Budget.** Document sent to Congress each year that outlines proposed revenues and spending for the coming fiscal year.

**Budget authority.** Authority given by Congress to spend funds.

**Budget reconciliation.** A step in the congressional budget process during which House and Senate committees are to bring actual spending by the federal government into conformity with congressional budget resolutions.

**Calendar.** Agenda or list of matters before either chamber.

**Calendar Wednesday.** A seldom-used procedure that allows House members to call for debate and a vote on bills that have been approved by a standing committee but not yet passed through the Rules Committee.

**Chamber.** The place where the membership of the House or Senate meets; also used to refer to each of these bodies in a general way.

**Clean bill.** A bill that has been revised and amended in committee and is then introduced to the floor, with all the amendments incorporated, as a new bill.

**Cloture.** A vote of at least sixty senators needed to close debate in the Senate. This is the device by which a filibuster can be ended.

**Committee.** A subgroup of either house that considers bills and prepares them for action by the whole chamber. After a bill is introduced, it is referred to a committee that has jurisdiction over the bill's subject matter. The committee is to make any necessary changes in the bill and then report it out, or send it back to the parent body. However, most bills are never reported out and they "die" in committee. (See also Ad hoc committee, Joint committee, Select committee, Standing committee.)

**Committee of the Whole.** Device used by the House of Representatives when considering bills presented to it by the Rules Committee. Under this procedure the House is permitted to operate under less formal rules than during normal procedures, and only 100 members are needed for a quorum.

**Concurrent resolution.** Resolution that must be passed by both chambers but is not signed by the president and thus is not law. Usually used to express the sense of the Congress on various issues or to set internal rules or procedures.

**Conference committee.** A temporary committee, consisting of representatives from both houses, created to reconcile different versions of the same bill, each passed by one of the houses.

**Consent Calendar.** Calendar on which noncontroversial bills from either the House or Union calendars may be placed. On the first and third Mondays of each month, bills on the Consent Calendar can become law without debate or vote on the floor if no member objects.

**Continuing resolution.** A joint resolution of Congress to permit the continued funding of an existing governmental department when the fiscal year begins but Congress has not yet appropriated funds for that fiscal year.

**Discharge Calendar.** House calendar or agenda for bills that are awaiting floor action after they have been forced out of, or "discharged" from, committees. (See Discharge petition.)

**Discharge petition.** Motion by which an absolute majority of House members (218) can force a bill out of committee. Used when a committee refuses to report out a bill the majority wishes to consider.

**Discharge resolution.** Motion by any senator to remove a bill from committee consideration. Such resolutions are voted upon by the Senate in the same manner as is other Senate business.

**Division vote.** See Standing vote.

**Engrossed bill.** The final copy of a bill as passed by one house of the Congress.

**Enrolled bill.** The final copy of a bill identical versions of which have been passed by both houses.

**Expenditures.** The actual spending of money that has been appropriated by Congress.

**Filibuster.** Device used in the Senate to delay or prevent a vote on a given bill. The Senate provision of unlimited debate enables a minority of senators to delay a vote as long as they are able to hold the floor. A filibuster can be ended through a motion of cloture. (See Cloture.)

**Hearings.** Special committee sessions during which witnesses are brought before the committee to offer expertise or opinions on pending bills or other matters at hand, as in the case of special congressional investigations.

**House Calendar.** Agenda for pending bills that do not involve appropriation of funds or raising of revenues.

**Joint committee.** Congressional committee including members from both houses. Some are standing committees; others are temporary. (See Standing committee, Ad hoc committee.)

**Joint resolution.** A piece of legislation similar to a bill that must be passed by both houses of Congress and signed by the president. Usually such resolutions deal with limited matters. This procedure is also used in proposing an amendment to the Constitution, in which case it does not require the signature of the president.

*Journal.* The official record of Senate and House proceedings. The *Journal* records the actions of each chamber but not the actual debate that takes place.

**Law.** An act of Congress, passed by both houses and signed by the president (or passed over a presidential veto by Congress), which is legally binding.

**Legislative day.** The period of time beginning when either house meets and ending when that house adjourns. Usually legislative days coincide with calendar days, but occasionally in the Senate one legislative day may encompass a number of calendar days.

**Lobby.** A group that seeks to influence legislators or other governmental officials regarding a topic or piece of legislation of particular interest to the group.

**Logrolling.** An informal process by which legislators agree in advance to support each other's bills.

**Mark-up.** The process under which legislative committees amend or even rewrite a piece of legislation before reintroducing it to the whole chamber.

**Morning hour.** A period of time set aside at the beginning of each legislative day for the consideration of routine business. In the House this period is of unlimited length but is seldom used. In the Senate this period is the first two hours of each legislative day.

**Motion.** A request by a member in either chamber to institute any one of a wide variety of parliamentary actions.

**Pairing.** An agreement between two legislators with opposing views on a legislative matter to withhold their votes on a given measure, so that the absence of one or the other from the chamber will not affect the outcome of the vote. Three types of pairs exist: a general pair, for which the two legislators are listed with no indication of how they would have voted; a simple pair, which indicates how the members would have voted; and a live pair, for which one member is present and votes on a measure, but later withdraws that vote and announces his/her pairing with an absent member.

**Pocket veto.** Presidential disapproval of a bill, effectively "killing" it by simply not signing it before Congress has adjourned. When Congress is in session, any bill the president does not sign within ten days automatically becomes law. However, if Congress adjourns within that ten-day period, the bill dies if the President does not sign it.

**Previous question.** A motion used in the House to prevent further debate or amendments and to force a vote on a pending measure.

**Private Calendar.** The agenda for private bills, i.e., those that deal with specific matters of individuals and not with matters of general legislation.

**Privilege.** The rights of members of Congress; also, the way in which their motions are prioritized within each chamber.

**Privileged questions.** The strict procedural rules that govern the order in which various legislative matters (bills, motions, etc.) are to be considered by the Congress.

**Quorum.** The minimum number of members of either chamber required to be present before business can be conducted. In both houses this number is an absolute majority (218 in the House and 51 in the Senate), but the House is often able to escape the requirement by resolving into the Committee of the Whole, for which the quorum is only 100. (See Committee of the Whole.)

**Readings of bills.** Each bill introduced in either chamber must be read before the chamber three times. The first reading occurs when a bill is introduced and is printed (by title only) in the *Congressional Record*. The second reading occurs when a bill is reintroduced to the floor after committee consideration. The third reading takes place when the bill is up for the final vote. Usually only the second (if any) reading is a full reading of the bill.

**Reconciliation.** See Budget reconciliation.

**Recorded vote.** A vote upon which each member's stand is made known and recorded.

**Referral.** The process of sending a bill to the committee or subcommittee that has jurisdiction over the subject matter of the bill.

**Report.** The act of a legislative committee sending a bill, along with the committee's findings and recommendations on it, to the parent chamber for consideration on the floor (or in the Rules Committee in the case of the House). Also, the actual document that contains the findings and recommendations.

**Resolution.** A measure passed by either chamber to deal with matters that are solely the prerogative of that chamber and do not require a vote by the other chamber. Usually simple resolutions deal with internal rules or procedures or express the sense of only one chamber. (See also Joint resolution.)

**Rules.** The set of standing procedures that govern the conduct of business in either chamber. Also, the set of procedures specified by the House Rules Committee for governing floor debate on a particular bill in the House.

**Select committee.** A special congressional committee set up to deal with a specific topic that does not fall under the jurisdiction of any standing committee. Select committees are usually established for a limited time period. They may be formed in either house or as joint committees. (See Joint committee.)

**Slip law.** The first official publication of an act of Congress after it has been passed by both houses and signed by the president (or passed by Congress over a presidential veto).

**Standing committee.** A permanent committee in either chamber that considers bills pertaining to a given subject area.

**Standing vote.** A type of vote in both the House and Senate for which the votes of individual members are not recorded. Instead, members who oppose a measure stand and are counted by the presiding officer, as are those who support a measure.

*Statutes at Large.* An annual bound volume of all of the laws passed by Congress in a given session.

**Suspending the rules.** A timesaving procedure used in the House to bring about a vote on noncontroversial bills. Under this procedure, debate is limited to forty minutes, no amendments may be added, and the vote of two-thirds of those present is required for passage.

**Tabling a bill.** A procedural motion in either house to effectively "kill" a bill on the floor.

**Treaties.** Executive proposals that must be approved by two-thirds of the senators present. Like other legislation, treaties must be read three times and are debated on the Senate floor before a vote is taken.

**Unanimous consent agreement.** A time-saving procedure in the Senate under which the members agree to adopt certain noncontroversial measures without a vote.

**Union Calendar.** Agenda for pending bills in the House that involve appropriation of funds or the raising of revenues.

*United States Code.* The record of laws of the United States, which is revised every six years and supplemented annually. Laws are arranged according to subject matter.

**Veto.** Presidential disapproval of a bill or joint resolution of Congress. When Congress is in session, the president must veto a bill within ten days of receiving it. Congress can override a presidential veto by a vote of two-thirds in each house, in which case the bill would become law without the president's signature. (See also Pocket veto.)

**Voice vote.** A type of vote in either house in which the members vote by answering "aye" or "nay" in chorus and the presiding officer determines the outcome by the volume of the responses.

# Author Index

ABC News, 205
ABC News/*Washington Post,* 205
Adams, James T., 117
Agranoff, Robert, 183, 209
Alexander, Herbert E., 174
Amer, Mildred L., 128
American Political Science Association, 155
Ames, John G., 6
Anderson, William S., 73
Andrews, Joseph L., 75
Andriot, John L., 4, 148
Austin, Eric W., 194

Barone, Michael, 151, 165
Bartley, Numan V., 204
Beach, William W., 188
Bemis, Samuel F., 111
Benton, Mildred, 211
Berelson, Bernard R., 203
Berman, Larry, 99
Bevans, Charles I., 109
Bitner, Harry, 3, 72
Black, Henry C., 74
Blandford, Linda A., 79
Boyd, Anne M., 3
Brightbill, George D., 215
Brock, Clifton, 5
Brown, Cecelia, 183
Brownson, Charles B., 164
Buchanon, William W., 8
Buhler, Michaela, 165
Burnham, Walter Dean, 204, 208

Burns, Richard D., 111
Bysiewicz, Shirley R., 3

Campbell, Angus, 201
Cannon, Clarence, 41
Casper, Gerhard, 79
CBS News, 200
CBS News/*New York Times,* 200, 201, 205
Center for Political Studies, 202
Center for the American Woman and Politics, 168
Chamberlin, Hope, 166
Chambliss, William J., 75
Chandler, Ralph C., 74
Christopher, Maurine, 166
Close, Arthur C., 178
Clubb, Jerome M., 204
Cohen, Morris L., 72
Coleman, James S., 205
Commission on the Operation of the Senate, 206
Common Cause, 175, 176
Congressional Information Service, 64
Congressional Quarterly, 40, 59, 113, 161, 165, 176, 192, 197, 200
Cook, Mary E., 128
Cook, Patsy, 159
Council of State Governments, 207
Cox, Edward F., 195, 196
C-SPAN, 156
Cummings, Frank, 40
Cummings, Milton C., 196

# Title Index

# Subject Index